A LITTLE PRIMER OF TU FU

A LITTLE PRIMER OF TU FU

by

DAVID HAWKES

A *RENDITIONS* Paperback

Renditions Paperbacks
are published by
The Research Centre for Translation,
The Chinese University of Hong Kong

General Editors
John Minford   T.L. Tsim   Eva Hung

Printed in Hong Kong

FOR JEAN

CONTENTS

viii   *Contents*

AUTHOR'S INTRODUCTION

I HAVE written this book in order to give some idea of what Chinese poetry is really like and how it works to people who either know no Chinese at all or know only a little. To write it I have taken all the poems by Tu Fu contained in a well-known Chinese anthology, *Three Hundred T'ang Poems*, arranged them chronologically, transliterated them, explained their form and historical background, expounded their meaning, and lastly translated them into English prose. The translations are intended as cribs. They are not meant to be beautiful or pleasing. It is my ardent hope that a reader who is patient enough to work his way through to the end of the book will, by the time he reaches it, have learned something about the Chinese language, something about Chinese poetry, and something about the poet Tu Fu.

Tu Fu (712–70) is regarded by many Chinese as their greatest poet, but his poems do not as a rule come through very well in translation, which makes him a particularly rewarding poet to study in the original. Partly for this reason, and partly because he lived in eventful times and often referred to them in his poems, he seemed a good poet to choose for the purposes of this book.

The anthology *Three Hundred T'ang Poems* dates from the late eighteenth century. It became the gateway through which generations of Chinese schoolboys were initiated into the pleasures of poetry, just as Palgrave's *Golden Treasury* became a schoolbook over here. Its selection of Tu Fu's poems (thirty-odd out of a total of more than fourteen hundred) is an intelligent one. The advantage of using it is that nearly all the poems of the anthology have been translated elsewhere, some several times over (see, for example, Soame Jenyns' *Selections from the Three Hundred Poems of the T'ang Dynasty* and *Further Selections*), and the venturesome reader of this book who wishes to extend his conquests should have little difficulty in obtaining a copy of the Chinese anthology—in which the Tu Fu poems will be familiar landmarks—and continuing his study with the help of translations.

When preparing this book I gave a good deal of thought to the problem of transliteration. T'ang phonology was quite unlike that of any Chinese spoken today: indeed, its sounds have to be reconstructed; and though scholars can get a very good idea of what they were like, their exact nature remains a learned guess. Moreover the reconstructed sounds are as a rule written in complicated and unfamiliar phonetic symbols. If we use the modern sound-values of the characters, many of the rhymes and much of the musical effect of the verse disappears. On the other hand, to insist that a reader who knows no Chinese or very little should begin with a kind of learned algebra unintelligible to the majority of Chinese living today would be to deprive him of the chance of relating whatever he might learn from this book with any Chinese he might succeed in learning subsequently. And the modern pronunciation will give him *some* idea of the sound and feel of Chinese verse. Even the different tones of Mandarin Chinese will give him a notion of the effect of tonality.

Having decided to transliterate into the sounds of Modern Chinese—i.e. Mandarin, which is the dialect most often learned by foreigners and most widely taught in Chinese schools—I was still faced with the problem of spelling. Which of the many systems should be used? In the end I decided to use *Pin-yin*, the system officially adopted by the Chinese Government, as being the most 'international' form and also the simplest (compare *Pin-yin* **quán** with Wade–Giles **ch'üan²**, for example). In the transliteration of T'ang verse it unexpectedly has the added advantage of producing eye-rhymes in many cases where the rhyme has been lost.

The most serious disadvantage in using *Pin-yin* is that in those cases where a reader is likely to know the Chinese word already—I am thinking particularly of place-names and personal names—*Pin-yin* will produce forms which are weird and unrecognizable. 'Kiangsi', for example, becomes *Jiāng-xī* and 'Chungking' *Chóngqìng*; whilst even Tu Fu himself is transmogrified into *Dù Fǔ*. The answer to this particular problem seemed to be to keep the familiar spellings in the notes and translations while using the *Pin-yin* forms for transliteration of the text. This may strike some people as confusing but is, I believe, less confusing than any alternative would have been.

I should like to have given the reader a gramophone record of the sounds of these poems. As this is not possible, I recommend him to seek, if he can, a Chinese speaker who will make the noises for him. I do not propose to undertake the impossible task of trying to explain them in unscientific language. There are, however, a few symbols in *Pin-yin* which are used in unaccustomed ways, and these I shall explain briefly and approximately in the following table.

x is used for a 'sh' sound made with the tongue-tip pressed against the lower teeth. *xī*, for example, is a sound midway between 'see' and 'he'.

q is used for a 'ch' sound made in exactly the same way.

c is like 'ts' in 'tsetse fly'.

z is like 'dz' in 'adze'.

zh can be achieved by omitting the first vowel from 'giraffe' and pronouncing the 'g'r' on its own.

After *s, z, c, zh, ch, sh*, and *r*, *i* contracts into a sound somewhat like the 'u' of 'suppose'.

After *j, q, x*, and *y*, *u* is narrowed into a sound like French 'u' or German 'ü'. (Elsewhere it is the Italian 'u'.) This sound is also found after *n* and *l*, when it is written with an umlaut: *nü, lü*.

After any of the above group of initials (*j, q, x*, and *y*) when labialized (i.e. when followed by a 'w' sound) or *any* initial when palatalized (i.e. when followed by a 'y' sound), *e* is pronounced like the 'e' in 'egg'. After any other initial an open *e* is a sound like French 'eu' or German 'ö', whilst a closed *e* (one followed by *n* or *ng*) is a short, neutral sound like the 'a' in 'ago'.

The four tones of Pekingese, high level (first tone), high rising (second tone), low rising (third tone), and falling (fourth tone) are written with the signs ¯, ´, ˇ, `. I shall not attempt to explain them here. The signs themselves can be regarded as crudely diagrammatic representations of the tonal cadences.

I think the only other really important point to bear in mind when reading these transliterations is that each cluster of letters represents only one syllable. Thus *piao* is a monosyllable consisting of a palatalized initial (py . . .) and a diphthong (. . . ow); NOT pee-ay-oh.

I make no apology for the inadequacy of this briefing, because I want the reader to meet Tu Fu straight away and to become acquainted with him through his poems. If, after reading them, he is still desirous of more information about Tu Fu's life and work, he cannot do better than turn to Dr. William Hung's excellent *Tu Fu* (Harvard, 1952), which contains a full biography of the poet and translations of many more of his poems than are contained in this little book.   D. H.

Oxford 1965

1

望嶽
Wàng yuè

岱宗夫如何

1. *Dài-zōng fū rú-hé?*

齊魯青未了

2. *Qí Lǔ qīng wèi liǎo.*

造化鍾神秀

3. *Zào-huà zhōng shén xiù,*

陰陽割昏曉

4. *Yīn yáng gē hūn xiǎo.*

盪胸生層雲

5. *Dàng xiōng shēng céng yún,*

決眥入歸鳥

6. *Jué zì rù guī niǎo.*

會當凌絕頂

7. *Huì-dāng líng jué dǐng,*

一覽衆山小

8. *Yì-lǎn zhòng-shān xiǎo!*

TITLE AND SUBJECT

Wàng means 'gaze at', 'look towards', and is commonly used in connexion with scenery or distant objects.

Yuè is a special word for 'mountain' used only of the Five Great Peaks of China: Sung-shan in the middle of China (Honan), T'ai-shan in the east (Shantung), Hua-shan in the west (Shensi), Heng-shan in the south (Hunan), and another Heng-shan in the north (on the borders of Hopei and Shansi). The *'yuè'* of this title is T'ai-shan, which was from earliest times regarded by the Chinese with special veneration. The god of T'ai-shan was a judge over the dead, and formerly stones representing him stood opposite the openings of side-streets to scare away demons.

This poem was written in 736 when Tu Fu was a young un-married man of twenty-four. His father was at the time assistant prefect of a city only a few miles from the foot of T'ai-shan. Tu Fu had recently returned there after failing the Civil Service examinations in Ch'ang-an.

'Gazing at T'ai-shan' is a typically Chinese title for a poem. Our titles are substantival: 'Lycidas', 'Home Thoughts From Abroad', 'The Rape of the Lock'. The Chinese are partial to verbal constructions: 'Mourning Lycidas', 'Thinking of My Homeland While in a Foreign Country', 'Raping the Lock', etc. I should feel no compunction in translating this title 'On a Distant Prospect of T'ai-shan', or something of the sort.

Note that although this poem is about a view and not an ascent of T'ai-shan, Tu Fu does, in lines 5 and 6, imagine himself up on the mountainside. He may of course have climbed it a bit already. The poem merely tells us that he had never been to the top.

FORM

Although this poem is eight lines long and observes strict verbal parallelism in the two middle couplets (lines 3–4 and 5–6), it is usually classed as a poem 'in the Old Style'. The reason why it is not thought of as being 'in the Modern Style' (or 'Regulated Verse' as it is more usual to call it) is that it does not follow the elaborate rules of euphony which have to be observed in Regulated Verse.

The metre is pentasyllabic (five syllables to the line). The rhyme is the same throughout, and is found in alternate lines. Chinese call this type of verse 'Five-word Old Style' or 'Five Old' for short.

EXEGESIS

In the parallel lines of Chinese text and English translation which follow it will be found that if every word or hyphenated compound or word-group is regarded as a single unit, there are as many units in each line of Chinese as in the corresponding English line; and since the English line follows the Chinese word order, the reader should experience no difficulty in correctly relating the English units to the Chinese units which correspond. The Chinese units will be found as separate entries in the Vocabulary section at the back of the book, the only exception being that hyphenated suffixes will sometimes be found as separate entries.

1. *Dai-zōng fū rú-hé*
   Tai-tsung then like-what?

2. *Qí Lǔ qīng wèi liǎo*
   Ch'i Lu green never ends

'Tai-tsung' is one of T'ai-shan's names as a god.

Ch'i and Lu were anciently the names of two states or principalities lying respectively north and south of the T'ai-shan mountain. Their combined area corresponded roughly to the modern province of Shantung. The names continued to be used as territorial designations long after these states had ceased to exist, rather as 'Wessex' and 'Provence' continue to be used although they long ago ceased to exist as political entities.

3. *Zào-huà zhōng shén xiù*
   Creator concentrated divine beauty

4. *Yīn yáng gē hūn xiǎo*
   Northside southside cleave dark dawn

Yin and *yang* are familiar enough not to need much explaining. They do not, of course, always mean 'northside' 'southside'. Their basic sense is 'dark' and 'sunny'. If you use them of river banks, *yin* rather confusingly becomes 'southside' and *yang* 'northside', since it is the north bank of a river which catches most of the sun.

5. *Dàng xiōng shēng céng yún*
   Heaving breast are-born layered clouds

6. *Jué zì rù guī niǎo*
   Bursting eye-sockets enter returning birds

Inversion is extremely rare in Chinese verse, for the obvious reason that the language contains no grammatical inflections and therefore depends on word-order as a means of expressing grammatical relationships. Any derangement of the usual order is liable to result in impossible ambiguities. These two lines look as if they *ought* to mean

'The heaving breast produces layered clouds,
The bursting eyes enter the returning birds';

but it has long been recognized that this is a case of poetical inversion. Tu Fu's poems contain several such instances. They are considered extremely daring and bizarre by Chinese critics.

7. *Huì-dāng líng jué dǐng*
   Really-must surmount extreme summit

8. *Yì-lǎn zhòng-shān xiǎo*
   Single-glance many-mountains little

zhòng-shān: literally 'the many mountains', 'the multitude of mountains'; i.e. 'all the other mountains'.

TRANSLATION

'On a Prospect of T'ai-shan'

How is one to describe this king of mountains? Throughout the whole of Ch'i and Lu one never loses sight of its greenness. In it the Creator has concentrated all that is numinous and beautiful. Its northern and southern slopes divide the dawn from the dark. The layered clouds begin at the climber's heaving chest, and homing birds fly suddenly within range of his straining eyes. One day I must stand on top of its highest peak and at a single glance see all the other mountains grown tiny beneath me.

2

兵車行
Bīng-chē xíng

車轔轔
1. *Chē lín-lín,*

馬蕭蕭
2. *Mǎ xiāo-xiāo,*

行人弓箭各在腰
3. *Xíng-rén gōng-jiàn gè zài yāo,*

爺孃妻子走相送
4. *Yé-niáng qī-zǐ zǒu xiāng-sòng,*

塵埃不見咸陽橋
5. *Chén-āi bú jiàn Xián-yáng-qiáo.*

牽衣頓足攔道哭
6. *Qiān yī dùn zú lán dào kū,*

哭聲直上干雲霄
7. *Kū-shēng zhí-shàng gān yún-xiāo.*

道旁過者問行人

8. *Daò-páng guò-zhě wèn xíng-rén,*

行人但云點行頻

9. *Xíng-rén dàn yún: 'Diǎn-xíng pín.*

或從十五北防河

10. *'Huò cóng shí-wǔ beǐ fáng Hé,*

便至四十西營田

11. *'Biàn zhì sì-shí xī yíng-tián.*

去時里正與裹頭

12. *'Qù shí lǐ-zhèng yǔ guǒ tóu,*

歸來頭白還戍邊

13. *'Guī-lái tóu bái huán shù-biān.*

邊亭流血成海水

14. *'Biān-tíng liú-xuè chéng hǎi-shuǐ,*

武皇開邊意未已

15. *'Wǔ-huáng kāi-biān yì wèi yǐ.*

君不聞漢家山東二百州

16. *'Jūn bù wén Hàn-jiā shān-dōng èr-bǎi zhōu,*

千村萬落生荆杞

17. *'Qiān cūn wàn luò shēng jīng qǐ.*

縱 有 健 婦 把 鋤 犁

18. 'Zòng yǒu jiàn fù bǎ chú lí,

禾 生 隴 畝 無 東 西

19. 'Hé shēng lǒng-mǔ wú dōng xī.

況 復 秦 兵 耐 苦 戰

20. 'Kuàng fù Qín bīng nài kǔ-zhàn,

被 驅 不 異 犬 與 雞

21. 'Bèi qū bú-yì quǎn yǔ jī.

長 者 雖 有 問

22. 'Zhǎng-zhě suī yǒu wèn,

役 夫 敢 申 恨

23. 'Yì-fū gǎn shēn-hèn?

且 如 今 年 冬

24. 'Qiě-rú jīn-nián dōng,

未 休 關 西 卒

25. 'Wèi xiū Guān-xī zú.

縣 官 急 索 租

26. 'Xiàn-guān jí suǒ zū,

租 稅 從 何 出

27. 'Zū-shuì cóng-hé chū?

信知生男惡

28. 'Xìn zhī shēng nán è,

反是生女好

29. 'Fǎn-shì shēng nǚ hǎo;

生女猶得嫁比鄰

30. 'Shēng nǚ yóu dé jià bǐ-lín,

生男埋沒隨百草

31. 'Shēng nán mái-mò suí bǎi-cǎo.

君不見青海頭

32. 'Jūn bú jiàn Qīng-hǎi tóu,

古來白骨無人收

33. 'Gǔ-lái bái-gǔ wú-rén shōu,

新鬼煩怨舊鬼哭

34. 'Xīn guǐ fán-yuàn jiù guǐ kū,

天陰雨溼聲啾啾

35. 'Tiān yīn yǔ shī shēng jiū-jiū.'

TITLE AND SUBJECT

Bīng means 'soldier', 'troops', 'arms', 'army'.

Chē is a general term for anything on wheels: car, cart, train, wheelbarrow, bicycle, or bus. Anciently it was the word for a chariot; but war-chariots went out of use with the introduction of cavalry before the beginning of the Christian era. The 'army carts' of the title are heavy baggage-wagons.

A *xíng* is a type of ballad. Poets of the T'ang era, in which Tu Fu lived, often wrote new words to existing tunes. Sometimes they wrote original lyrics which were set to new tunes, like Po Chü-i's famous 'Song of Everlasting Grief' which was sung in every wine-shop and teahouse of the Empire. Others again borrowed the themes of earlier folk-songs whose melodies had long since been forgotten, in order to write ballad-style poems which were not intended to be sung at all. For example, Li Po's moving poem 'Fighting South of the Wall' imitates an ancient ballad which was at least seven centuries old in Li Po's own day. Tu Fu's 'Ballad of the Army Carts' falls into none of these categories: it was not written to an existing tune; it was not written to be sung to a new tune; and finally it was not written in imitation of the words of any previously existing ballad. Rather it is a completely original poem written in the ballad style. I shall point out some of the features of that style in the following section. Let me for the moment explain why I think Tu Fu elected to write this poem about soldiers in a form which would remind his readers of the old ballads they had read in popular anthologies, probably while they were still school children.

Clearly one reason is that he wanted to put most of the poem into the mouths of his conscripts, and the popular ballad form would suit their homely, unsophisticated language. Kipling's *Barrack Room Ballads* is a parallel which readily suggests itself.

There is another reason, however, '*Vox populi, vox Dei*' was from very early times a cardinal tenet of Chinese political thought, and it was held that the *vox populi* expressed itself nowhere so effectively as in the people's songs and ballads. According to a view commonly held in Tu Fu's time, much of the *Book of Songs*, the most ancient surviving corpus of Chinese poetry, consisted of songs and ballads which had been deliberately collected from among the peasantry by rulers who wished to determine the temper of their people. The enormous prestige of the *Book of Songs* meant that poetry had—in theory at any rate—to resemble it as much as possible, if not formally, then at least in spirit. Now much of the poetry in the *Book of Songs* was thought to contain criticism of rulers by their subjects. It followed from all this that the best poetry ought to be critical and didactic and that it ought, in some way or other, to resemble the songs sung by the peasantry of North China in ancient times. This, then, is the reason why a Chinese poet wishing to write satirical verses on a contemporary theme would be almost certain to employ the ballad form as a medium.

The 'Ballad of the Army Carts' was probably written in 750 (when the poet was thirty-eight) on the occasion of a new drafting of reservists and 'volunteers' to fight against the Tibetans. The 'passer-by' of line 8 is, of course, the poet himself.

The old system of militia service which took the peasants away for regular periods of unpaid National Service was superseded a generation before the date of this poem by the recruitment of paid regulars who were kept on reserve and called out intermittently as occasion arose. Unfortunately the new system did not produce an adequate intake of recruits, and press-gang methods were frequently resorted to in order to raise armies for unpopular campaigns. The most notorious recruiting campaign of this sort was that of 751. In order to raise troops to fight against the kingdom of Nan-chao in Yunnan, which was popularly thought of (and with some justification) as the graveyard of any soldier unlucky enough to be drafted there, commissioners were sent out into all the northern prefectures who marched back their quotas of forcibly conscripted men tied up in files one behind the other, and with wooden collars or 'cangues' round their necks like common criminals. The historian's account of the distressing scenes witnessed on that occasion closely resembles the description contained in the opening lines of this poem.

FORM

The Chinese ballad style differs from other kinds of Old Style verse in admitting a certain amount of metrical variety. Most of this poem is in heptasyllabics (lines of seven syllables), but the first two lines contain only three syllables each, and there is quite a long passage in pentasyllabics beginning at line 22.

Chinese ballad style also admits the insertion of certain stock phrases which are either outside the metre altogether or else, if they are in it, have a metrical value less than their syllabic content. '*Jūn bū wén*' in line 16 is outside the heptasyllabic metre altogether. It is a sort of enclitic introduction to the seven-syllable line which follows it. In line 32 the '*bū*' is clipped so short that '*Jūn bū jiàn*' reads like two syllables and the line counts metrically as a pentasyllabic. The stock phrases used in this way are very limited in number and all similar in meaning: 'Don't you know?', 'Haven't you heard?', 'Can you really be unaware?', etc.

Another feature of Chinese ballad poetry—as of ballad poetry all over the world, I suppose—is its partiality for iteration: the repetition of words or phrases for deliberate effect. A favourite form of this, which for want of a term I call 'linking iteration', is where the beginning of one line echoes the end of the line before —the sort of effect Keats used in his 'Ode to a Nightingale':

.. in faery lands forlorn.
Forlorn! the very word is like a bell. . .

'*Xíng-rén*' in lines 8 and 9 is an example of this. Other examples are the repetition of '*kū*' in lines 6 and 7, of '*biān*' in lines 13 and 14, and of '*zǔ*' in lines 26 and 27. Another kind of repetition is found in lines 28–31: all those '*shēng nán*' and '*shēng nǚ*'. This kind of effect would as a rule be avoided in more formal types of verse, but is extremely common in ballads, traditional and imitation ones alike.

Finally the dialogue form, really a dramatic monologue provoked by the initial query of a lay-figure whom the reader identifies with the poet himself (Coleridge's 'wedding guest', Tu Fu's 'passer-by'), is also characteristic of Chinese ballad style. But this again, I imagine, is a common feature of all ballad poetry. Sometimes the poet does not bother to assume any 'persona' when addressing the 'provoking' question to his chief character:

O what can ail thee, knight-at-arms, . . .?

A rather interesting example of this is to be found in No. 5 in this selection, which I shall explain when we get to it.

EXEGESIS

1. *Chē lín-lín*
Carts rattle-rattle

2. *Mǎ xiāo-xiāo*
   Horses whinny-whinny

3. *Xíng-rén gōng-jiàn gè zài yāo*
   Service-men bows-arrows each at waist

Lín-lín and *xiāo-xiāo* are onomatopoeic expressions.

Gè: Chinese syntax often treats distributives (words like 'all', 'each', 'no', 'some', 'every') as adverbs modifying the verb rather than as adjectives qualifying the subject or object. It is as if, instead of saying 'No soldiers enjoy route-marching' or 'Every lassie has her laddie' we were to say 'Soldiers no-case enjoy route-marching', 'Lassies each-wise have laddies.'

4. *Yé-niáng qī-zǐ zǒu xiāng-sòng*
   Fathers-mothers wives-children run see-off

5. *Chén-āi bú jiàn Xián-yáng-qiáo*
   Dust not see Hsien-yang Bridge

Xiāng-sòng: *sòng* on its own means to see someone off, whether for a mere twenty paces to the front gate or for a distance of eighty miles to a station or port of embarkation. *Xiāng* is a pronoun-prefix used with verbs which normally have a personal noun or pronoun for their object, when the person of the object is unspecified. Its translation has to be determined by the context. In 'Please don't bother to *xiāng-sòng!*' it would probably be 'see *me* off'. In 'Oh, but I insist on *xiāng-sòng!*' it would be 'seeing *you* off'. Here it is 'seeing *them* off'.

Xián-yáng-qiáo: the Hsien-yang Bridge crossed the R. Wei to the south-west of the city. We are meant to infer that the troops are setting out for a westerly or south-westerly destination.

6. *Qiān yī dùn zú lán dào kū*
   Pull clothes stamp feet stand-in way weep

7. *Kū-shēng zhí-shàng gān yún-xiāo*
   Weep-sound straight-ascend assail cloud-welkin

Yún-xiāo: *yún* on its own means 'cloud'. The compound word is one of a large number of poetic synonyms for 'sky'.

8. *Dào-páng guò-zhě wèn xíng-rén*
Road-side passer-by asks service-men

9. *Xíng-rén dàn yún: Diǎn-xíng pín*
Service-men only say: Mobilizing frequent

The *dào-páng guò-zhě* is, of course, Tu Fu himself.
Diǎn-xíng: diǎn on its own means 'prick off', 'mark down'. Here
diǎn-xíng is to mark down for service, i.e. to mobilize reservists.

10. *Huò cóng shí-wǔ běi fáng Hé*
Some from fifteen north guard River

11. *Biàn zhì sì-shí xī yíng-tián*
Even reaching forty west army-farm

Hé: the 'River' referred to here is the Yellow River. Its upper,
western reaches were at this time under constant threat from the
Tibetans.

Yíng-tián: a system of military colonies or settlements first used
by the Chinese during the Han period (206 B.C.–A.D. 220) as a
means of holding down their remote north-western conquests. The
soldiers worked on the farms when they were not engaged in military duties, so that these outposts could be self-supporting and did
not have to rely on the maintenance of long lines of supply. The
expression is used here verbally: 'to do frontier duty in a military
settlement'.

12. *Qù shí lǐ-zhèng yǔ guǒ tóu*
Went time village-headman for-them wrapped head

13. *Guī-lái tóu bái huán shù-biān*
Come-back head white still garrison-frontier

Guǒ tóu: the common soldiers of this period wore a sort of head-
cloth or turban, rather like the headcloths of white towelling still
sometimes worn by the peasants of North China in modern times.
The point of this line is, I think, that the new recruits were so
pathetically young that they still didn't know how to tie up their
own head-cloths properly.

14. *Biān-tíng liú-xuè chéng hǎi-shuǐ*
    Frontier-posts run-blood form sea-water

15. *Wǔ-huáng kāi-biān yì wèi yǐ*
    Martial-emperor's expand-frontier notions not-yet ended

Wǔ-huáng: the 'Martial Emperor' is Wu-ti of the Han dynasty (reigned 140–87 B.C.). It was a well-established convention among the poets of Tu Fu's time to substitute the names of Han persons and institutions when they were talking about contemporary affairs. Nobody was deceived by this convention, and yet for some reason it emboldened poets to be somewhat more outspoken in their criticisms than they might otherwise have been. Here *Wǔ-huáng* really refers to the reigning emperor Hsüan-tsung (sometimes called *Ming-huang*, the 'Brilliant Emperor'), just as '*Hàn-jiā*' in the next line really refers to the 'land of T'ang', i.e. contemporary China.

16. *Jūn bù wén Hàn-jiā shān-dōng èr-bǎi zhōu*
    My-lord not hear Han-land east-of-mountains two-hundred prefectures

17. *Qiān cūn wàn luò shēng jīng qǐ*
    Thousand villages ten-thousand hamlets grow briers thorns

Qiān cūn wàn luò: this type of hendiadys is very common in Chinese both in verse and in prose. *Cūn* and *luò* are exactly synonymous: in fact, *cūn-luò* regularly features as a compound word meaning 'village'. *Qiān cūn wàn luò* is simply a rhetorical way of saying 'very many villages'.

18. *Zòng yǒu jiàn fù bǎ chú lí*
    Even-if there-is sturdy wife handle hoe plough

19. *Hé shēng lǒng-mǔ wú dōng xī*
    Crops grow fields not-have east west

Lǒng-mǔ: *lǒng* on its own is used of the baulks of earth which divide the fields in the Chinese countryside. *Lǒng-mǔ* literally, then, means something like 'bordered fields'. I think the soldiers mean that the women can't plough straight and can't in any case manage to scratch up more than a few patches here and there. The edges of the fields are all overgrown, and you can no longer see where one ends and the next begins.

20. *Kuàng fù Qín bīng nài kŭ-zhàn*
    Still-more also Ch'in soldiers capable-of hard-fighting

21. *Bèi qū bú-yì quăn yŭ jī*
    Subjected-to driving just-like dogs or chickens

Qín, like Ch'i and Lu in No. 1, line 2, was the name of an ancient principality. It was used in Tu Fu's time to designate a geographical area corresponding very roughly to the modern province of Shensi.

22. *Zhăng-zhĕ suī yŏu wèn*
    You-sir though have asking

23. *Yì-fū găn shēn-hèn*
    Conscripted men dare state-resentment?

Zhăng-zhĕ: literally 'superior', is used here as a polite expression: 'sir'. Tu Fu would be wearing the long gown of a scholar and is addressed by the soldiers as a member of the officer class.

Yŏu wèn is also a polite form, more respectful than a simple *wèn* 'you ask' would be. 'Though you are good enough to ask, sir' is roughly the tone.

Yì-fū: 'conscripted man', i.e. 'I', 'we'. In polite language first and second person pronouns are seldom used, various substantival formulas being substituted, according to the status and relationship of the speakers.

Note that Chinese frequently uses a rhetorical question where in English we would use a negative statement. The oddity of much translation from the Chinese is due to the failure of translators to make allowance for this fact. It isn't English to say 'Dare I tell you?' when we mean 'I dare not tell you'.

24. *Qiĕ-rú jīn-nián dōng*
    Take-for-example this-year winter

25. *Wèi xiū Guān-xī zú*
    Not yet demobilize Kuan-hsi troops

Guān-xī: the 'Land West of the Passes', i.e. the metropolitan area around Ch'ang-an: Shensi (which does, in fact, have the same sense as 'Kuan-hsi').

26. *Xiàn-guān jí suǒ zū*
    District-officers urgently seek land-tax

27. *Zū-shuì cóng-hé chū*
    Land-taxes from-what proceed?

28. *Xìn zhī shēng nán è*
    Truly know bear son bad

29. *Fǎn-shì shēng nǚ hǎo*
    On-the-contrary bear daughter good

30. *Shēng nǚ yóu dé jià bǐ-lín*
    Bear daughter still can marry neighbour

31. *Shēng nán mái-mò suí bǎi-cǎo*
    Bear son bury-lost along-of hundred-grasses

Bǎi-cǎo: the 'hundred' in such expressions is really little more than a plural prefix: 'the grasses of the field'. Compare Mao Tsetung's famous dictum 'Let the hundred flowers bloom' in which the '*bǎi-huā*' could more accurately have been translated 'all the flowers' or 'every flower'.

32. *Jūn bú jiàn Qīng-hǎi tóu*
    My-lord not see Kokonor shores

33. *Gǔ-lái bái-gǔ wú-rén shōu*
    From-of-old white-bones no-man collect

Qīng-hǎi, literally 'Blue Sea', is the Chinese name for the Kokonor.

34. *Xīn guǐ fán-yuàn jiù guǐ kū*
    New ghosts complain old ghosts weep

35. *Tiān yīn yǔ shī shēng jiū-jiū*
    Sky overcast rain wet voices twitter-twitter

Jiū-jiū: onomatopoeic expression normally used of bird-cries. The weeping and complaining of the multitudinous ghosts makes a thin, twittering sound.

'Ballad of the Army Carts'

The carts squeak and trundle, the horses whinny, the conscripts go by, each with a bow and arrows at his waist. Their fathers, mothers, wives, and children run along beside them to see them off. The Hsien-yang Bridge cannot be seen for dust. They pluck at the men's clothes, stamp their feet, or stand in the way weeping. The sound of their weeping seems to mount up to the blue sky above. A passer-by questions the conscripts, and the conscripts reply:

'They're always mobilizing now! There are some of us who went north at fifteen to garrison the River and who are still, at forty, being sent to the Military Settlements in the west. When we left as lads, the village headman had to tie our head-cloths for us. We came back white-haired, but still we have to go back for frontier duty! On those frontier posts enough blood has flowed to fill the sea; but the Martial Emperor's dreams of expansion remain unsatisfied. Haven't you heard, sir, in our land of Han, throughout the two hundred prefectures east of the mountains briers and brambles are growing in thousands of little hamlets; and though many a sturdy wife turns her own hand to the hoeing and ploughing, the crops grow just anywhere, and you can't see where one field ends and the next begins? And it's even worse for the men from Ch'in. Because they make such good fighters, they are driven about this way and that like so many dogs or chickens.

'Though you are good enough to ask us, sir, it's not for the likes of us to complain. But take this winter, now. The Kuan-hsi troops are not being demobilized. The District Officers press for the land-tax, but where is it to come from? I really believe it's a misfortune to have sons. It's actually better to have a daughter. If you have a daughter, you can at least marry her off to one of the neighbours; but a son is born only to end up lying in the grass somewhere, dead and unburied. Why look, sir, on the shores of the Kokonor the bleached bones have lain for many a long year, but no one has ever gathered them up. The new ghosts complain and the old ghosts weep, and under the grey and dripping sky the air is full of their baleful twitterings.'

3

麗人行

Lì-rén xíng

三月三日天氣新

1. *Sān-yuè sān-rì tiān-qì xīn,*

長安水邊多麗人

2. *Cháng-ān shuǐ-biān duō lì-rén.*

態濃意遠淑且真

3. *Tài nóng yì yuǎn shū qiě zhēn,*

肌理細膩骨肉勻

4. *Jī-lǐ xì-nì gǔ-ròu yún.*

繡羅衣裳照暮春

5. *Xiù-luó yī-shāng zhào mù-chūn,*

蹙金孔雀銀麒麟

6. *Cù-jīn kǒng-què yín qí-lín.*

頭上何所有

7. *Tóu-shàng hé-suǒ yǒu?*

翠微匎葉垂鬢唇

8. *Cuì-wēi è-yè chuí bìn-chún.*

背後何所見

9. *Bèi-hòu hé-suǒ jiàn?*

珠壓腰衱穩稱身

10. *Zhū yà-yāo-jié wěn chèn shēn.*

就中雲幕椒房親

11. *Jiù-zhōng yún-mù jiāo-fáng qīn,*

賜名大國虢與秦

12. *Sì-míng dà guó Guó yǔ Qín.*

紫駝之峯出翠釜

13. *Zǐ tuó zhī fēng chū cuì fǔ,*

水精之盤行素鱗

14. *Shuǐ-jīng zhī pán xíng sù lín,*

犀箸厭飫久未下

15. *Xī-zhù yàn-yù jiǔ wèi xià,*

鸞刀縷切空紛綸

16. *Luán-dāo lǚ-qiē kōng fēn-lún.*

3. *Ballad of Lovely Women*

黄門飛鞚不動塵

17. *Huáng-mén fēi kòng bú dòng chén,*

御厨絡繹送八珍

18. *Yù-chú luò-yì sòng bā-zhēn.*

簫鼓哀吟感鬼神

19. *Xiāo gǔ āi yín gǎn guǐ-shén,*

賓從雜遝實要津

20. *Bīn-cóng zá-tà shí yào-jīn,*

後來鞍馬何逡巡

21. *Hòu lái ān-mǎ hé jùn-xún!*

當軒下馬入錦茵

22. *Dāng xuān xià-mǎ rù jǐn-yīn.*

楊花雪落覆白蘋

23. *Yáng-huā xuě luò fù bái-pín,*

青鳥飛去銜紅巾

24. *Qīng-niǎo fēi-qù xián hóng jīn,*

炙手可熱勢絶倫

25. *Zhì-shǒu kě rè shì jué-lún,*

慎莫近前丞相瞋

26. *Shèn-mò jìn-qián chéng-xiàng chēn!*

TITLE AND SUBJECT

Lì-rén means 'lovely woman' or 'lovely women'.

Xíng means 'ballad', as in the title of the last poem. The 'lovely women' are the great ladies of the court: Yang Kuei-fei, now Empress in all but name, and her sisters the Duchess of Kuo, the Duchess of Ch'in, and the Duchess of Han. Tu Fu, along with many other holidaymakers, watched them at a sort of *fête champêtre* by the lakeside in Ch'ang-an's principal park on the day of the Spring Festival in April 753. Yang Kuei-fei's cousin, Yang Kuo-chung, had become Chief Minister following the death of the dictator Li Lin-fu in 752. He was extremely unpopular, and the blatant extravagance of the Yang sisters was already a public scandal. Tu Fu's description of the scene contains just that mixture of admiration, envy, and disgust which exhibitions of high living and conspicuous consumption are liable to arouse in the bourgeois breast.

FORM

Like the 'Ballad of the Army Carts', this is mainly in heptasyllables. The 'interpolated' questions of lines 7 and 9 are typical of the ballad style.

Although Chinese editors do not as a rule divide this poem, I am almost sure that it is meant to be read as three stanzas of equal length. This is possible if one regards the questions of lines 7 and 9 as being outside the prosodic structure. We then have three stanzas of eight lines each: lines 1–10, lines 11–18, and lines 19–26. Many readers have found lines 19–20 of this poem puzzling. They understand the music of line 19 as part of the entertainment being offered to the ladies, and then experience great difficulty in extracting any sense from line 20, which seems totally unconnected. In fact, if you take lines 19–26 as a separate stanza, it is at once plain that the *whole* of this passage is about Yang Kuo-chung, who has just arrived on the scene preceded by a mounted fife-and-drum band. There is then no difficulty whatever about line 20.

Read in this light the whole poem very cleverly unfolds the scene as it must have appeared to the crowded onlookers. The first stanza describes the expensive dresses, beautiful complexions, and haughty manners of the court ladies; the second watches them eating—or wasting—a great deal of very rich and expensive food, and identifies various mounted couriers who come galloping up as palace eunuchs bearing additions to the feast from the imperial kitchens; and finally, in the last stanza, a sound of music is heard and the crowd watches the arrival of a mounted procession: Yang Kuochung and other male courtiers coming to join the ladies. Yang Kuo-chung himself appears last of all, looking very proud and grand. The onlookers, who would boo if they dared, shuffle their feet and move back a step or two.

EXEGESIS

1. *Sān-yuè sān-rì tiān-qì xīn*
   Third-month third-day weather new

2. *Cháng-ān shuǐ-biān duō lì-rén*
   Ch'ang-an water-side many lovely-women

Sān-yuè sān-rì: *not* 3 March. In the Chinese calendar this day corresponded to 10 April 753. The third day of the third month was a festival on which everyone went out walking in their best clothes and picnicked in the open air, if possible beside some water. It may have been connected anciently with some ceremony of ritual purification. (The importance of the water suggests ritual lustrations.) In Ch'ang-an, the fashionable place to go to on this day was the *Qū-jiāng*, the Serpentine Lake in the large park which occupied the south-east corner of the city. The *shuǐ-biān* of line 2 refers to this lake.

3. *Tài nóng yì yuǎn shū qiě zhēn*
   Appearance gorgeous thoughts remote pure and true

4. *Jī-lǐ xì-nì gǔ-ròu yún*
   Complexions delicate bones-flesh well-proportioned

Shú qiě zhēn: I don't think Tu Fu is referring to their morals: it is their breeding and refinement that he finds so impressive—like those of the princess in the fairy-tale who was a *real* princess because she could feel a dried pea through several thicknesses of mattress.

5. *Xiù-luó yī-shāng zhào mù-chūn*
   Embroidered-silk clothing shine late-spring

6. *Cù-jīn kŏng-què yín qí-lín*
   Gold-passement peacocks silver ch'i-lins

Cù-jīn was work done in gold thread on top of a silk ground.
I think *passement* is about the nearest equivalent.

Qí-lín: a mythical beast, combining features of deer, ox, and
unicorn.

7. *Tóu-shàng hé-suŏ yŏu*
   On-heads what-that-which there-is

8. *Cuì-wēi è-yè chuí bìn-chún*
   Greenish-blue bandeaux hanging-down-to hair-line

9. *Bèi-hòu hé-suŏ jiàn*
   Behind-back what-that-which seen

10. *Zhū yà-yāo-jié wĕn chèn shēn*
    Pearl press-waist-aprons firmly fitting body

It is virtually impossible to get much idea of the clothing and
jewellery described in the last few lines. We can be sure that they
represent the height of fashion at the Chinese capital in spring 753,
and the terms used must have been thoroughly familiar to Tu Fu's
contemporary readers. Unfortunately the modern reader can only
guess their meaning. I think *è-yè* may perhaps have resembled
those jewelled head-dresses worn by players of female roles in the
Peking opera which cover the hair almost down to the brows but
leave the chignon exposed.

11. *Jiù-zhōng yún-mù jiāo-fáng qīn*
    There-among cloud-curtain pepper-chamber kin

12. *Sì-míng dà guó Guó yŭ Qín*
    Granted-as-titles great-countries, Kuo and Ch'in

Yún-mù: bed-curtains embroidered with cloud-patterns.

Jiāo-fáng refers to the apartments of the Empress. In the
palaces of the Han era the Empress's apartments had their walls
plastered with a paste in which dried pepper-flowers had been
pounded. It was said to impart a subtle fragrance to the air.

'Cloud curtains and pepper-scented chamber' are used here by metonymy for their occupant, the Empress, i.e. Yang Kuei-fei, who at this time was Empress in all but name. *Yún-mù jiāo-fáng qīn* therefore means 'the kinswomen of the Empress', i.e. Yang Kuei-fei's sisters, the Duchesses of Kuo, Ch'in, and Han.

13. *Zǐ tuó zhī fēng chū cuì fǔ*
    Purple camel-hump emerges-from green cauldron

14. *Shuǐ-jīng zhī pán xíng sù lín*
    Crystal plate is-served white scales

Zhī is an unstressed particle which connects a noun with the preceding word or words that qualify it. In T'ang poetry it is very unusual to find the particle used (it is virtually *never* used in Regulated Verse), but it is extremely common in prose. For example, *hòu lái ān-mǎ* ('the rider who comes last') in line 21 of this poem would quite certainly become *hòu lái zhī ān-mǎ* in prose.

Roasted camel-hump was at this time a delicacy much in demand at the tables of the great.

I don't think the 'green cauldron' is a metal one. The word used for 'green' suggests the green glaze typical of T'ang pottery.

Sù lín ('white scales') is used by synecdoche for 'fish'.

15. *Xī-zhù yàn-yù jiǔ wèi xià*
    Rhinoceros-chopsticks sated long have-not descended

16. *Luán-dāo lǚ-qiè kōng fēn-lún*
    Belled-knife thread-cutting vainly busy

Rhinoceros horn is well known for its aphrodisiac and magical properties. Its use for chopsticks would be as a poison-detector. Spoons and chopsticks of rhinoceros-horn were among the lavish gifts sent on one occasion by the Emperor Hsüan-tsung to An Lu-shan.

The carvers had tiny bells on their knives and executed a kind of ballet as they carved.

17. *Huáng-mén fēi-kòng bú dòng chén*
    Eunuchs' flying-steeds do-not stir dust

18. *Yù-chú luò-yì sòng bā-zhēn*
    Imperial-kitchen in-succession sends eight-precious-foods

Kòng 'bridle': here by synecdoche for the horse itself. Tu Fu means they gallop so fast that their hooves hardly touch the ground. *Bā-zhēn*: the Chinese have a passionate weakness for numbered categories. There is an ancient text which enumerates eight particularly delicious and costly dishes; but the expression is used here to mean simply 'delicacies'. The number is not meant to be taken seriously.

19. *Xiāo-gǔ āi yín gǎn guǐ-shén*
    Flutes-drums' mournful sound would-move demons-gods

20. *Bīn-cóng zá-tà shí yào-jīn*
    Guest-followers numerous-thronging truly-is power-path

The band and the shoal of followers, as I have explained in the introductory section, belong not to the great ladies but to Yang Kuo-chung, whose party is just arriving on the scene.

21. *Hòu lái ān-mǎ hé jùn-xún*
    After-coming saddle-horse how dawdlingly-advances

22. *Dāng xuān xià-mǎ rù jǐn-yīn*
    In-front-of balustrade dismounts enters patterned-carpet

Ān-mǎ: the horse is used by metonymy for the rider, Yang Kuo-chung. *Rù jǐn-yīn*: i.e. took his place among the other picnickers, who were sitting on carpets. In the T'ang period the Chinese still sat on the floor, as the Japanese do to this day.

23. *Yáng-huā xuě luò fù bái-pín*
    Willow-down snow-like falls covers white water-weed

24. *Qīng-niǎo fēi-qù xián hóng jīn*
    Blue-bird flies-off bearing-in-beak red handkerchief

There is a double meaning in these lines. They can be taken at their face value as a description of the scenery in the park. But *Yáng*, as well as meaning 'willow', is the surname of Yang Kuo-chung, the subject of this stanza. According to an ancient bit of Chinese folklore, frogbit (the *bái-pín* of line 23) was generated by the mutation of willow-down when it fell into water. Now there was a popular rumour, apparently believed by Tu Fu, that Yang

Kuo-chung was carrying on an incestuous relationship with his cousin, the Duchess of Kuo. The 'Yang flower covering the frogbit' therefore has an indecent meaning concealed beneath its harmless exterior.

As for *qīng-niǎo*, in Chinese mythology the blue-bird is the messenger of Hsi Wang Mu, the Fairy Queen who rules over the Garden of Paradise in the Mountain of Kunlun. Red silk handkerchiefs about a yard long were much in vogue among Chinese ladies of this period. They were held in the hand, twisted, fluttered, played with, and used in a hundred decorous and becoming ways, rather as fans were at a later period in Europe. The blue-bird carrying a red handkerchief therefore suggests a secret assignation being arranged by the exchange through an intermediary of *billets-doux* and love-tokens.

The ambiguity of these lines is, of course, quite deliberate.

25. *Zhì-shǒu kě rè shì jué-lún*
    Toast-hands could-be warmed-at power without-a-match

26. *Shèn-mò jìn-qián chéng-xiàng chēn*
    Mind-don't approach-before Prime-Minister's anger

Chēn literally means 'an angry glance'. The implication is that Yang Kuo-chung is so powerful and so vengeful that a single angry look from him could spell one's doom.

TRANSLATION

'Ballad of Lovely Women'

On the day of the Spring Festival, under a new, fresh sky, by the lakeside in Ch'ang-an are many lovely women. Their breeding and refinement can be seen in their elegant deportment and proud aloofness. All have the same delicate complexions and exquisitely proportioned figures. In the late spring air the peacocks in *passement* of gold thread and unicorns of silver thread glow on their dresses of embroidered silk. What do they wear on their heads? Bandeaux of kingfisher-feather jewellery which reach down to the front edges of their hair. And what do we see at their backs? Overskirts of pearl net, clinging to their graceful bodies.

Amongst these ladies are to be seen the relations of the Mistress of the Cloud Curtains and the Pepper-flower Apartments, ladies dignified by imperial favour with titles that were once the names of great states: Kuo and Ch'in. Purple camel-humps rise like hillocks from green-glazed cauldrons, and fish with gleaming scales are served on crystal dishes. But the chopsticks of rhinoceros-horn, sated with delicacies, are slow to begin their work, and the belled carving-knife which cuts those threadlike slices wastes its busy labours. Palace eunuchs gallop up in continuous succession, bearing delicacies from the imperial kitchens, the flying hooves of their horses seeming scarcely to touch the dust beneath them.

And now, with music of flutes and drums mournful enough to move the very gods, surrounded by a shoal of clients and followers, the very fountain-head of power, with what disdainful steps this last rider comes pacing! Arrived at the balustrade surrounding the pavilion, he dismounts and takes his place among the diners sitting on the patterned carpet. The willow-down falls like snow and settles on the white water-weed. A blue-bird flies off, bearing a lady's red handkerchief in its beak. He wields a power you could warm your hands against, a power unequalled by any other man: beware of pressing forward within range of the Chief Minister's displeasure!

4

月夜

Yuè-yè

今夜鄜州月

1. Jīn-yè Fū-zhōu yuè,

閨中只獨看

2. Guī-zhōng zhǐ dú kān

遙憐小兒女

3. Yáo lián xiǎo ér-nǚ

未解憶長安

4. Wèi jiě yì Cháng-ān.

香霧雲鬟溼

5. Xiāng wù yún-huán shī

清輝玉臂寒

6. Qīng huī yù-bì hán.

何時倚虛幌

7. Hé-shí yǐ xū huǎng,

雙照淚痕乾

8. Shuāng zhào lèi-hén gān?

TITLE AND SUBJECT

Yuè means 'moon'; *yè* means 'night'.

Yuè-yè, therefore, is 'Night of Moon' or 'Moonlit Night'.

In order to understand the circumstances in which this poem came to be written, it is necessary to know quite a lot about the history of this period and the part that Tu Fu played during it.

On 17 December 755, two and a half years after the date of the last poem, An Lu-shan, the illiterate barbarian soldier who in 751, as trusted favourite of the Emperor and protégé of the dictator Li Lin-fu, had become Military Governor over the whole eastern half of the northern frontier of China, raised the standard of revolt in Fan-yang (near present-day Peking), ostensibly to 'punish' his rival, the Chief Minister, Yang Kuo-chung. When T'ung-kuan, the pass controlling the approaches to the capital, was captured by a rebel army in July 756, the Emperor and his immediate entourage slipped out of the city during the night, and Ch'ang-an shortly afterwards fell into enemy hands. At Ma-wei, about forty miles west of the capital, the Emperor's military escort mutinied, killing Yang Kuo-chung and demanding the death of Yang Kuei-fei, who was strangled in order to placate them.

On continuing his journey to his destination in Szechwan—refuge, it will be remembered, of the Chinese Government throughout most of the Second World War—the Emperor, in response to popular representations, left the Crown Prince behind him to organize resistance in the North. In early August, while his father was still making his way down to Ch'eng-tu, the Crown Prince set up court at Ling-wu beyond the Great Wall, more than four hundred miles north-west of Ch'ang-an. Shortly afterwards he was proclaimed Emperor, the Imperial Seal was sent to him from Szechwan, and historians record the beginning of a new reign, that of the Emperor Su-tsung.

About the time when the T'ung-kuan pass fell, Tu Fu, who at forty-four, after long years of unemployment, had just received a small appointment in the capital, appears to have been visiting his wife and children at a place near Feng-hsien, eighty miles north of Ch'ang-an, where they were living in great poverty. Military operations made it impossible for him to return to the capital, and after its fall and the setting up of a new Imperial government at Ling-wu, he seems to have decided to move his family to a place of greater safety and from there make his own way north and offer his services to the Crown Prince. After a nightmarish journey made mostly on foot, leading and carrying their hungry children through country infested with marauding bands of rebels, Tu Fu and his wife finally reached Fu-chou, some 130 miles north of Feng-hsien.

When he had deposited his family in Fu-chou, Tu Fu, disguised as a peasant, began the long journey north-west to Ling-wu, but on the way was captured by a band of rebel soldiers. Probably used by them as a porter to carry the forage or loot which had no doubt been the object of their expedition, he would appear to have been released when the party reached its destination in Ch'ang-an; for although, like other residents of the occupied city, he was not at liberty to leave it, he does not seem to have been harmed or imprisoned, which he certainly would have been if he had been identified as an official and a partisan of the Imperial government. It is not known where or how he lived in the occupied city during the several months which elapsed before he succeeded in making his escape from it, but one would assume that he found some relation or friend with whom to stay.

This poem was probably written in September 756, a month or two after Tu Fu's forcible re-entry into Ch'ang-an. The Mid-Autumn Festival fell in mid September that year. This is a festival traditionally celebrated by eating 'moon-cakes' and crabs and drinking wine and, of course, looking at the moon, and tends to be a family affair. The sight of the full moon on this occasion would therefore lend an added poignancy to Tu Fu's feelings of anxiety and nostalgia, and he could be almost certain that his wife would be looking at it too and experiencing the same feelings. There is nothing to indicate that the poem was in fact written on the night of the festival, or even that it was written at the full moon; but the assumption he makes in it that his wife would be watching too does make it seem rather probable.

FORM

This is a pentasyllabic poem in Regulated Verse. I propose not to explain the complicated rules of euphony which govern the pattern of tones which have to be used in writing this kind of verse, for the simple reason that the tones of Modern Chinese are often not the same as the ones used in Tu Fu's day. One of the rules is that the rhyme—which must be the same throughout the poem—must always come on a syllable with a level tone. The rhymes of this poem are still recognizable as rhymes in Modern Chinese, but they are no longer all level-tone syllables: *ān* and *gān* in lines 4 and 8 are level-tone syllables, but *kàn* and *hán* in lines 2 and 6 are not.

The rules that we do need to remember when reading poems in Regulated Verse are (1) that the poem must be one of eight lines in four couplets; and (2) that the two middle couplets (lines 3–4 and lines 5–6) must each be antithetically arranged: i.e. line 4 must parallel line 3 in both grammar and meaning, and line 6 must parallel line 5 in the same way.

Having said that, one has at once to observe that great poets do not always bother about the rules quite as much as their admirers and imitators; and this poem is in fact a rare exception to the general Rule of Parallelism in not having any antithesis in the second couplet (lines 3–4).

EXEGESIS

1. *Jīn-yè Fū-zhōu yuè*
   To-night Fu-chou moon

2. *Guī-zhōng zhǐ dú kàn*
   My-wife can-only alone watch

   Guī-zhōng, literally 'in the women's apartments', is a synonym for 'wife'. According to the traditional Chinese way of thinking, a wife is the 'person inside'.

3. *Yáo lián xiǎo ér-nǚ*
   Distant sorry-for little sons-daughters

4. *Wèi jiě yì Cháng-ān*
   Not-yet understand remember Ch'ang-an

   Cháng-ān: used by metonymy for Tu Fu himself: 'me in Ch'ang-an'.

5. *Xiāng wù yún-huán shī*
   Fragrant mist cloud-hair wet

6. *Qīng huī yù-bì hán*
   Clear light jade-arms cold

Xiāng wù: 'fragrant mist' is, of course, a poetic conceit. It is the woman's hair which is fragrant and which imparts some of its fragrance to the mist.

Yún 'cloudlike' and *yù* 'jadelike' are stock epithets for women's hair and arms.

Notice the parallelism in this couplet: 'fragrant mist' parallels 'clear light', 'cloud hair' parallels 'jade arms', and 'wet' parallels 'cold'.

7. *Hé-shí yǐ xū huǎng*
   What-time lean empty curtain

8. *Shuāng zhào lèi-hén gān*
   Double-shine tear-marks dry

Yǐ xū huǎng, literally 'lean at the empty curtain', presumably means lean on the open casement from which the curtains have been drawn back.

The *shuāng zhào* of line 8 contrasts with the *dú kàn* of line 2.

The picture which this last couplet is meant to convey is of Tu Fu and his wife leaning side by side at the open window and gazing up at the moon while the tears of happiness slowly dry on their cheeks.

TRANSLATION

'Moonlit Night'

Tonight in Fu-chou my wife will be watching this moon alone. I think with tenderness of my far-away little ones, too young to understand about their father in Ch'ang-an. My wife's soft hair must be wet from the scented night-mist, and her white arms chilled by the cold moonlight. When shall we lean on the open casement together and gaze at the moon until the tears on our cheeks are dry?

5

哀王孫
Āi wáng-sūn

長安城頭頭白烏

1. *Cháng-ān chéng-tóu tóu-bái wū,*

夜飛延秋門上呼

2. *Yè fēi Yán-qiū-mén-shàng hū.*

又向人家啄大屋

3. *Yòu xiàng rén-jiā zhuó dà-wū,*

屋底達官走避胡

4. *Wū-dǐ dá-guān zǒu bì hú.*

金鞭斷折九馬死

5. *Jīn biān duàn-zhé jiǔ mǎ sǐ,*

骨肉不得同馳驅

6. *Gǔ-ròu bū-dé tóng chí-qū.*

腰下寶玦青珊瑚

7. *Yāo-xià bǎo-jué qīng shān-hú,*

可憐王孫泣路隅

8. *Kě-lián wáng-sūn qì lù-yú.*

問 之 不 肯 道 姓 名

9. *Wèn zhī bù-kěn dào xìng-míng,*

但 道 困 苦 乞 為 奴

10. *Dàn dào kùn-kǔ qǐ wéi nú.*

巳 經 百 日 竄 荆 棘

11. *Yǐ-jīng bǎi-rì cuàn jīng-jí,*

身 上 無 有 完 肌 膚

12. *Shēn-shàng wú-yǒu wán jī-fū.*

高 帝 子 孫 盡 隆 準

13. *Gāo-dì zǐ-sūn jìn lóng-zhǔn,*

龍 種 自 與 常 人 殊

14. *Lóng-zhǒng zì yǔ cháng-rén shū.*

豺 狼 在 邑 龍 在 野

15. *Chái-láng zài yì lóng zài yě,*

王 孫 善 保 千 金 軀

16. *Wáng-sūn shàn bǎo qiān-jīn qū!*

不 敢 長 語 臨 交 衢

17. *Bù-gǎn cháng-yǔ lín jiāo-qú,*

且 為 王 孫 立 斯 須

18. *Qiě wèi wáng-sūn lì sī-xū.*

昨夜東風吹血腥

19. *Zuó-yè dōng-fēng chuī xuè-xīng,*

東來橐駝滿舊都

20. *Dōng-lái tuó-tuó mǎn jiù-dū.*

朔方健兒好身手

21. *Shuò-fāng jiàn-ér hǎo shēn-shǒu,*

昔何勇銳今何愚

22. *Xī hé yǒng-ruì jīn hé yú!*

竊聞天子巳傳位

23. *Qiè-wén tiān-zǐ yǐ chuán-wèi,*

聖德北服南單于

24. *Shèng-dé běi fú Nán-chán-yú,*

花門剺面請雪恥

25. *Huā-mén lí-miàn qǐng xuě-chǐ.*

慎勿出口他人狙

26. *Shèn-wù chū-kǒu tā-rén jū!*

哀哉王孫慎勿疏

27. *Āi-zāi wáng-sūn shèn-wù shū!*

五陵佳氣無時無

28. *Wǔ-líng jiā-qì wú-shí wú!*

TITLE AND SUBJECT

Āi means 'mourn', 'lament', 'grieve for'.

Wáng-sūn literally 'king's grandson': here 'young prince'.

Āi wáng-sūn therefore means 'Lamenting a Young Prince'; but in the light of what I have said on page 2, I propose to translate it 'The Unfortunate Prince'.

Tu Fu wrote this poem in occupied Ch'ang-an, probably in October 756, a month or so after the date of the last poem.

In July 756 the rebel leader An Lu-shan sent his lieutenant Sun Hsiao-che to Ch'ang-an to supervise the conveyance to his headquarters at Fan-yang of everything of value that could still be looted from the imperial palaces, parks, and treasuries. The eunuchs, officials, and palace ladies who had remained in the city were rounded up and sent under military escort to Loyang in batches of several hundred at a time, and the families of princes, officials, and high-ranking officers who had accompanied the Emperor in his flight were hunted down and massacred, down to the smallest infant.

In mid August Sun Hsiao-che received further orders from his master enjoining him to execute the Princess of Huo and various other royal ladies and their consorts who were being held in custody in Ch'ang-an. The executions were carried out publicly, the hearts of the condemned being torn from their bodies and offered in sacrifice to the ghost of An Ch'ing-tsung, a son of An Lu-shan who had been married to a princess of the imperial family, and whom the Emperor had put to death as a reprisal when An Lu-shan rebelled. Eighty-three of the partisans of Yang Kuo-chung and other persons especially obnoxious to An Lu-shan were also publicly executed, some of them by having the tops of their heads prised off with iron claws. The street in the Ch'ung-jen Ward where the executions were carried out ran with blood.

It is quite possible that Tu Fu may have been a witness of this butchery. In any case, this account of his encounter in a Ch'ang-an street with a terrified young prince must be read in the light of the above events. The young prince was one of the many members of the imperial family who, because they did not live inside the Palace City or did not happen to be there on the night of 13 July, were simply abandoned by the fleeing court. He had gone into hiding in the countryside outside Ch'ang-an, or perhaps in one of its parks, and had emerged on to the streets in order to look for food and to find out what had been happening during the weeks he had lain concealed.

To Tu Fu, and no doubt to many others, it was a source of indignation that persons of ignoble birth like Yang Kuo-chung and his cousins should have been chosen to attend the Emperor in his precipitate flight while princes and princesses of the blood were callously left behind to face the cruel rage of the rebels.

In order to enhance the pathos of the prince's predicament, Tu Fu assigns himself a very unflattering role in this poetic record of his encounter. He appears first of all as rather pleased with himself for having spotted, from the T'ang equivalent of the 'Hapsburg lip', a member of the imperial family; then rather proud to be talking to a real prince; then scared for his own safety; then garrulously retailing the rumours, which in an enemy-occupied city must pass for news; and then apparently abandoning him, after a lot of completely valueless admonitions, to fend for himself. There is no evidence in the poem that the assistance of which the unfortunate prince was so manifestly in need was forthcoming.

Of course, there is no reason to suppose that Tu Fu really behaved like this in the encounter, or even that the encounter really took place—though I should guess that he *was* inspired to write this poem by an actual experience of the kind he describes. The point is that Tu Fu is perfectly capable of *inventing* an unsympathetic first person if he can make a more effective poem by doing so. In this poem the timid, selfish, self-important, garrulous, clucking interlocutor tells us far more about the prince and his predicament and the state of affairs inside the occupied city than a wholly noble and wholly sympathetic one would have done. This is a device which was several times made use of by Browning—though in Browning we tend to learn more about the anonymous 'I' than about the nominal subject of the poem.

FORM

This heptasyllabic 'Old Style' poem is usually classified as a poem in ballad style, though bearing no relation to either the words or the tune of any existing ballad. The dialogue which is really a monologue, and the iteration (*tóu* in line 1 and *wū* in lines 3 and 4) are, of course, features of ballad style.

Note that the same rhyme is sustained throughout the whole of this longish poem—altogether eighteen times. This is by no means unusual in Chinese poetry, in which a sequence of thirty instances of the same rhyme can be achieved with comparative ease.

EXEGESIS

1. *Cháng-ān chéng-tóu tóu-bái wū*
   Ch'ang-an wall-top white-headed crows

2. *Yè fēi Yán-qiū-mén-shàng hū*
   Night fly Welcome-autumn-gate-over caw

The sixth-century rebel Hou Ching succeeded for a time in usurping the power of the Liang emperors who reigned in Nanking. Flocks of 'white-headed' (i.e. hooded) crows made an ominous appearance above the south gate of the Palace City at the time of his usurpation. Tu Fu is making use of this historical tale when he imagines hooded crows coming as messengers of doom to warn the Emperor and his courtiers of the impending fall of Ch'ang-an to the forces of the rebel An Lu-shan.

The *Yán-qiū-mén* was the west gate of the Imperial Park which lay outside the western city wall of Ch'ang-an. 'Welcoming Autumn', because autumn is associated with the west, just as spring is with the east, winter with the north, and summer with the south. It was through this gate that the Emperor and his entourage made their getaway just before dawn on 14 July 756.

Notice that in Chinese verse it is usually the *couplets* not the *lines* which are end-stopped. Translators often come unstuck through ignorance of this simple rule. Here line 1 is the subject of a sentence whose verbs are in line 2. I say 'usually' because many exceptions will be found in Old Style verse. There is in fact an exception, as will be seen later, in lines 23–25 of this poem.

3. *Yòu xiàng rén-jiā zhuó dà-wū*
   Also go-towards people's-households peck-at great roofs

4. *Wū-dǐ dá-guān zǒu bì hú*
   Roof-beneath high-officials run escape barbarians.

Dá-guān: e.g. Yang Kuo-chung.

5. *Jīn biān duàn-zhé jiǔ mǎ sǐ*
   Gold whip broken-in-two nine horses die

6. *Gǔ-ròu bū-dé tóng chí-qū*
   Bones-flesh not-able together gallop

Jiǔ mǎ: the number of horses involved in the Emperor's flight was more like nine hundred than nine. The 'nine horses' here is an allusion to the story of the race to Ch'ang-an in time to be proclaimed Emperor of the Prince of Tai, known in history as Emperor Wen of the Han dynasty, in the second century B.C.

There is an implied reproach in this couplet. Horse after horse from the imperial stables dropped exhausted beneath the flailing whips of the flying ministers, yet there were supposed not to have been enough horses to take members of the imperial family like the unfortunate prince of the title.

Gǔ-ròu, literally 'bone and flesh', is the Chinese equivalent of our 'flesh and blood' in expressions like 'his own flesh and blood turned against him'.

7. *Yāo-xià bǎo-jué qīng shān-hú*
   Waist-below precious-*chüeh* blue coral

8. *Kě-lián wáng-sūn qì lù-yú*
   Pitiful prince weeps road-corner

Jué in this context means a C-shaped disk of jade or nephrite suspended from the belt as an ornament. The 'blue coral' presumably refers to another ornament that he is wearing. It would have been more prudent to hide these objects, under the circumstances; but a certain amount of dim helplessness would no doubt have been expected of royal personages deprived of their servants. The prince, for example, would probably have been quite incapable of dressing himself without assistance.

9. *Wèn zhī bù-kěn dào xìng-míng*
   Ask him not-willing tell surname-name

10. *Dàn dào kùn-kǔ qǐ wéi nú*
    Only tells distress begs become slave

11. *Yǐ-jīng bǎi-rì cuàn jīng-jí*
    Already hundred-days lie-low-in thorn-bushes

12. *Shēn-shàng wú-yǒu wán jī-fū*
    Body-on not-have whole skin

This couplet continues to report what the prince said. The character for *cuàn* represents a rat in a hole.

Shēn-shàng: the reader will no doubt have deduced by now that the Chinese equivalent of our prepositions is very often a word which comes *after* the noun, e.g. line 2 *Yán-qiū-mén-shàng* 'over the Gate of Autumn', line 4 *wū-dǐ* 'below the roof', line 7 *yāo-xià* 'below (i.e. 'at') the waist'. Compare also No. 3, line 2 *shǔi-biān* 'beside the water' and line 7 in the same poem *tóu-shàng* 'on the head'. Strictly speaking these words are nouns. The Chinese way of saying 'There are books on the table' is 'Table-top has books'.

13. *Gāo-dì zǐ-sūn jìn lóng-zhǔn*
    Kao-tsu's sons-grandsons all aquiline-noses

14. *Lóng-zhǒng zì yǔ cháng-rén shū*
    Dragon-seed naturally from ordinary-men different

Kao-tsu, or Kao-ti (*Gāo-dì*) was the founder of the Han dynasty, and his *lóng-zhǔn* was one of his distinctive features. But there is no suggestion here that the T'ang house was descended from the ruling house of Han. This is simply another instance of the familiar convention already encountered in No. 2 whereby a Han parallel is regularly employed by a T'ang poet when he wishes to speak of the T'ang sovereign or his family or affairs. The nominal founder of the T'ang dynasty was as a matter of fact also called Kao-tsu, but I don't think he had a particularly famous nose.

In this couplet the poet is addressing himself or the reader.

15. *Chái-láng zài yì lóng zài yě*
    Jackals-wolves in city dragon in wilds

16. *Wáng-sūn shàn bǎo qiān-jīn qū*
    Prince take good care of thousand-tael body

The jackals and wolves symbolize the rebels who are in control of the capital; the dragon symbolizes the Emperor who has fled into the 'wilds'.

Qiān-jīn qū: i.e. 'your precious person'. *Jīn* 'metal' without any qualifying word anciently meant bronze. In Tu Fu's time, however, when used in connexion with price or value, it frequently stands for ounces or 'taels' of silver, the metal mainly used for making large purchases with.
This couplet and all the rest of the poem is addressed to the prince.

17. *Bù-gǎn cháng-yǔ lín jiāo-qú*
    Not-dare long-talk overlooking cross-roads
18. *Qiě wèi wáng-sūn lì sī-xū*
    Will-however for-sake-of prince stand just-a-moment

19. *Zuó-yè dōng-fēng chuī xuè-xīng*
    Last-night east-wind blew blood-stink
20. *Dōng-lái tuó-tuó mǎn jiù-dū*
    From-the-east camels filled late-capital

The camels, as explained above, were sent to Ch'ang-an by An Lu-shan to carry off the loot of the imperial treasuries.
Jiù-dū: Ch'ang-an was no longer the capital under the rebel régime, whilst from a loyalist point of view the capital was where the Emperor happened to be.

21. *Shuò-fāng jiàn-ér hǎo shēn-shǒu*
    The Shuo-fang veterans were-good-at military-skills
22. *Xī hé yǒng-ruì jīn hé yú*
    Formerly how bold-and-keen now how foolish

Shuo-fang was the name of the frontier command immediately to the north of the metropolitan area, comprising the territories inside and to the north of the great 'Ordos loop' of the Yellow River. The reference here is to the army raised for the defence of the T'ung-kuan pass, the key to the capital, under Ko-shu Han, famous T'ang general of foreign extraction who was called out of semi-retirement at the time of the An Lu-shan rebellion to command the Imperial troops. Ko-shu Han was an invalid, having ruined his health by drinking and dissipation; but he might have held T'ung-kuan if the intrigues of jealous courtiers, particularly

Yang Kuo-chung, had not driven him into an offensive which he knew to be unwise. Under the circumstances, Tu Fu's irony seems a trifle misplaced. But one must remember that at the time he probably knew far less about the true circumstances surrounding the fall of T'ung-kuan than we do today.

23. *Qiè-wén tiān-zǐ yǐ chuán-wèi*
    I-have-heard-that Son-of-Heaven has-already abdicated

24. *Shèng-dé běi fú Nán-chán-yú*
    Imperial-virtue in-the-north has-won-over Southern-ch'an-yü

25. *Huā-mén lí-miàn qǐng xuě-chǐ*
    Hua-men gashed faces begged wipe-out-disgrace

26. *Shèn-wù chū-kǒu tā-rén jū*
    Mind-don't utter some-one-else lie-in-wait

Qiè-wén, literally 'furtively heard', is polite language for 'I hear that'. The honorifics and humilifics in which Chinese speech once abounded are not, of course, to be translated literally unless one is deliberately aiming at an exotic, 'Kai Lung' effect. The rest of line 23 and the whole of lines 24 and 25 are all the object of *qiè-wén*. This is therefore one of the exceptions, found in Old Style but not in Regulated Verse, as already stated above, to the rule that the couplet in Chinese verse is end-stopped.

Tiān-zǐ 'Son of Heaven' was an archaic title of the Chinese emperors. Sometimes they are referred to in ancient texts as 'Heavenly King'.

Nán-chán-yú: *'ch'an-yü'* was the title of the Hunnish kings who ruled over the steppelands north of China at the time of the Han dynasty. About the beginning of the Christian era these Huns had divided into a northern and a southern group, each with its own *ch'an-yü*, and in A.D. 49 the *ch'an-yü* of the southern group made his submission to the Han emperor. Here we have yet another instance of the convention whereby Han equivalents were used by T'ang poets when they were speaking of contemporary events. The southern *ch'an-yü* stands for the Uighur khan, whose help as an ally was in large measure responsible for the eventual defeat of the rebel forces by the Imperial army. When Hsüan-tsung took leave of the Crown Prince before continuing his flight into Szechwan, he recommended him to seek Uighur help; and it was the Uighurs who, in their camp at Hua-men, responded to the appeal of Su-tsung's envoy by slashing their faces and vowing their devotion to the Chinese Emperor.

Shèng-dé: literally 'sacred virtue'. It was a convention of Chinese court language that barbarian tribes were subdued not by force of arms or costly bribes, but by moral power personally exercised by the Emperor.

27. *Āi-zāi wáng-sūn shèn-wù shū*
Alas prince mind-don't be-remiss

28. *Wǔ-líng jiā-qì wú-shí wú*
Five-mounds lucky-emanation no-time not-be-there

Wǔ-líng, the 'Five Tumuli', were the tombs of the early Han emperors. Subsequently the name Wu-ling was given to the fashionable suburb which grew up in the place where they were situated. Here the Han term is used for a T'ang parallel: it refers to the tombs of the early T'ang emperors. Tu Fu means, 'Wherever you go, may the spirits of your imperial ancestors watch over you!'

TRANSLATION

'The Unfortunate Prince'

Hooded crows from the battlements of Ch'ang-an flew cawing by night over the Gate of Autumn and thence to the homes of men, pecking at the great roofs, warning the high ministers who dwelt beneath to flee from the barbarian. Golden whips were flailed until they snapped and the royal horses sank dead with exhaustion beneath them; but many of the Emperor's own close kin were unable to gallop with him.

With a precious jade emblem and blue coral pendant at his waist, a pitiful young prince stands weeping at the corner of the street. Questioned, he is unwilling to tell me his name; he will only say that he is in great distress, and begs me to take him as my slave. He has already been lying in concealment for a hundred days amongst the thorn-bushes and has not a whole piece of skin on his body; but descendants of the August Emperor all have the imperial nose; the Seed of the Dragon are not as other men are.

Wolves and jackals now occupy the city; the dragons are out in the wilds: Your Highness must take care of his precious person! I dare not talk very long with you here beside the crossroads, but I will stand with Your Highness just a little while.

Last night the east wind carried a stench of blood and the 'former capital' was full of camels from the east. The Shuo-fang veterans were splendid soldiers. How bold and keen they were a while ago, and how foolish they look today! I've heard tell that the Son of Heaven has abdicated. And they say that in the North the Khan is so indebted for the favours shown him by his Sacred Majesty that at Hua-men he and all his warriors slashed their faces and vowed to wipe out this humiliation. But we must mind what we say, with so many spies about. Alas, poor prince! Be on your guard! May the protecting power that emanates from the Imperial Tombs go always with you!

6

春望

Chūn wàng

國破山河在
1. Guó pò shān-hé zài,

城春草木深
2. Chéng chūn cǎo-mù shēn.

感時花濺淚
3. Gǎn shí huā jiàn lèi,

恨別鳥驚心
4. Hèn bié niǎo jīng xīn

烽火連三月
5. Fēng-huǒ lián sān yuè,

家書抵萬金
6. Jiā-shū dǐ wàn jīn.

白頭搔更短
7. Bái tóu sāo gèng duǎn,

渾欲不勝簪
8. Hún yù bù-shēng zān.

6. *Spring Scene*

TITLE AND SUBJECT

Chūn means 'spring'.

Wàng, as in the first poem in this selection, means 'gaze at'.

Chūn wàng is 'Spring Gazing': i.e. 'View in Spring' or 'Spring Scene'.

This poem was written in occupied Ch'ang-an in the spring of 757, half a year after Tu Fu's encounter with the hunted prince. Its occasion may well have been a walk in the deserted Serpentine Park, which is the subject of the next poem in this book. From contemplation of public disasters—so much in contrast with the joyful exuberance of the season—Tu Fu turns to contemplation of his personal griefs and worries.

Note the skilful way in which this poem exploits the ambivalence of its images. It is stated

(1) that nature, continuing unchangingly in its annual cycle, is indifferent to human sorrows and disasters;

(2) that, on the contrary, nature is grieving in sympathy with the beholder at the ills which beset him.

The propositions stating this thesis and antithesis are themselves couplets containing antithetical lines. It is partly this involutedness which gives Chinese poetry the extraordinary richness of texture we sometimes find in it.

Notice also the sudden shifting of mood which takes place in the poem. The sombre anguish of the first part ends, as the tragic figure of the opening lines turns into a comic old man going bald on top, on a note of playful self-mockery which is nevertheless infinitely pathetic.

FORM

This is a formally perfect example of a pentasyllabic poem in Regulated Verse. Not only the middle couplets, but the first couplet, too, contain verbal parallelism. It is amazing that Tu Fu is able to use so immensely stylized a form in so natural a manner. The tremendous spring-like compression which is achieved by using very simple language with very complicated forms manipulated in so skilful a manner that they don't show is characteristic of Regulated Verse at its best. Its perfection of form lends it a classical grace which unfortunately cannot be communicated in translation. That is the reason why Tu Fu, one of the great masters of this form, makes so comparatively poor a showing in foreign languages.

EXEGESIS

1. *Guó pò shān-hé zài*
   State ruined mountains-rivers survive

2. *Chéng chūn cǎo-mù shēn*
   City spring grass-trees thick

3. *Gǎn shí hūa jiàn lèi*
   Moved-by times flowers sprinkle tears

4. *Hèn bié niǎo jīng xīn*
   Hating separation birds startle heart

Since this is a poem in Regulated Verse, every word and every phrase in this and the following couplet must be arranged antithetically. Notice the skill with which monotony is avoided by a change of grammatical construction. In this couplet the subjects ('flowers', 'birds') come in the third place in the line, whilst in the following couplet the compound subjects ('beacon-fires', 'letter from home') come at the beginning of the line.

5. *Fēng-huǒ lián sān yuè*
   Beacon-fires have-continued-for three months

6. *Jiā-shū dǐ wàn jīn*
   Home-letter worth ten-thousand taels

In our own history beacons were generally used in order to give warning of invasion. The Chinese used them a good deal in time of emergency, however, as a routine means of maintaining contact between garrisons. For example, two garrisons established at a distance of ten miles apart would light a beacon every evening, and each would know that the other was all right if it saw the fire burning at the appointed hour. To say that the beacons have been burning for three months running is therefore only another way

6. *Spring Scene*

of saying that a state of military emergency has existed throughout that time.

7. *Bái tóu sāo gèng duǎn*
   White hair scratch even shorter
8. *Hún yù bù-shēng zān*
   Quite will-be unequal-to hatpin

Until their conquest by the Manchus in the seventeenth century, the Chinese, like the Japanese and Koreans and other Far Eastern peoples, dressed their hair in a top-knot on the crown of the head. Their hats, like those of our grandmothers, were anchored to their heads by large hatpins which passed through the knot of hair.

TRANSLATION
'Spring Scene'

The state may fall, but the hills and streams remain. It is spring in the city: grass and leaves grow thick. The flowers shed tears of grief for the troubled times, and the birds seem startled, as if with the anguish of separation. For three months continuously the beacon-fires have been burning. A letter from home would be worth a fortune. My white hair is getting so scanty from worried scratching that soon there won't be enough to stick my hatpin in!

7

哀江頭
Āi jiāng-tóu

少陵野老吞聲哭
1. Shào-líng yě-lǎo tūn-shēng kū,

春日潛行曲江曲
2. Chūn-rì qián-xíng Qū-jiāng qū.

江頭宮殿鎖千門
3. Jiāng-tóu gōng-diàn suǒ qiān mén,

細柳新蒲為誰綠
4. Xì liǔ xīn pú wèi shuí lǜ?

憶昔霓旌下南苑
5. Yì xī ní-jīng xià Nán-yuàn,

苑中萬物生顏色
6. Yuàn-zhōng wàn-wù shēng yán-sè.

昭陽殿裏第一人
7. Zhāo-yáng-diàn-lǐ dì-yī rén,

同輦隨君侍君側
8. Tóng-niǎn suí jūn shì jūn cè.

輦前才人帶弓箭

9. *Niǎn-qián cái-rén dài gōng-jiàn,*

白馬嚼齧黃金勒

10. *Bái mǎ jué-niè huáng-jīn lè;*

翻身向天仰射雲

11. *Fān-shēn xiàng tiān yǎng shè yún,*

一笑正墜雙飛翼

12. *Yí xiào zhèng zhuì shuāng fēi yì.*

明眸皓齒今何在

13. *Míng-móu hào-chǐ jīn hé zài?*

血污遊魂歸不得

14. *Xuè-wū yóu-hún guī-bù-dé.*

清渭東流劍閣深

15. *Qīng Wèi dōng liú Jiàn-gé shēn,*

去住彼此無消息

16. *Qù zhù bǐ-cǐ wú xiāo-xī.*

人生有情淚霑臆

17. *Rén-shēng yǒu qíng lèi zhān yì,*

江水江花豈終極

18. *Jiāng-shuǐ jiāng-huā qǐ zhōng jí?*

黄 昏 胡 騎 塵 滿 城

19. *Huáng-hūn hú-jì chén mǎn chéng,*

欲 往 城 南 望 城 北

20. *Yù wǎng chéng-nán wàng chéng-běi.*

TITLE AND SUBJECT

Jiāng-tóu: 'river-side'. The 'river' is the *Qū-jiāng* of line 2—the Serpentine lake of Ch'ang-an's main park.

For *āi* 'lamenting', 'grieving at' see the explanation of *Āi wáng-sūn* on page 36. For some reason 'Lament fór the Serpentine' strikes me as comical and I propose to translate this title simply as 'By the Lake'.

This poem was written in the spring of 757 about the same time as 'Spring Scene' (No. 6)—possibly even on the same occasion. Tu Fu has slipped into the deserted park. As he glides furtively along its walks, past the desolate, shuttered palaces that line the waterside, he thinks of the gay and jostling scenes—like the one so brilliantly described in the 'Ballad of Lovely Women' (No. 3)— witnessed so often in the park at this time of year, and he thinks of the tragedy at Ma-wei in which all the light-hearted extravagance of those days has ended. Tears fill his eyes, and he hurries back to his lodgings in the gathering dusk.

FORM

This is written in the ballad style, like No. 5, which has a similar title. Instances of the iteration which so often occurs in this kind of poetry are to be found in line 2 (*Qū* . . . *qū*), in lines 5 and 6 (*yuàn*), in line 18 (*jiāng* . . . *jiāng* . . .), and in line 20 (*chéng* . . . *chéng* . . .).

The rhyme-scheme is more interesting than the Modern Chinese phonology I have used in transliterating these poems allows it to appear. Actually the same rhyme is sustained from line 5 to the end of the poem (*sè, cè, lè, yì, dé,* etc.), whilst lines 1–4 have a different rhyme (*kū, qū, lù*). A change of rhyme often accompanies some important break in the meaning. Here I think it is used because lines 1–4 are a sort of verse introduction to the main part of the poem. It is even possible that lines 5–20 may have been the original poem to which Tu Fu later added lines 1–4 as an afterthought. At least three poems in his collected works begin with the words *Yì xí*, and this may have been a fourth.

EXEGESIS

1. *Shào-líng yě-lǎo tūn-shēng kū*
   Shao-ling old-countryman swallowing-sound weeps

2. *Chūn-rì qián-xíng Qū-jiāng qū*
   Spring-day secretly-walks Serpentine's bends

Shao-ling was the name of a hill in Tu-ling, a village in the neighbourhood of Ch'ang-an in which Tu Fu had acquired some land five or six years before the date of this poem.

3. *Jiāng-tóu gōng-diàn suǒ qiān mén*
   River-side palaces have-locked thousand doors

4. *Xì liǔ xīn pú wèi shuí lǜ*
   Tender willows new rushes for whom are-green

Xì literally means 'thin', 'fine'. Tu Fu is referring to the long, thin, yellowish shoots which trail from weeping willows in the spring-time.

5. *Yì xī ní-jīng xià Nán-yuàn*
   I remember formerly rainbow-banner descending-to South-park

6. *Yuàn-zhōng wàn-wù shēng yán-sè*
   Park-within all-things put-forth colour

Ní-jīng: the rainbow-coloured banner borne before the Emperor's litter, here used by metonymy for the Emperor and his train.

Nán-yuàn refers to the Lotus Pool Garden adjacent on the south side to the park of the Serpentine.

Wàn-wù: literally 'the ten thousand creatures', which includes human beings. Here it obviously refers to the flora of the park.

7. *Zhāo-yáng-diàn-lǐ dì-yī rén*
   Chao-yang-palace-in number-one person

8. *Tóng-niǎn suí jūn shì jūn cè*
   Same-carriage attend lord serve-at lord's side

The First Lady of the Chao-yang Palace was Lady Flying Swallow, the favourite, and subsequently the Empress, of Emperor Ch'eng of the Han dynasty who reigned from 32 to 7 B.C. Tu Fu and his contemporaries used her name in their verses as a substitute when they wanted to refer to Yang Kuei-fei. The substitution was made more piquant by the fact that Yang Kuei-fei was plump and curvaceous, like the favourites of Charles II, whilst Flying Swallow had been extremely thin and frail.

It is a cardinal rule of Chinese grammar that the modifier precedes the thing it modifies. Here 'in the Chao-yang Palace' modifies 'number one person', so line 7 means 'the First Lady in (i.e. 'of') the Chao-yang Palace'.

9. *Niǎn-qián cái-rén dài gōng-jiàn*
   Carriage-before maids-of-honour carried bows-arrows

10. *Bái mǎ jué-niè huáng-jīn lè*
    White horses champed yellow-metal bridles

The 'yellow metal' is, of course, gold.

11. *Fān-shēn xiàng tiān yǎng shè yún*
    Bend-back-body face sky look-up shoot clouds

12. *Yí xiào zhèng zhuì shuāng fēi yì*
    One laugh fair-and-square bring-down pair-of flying wings

Yí xiào 'one laugh' is verbal: 'have a laugh'. The Modern Chinese equivalent would be *xiào-yí-xiào* 'laugh a laugh'. As a poetic conceit the 'one' or 'single' of *yí xiào* is contrasted with the 'double' or 'pair' of *shuāng fēi yì*; but this is a bit of word-play which cannot be reproduced in translation.

13. *Míng-móu hào-chǐ jīn hé zài*
    Bright-eyes gleaming-teeth now where are-they

14. *Xuè-wū yóu-hún guī-bù-dé*
    Blood-polluted wandering-soul return-not-able

Half a century of tooth-paste advertisement has made it impossible for us to admire a woman's teeth without risk of absurdity.

To the Chinese, however, a smile full of gleaming white teeth was, from ancient times, regarded as one of the most important marks of beauty in a woman.

Yang Kuei-fei's death was in point of fact a bloodless one. She was strangled in the courtyard of the Buddhist chapel at the post-station of Ma-wei, where the Emperor happened to be staying at the time of the army's mutiny. But the other members of her family met their ends in a more sanguinary fashion; and since she could be regarded as in some sense partly responsible for their deaths, it would be poetically justifiable to speak of her soul as being stained with the blood of others. A simpler explanation would be, of course, that Tu Fu had been misinformed about the manner of her death.

15. *Qīng Wèi dōng liú Jiàn-gé shēn*
　　 Clear Wei eastward flows Chien-ko is-remote

16. *Qù zhù bǐ-cǐ wú xiāo-xī*
　　 One-who-went one-who-stayed mutually have-not news

The waters of the river Wei flow eastward below the Ma-wei station where Yang Kuei-fei was buried. Chien-ko is the name of a dangerous pass in Szechwan which Hsüan-tsung traversed on his way to Ch'eng-tu.

The 'one who went' is the Emperor and the 'one who stayed' is Yang Kuei-fei.

17. *Rén-shēng yǒu qíng lèi zhān yì*
　　 Human-nature have feelings tears wet bosom

18. *Jiāng-shuǐ jiāng-huā qǐ zhōng-jí*
　　 River-water river-flowers how come-to-an-end

The 'river' is the Serpentine lake beside which Tu Fu is walking. Compare the *Jiāng* in the title of this poem.

In Chinese idiom a rhetorical question is often used where we should use a negative statement: 'will never come to an end' is the sense of *qǐ zhōng-jí*.

19. *Huáng-hūn hú-jì chén mǎn chéng*
　　 Twilight barbarian-horsemen's dust fills city

20. *Yù wǎng chéng-nán wàng chéng-běi*
　　 Want go-to city-south gaze-at city-north

Tu Fu's eyes turn northwards in the direction of the exiled court of Su-tsung, on which the loyalists pin all their hopes.

TRANSLATION

'By the Lake'

The old fellow from Shao-ling weeps with stifled sobs as he walks furtively by the bends of the Serpentine on a day in spring. In the waterside palaces the thousands of doors are locked. For whom have the willows and rushes put on their fresh greenery?

I remember how formerly, when the Emperor's rainbow banner made its way into the South Park, everything in the park seemed to bloom with a brighter colour. The First Lady of the Chao-yang Palace rode in the same carriage as her lord in attendance at his side, while before the carriage rode maids of honour equipped with bows and arrows, their white horses champing at golden bits. Leaning back, face skywards, they shot into the clouds; and the Lady laughed gaily when a bird fell to the ground transfixed by a well-aimed arrow. Where are the bright eyes and the flashing smile now? Tainted with blood-pollution, her wandering soul cannot make its way back. The clear waters of the Wei flow eastwards, and Chien-ko is far away: between the one who has gone and the one who remains no communication is possible. It is human to have feelings and to shed tears for such things; but the grasses and flowers of the lakeside go on for ever, unmoved. As evening falls, the city is full of the dust of foreign horsemen. My way is towards the South City, but my gaze turns northwards.

8

春宿左省

Chūn sù zuǒ-shěng

～～～～～～～～～～～～～～～

花隱掖垣暮

1. *Huā yǐn yì-yuán mù,*

啾啾棲鳥過

2. *Jiū-jiū xī niǎo guò.*

星臨萬戶動

3. *Xīng lín wàn-hù dòng,*

月傍九霄多

4. *Yuè bàng jiǔ-xiāo duō.*

不寢聽金鑰

5. *Bù-qǐn tīng jīn-yuè,*

因風想玉珂

6. *Yīn fēng xiǎng yù-kē.*

明朝有封事

7. *Míng-zhāo yǒu fēng-shì,*

數問夜如何

8. *Shuò wèn yè rú-hé.*

TITLE AND SUBJECT

Chūn: 'spring', as in the title of No. 6.

Sù: 'spend the night at'.

Zuŏ-shĕng literally means 'Department of the Left': i.e. the Imperial Chancellery, so called because of the position occupied by its offices inside the Palace City. The whole title therefore means, 'On spending a spring night in the Imperial Chancellery'.

This poem was written in the spring of 758, when Tu Fu was forty-six years old.

In the early summer of 757 Tu Fu had escaped from occupied Ch'ang-an and made his way a hundred miles west to Feng-hsiang, whither the Imperial court had moved in the spring of that year, appearing before the Emperor Su-tsung in hemp sandals and a gown which was out at elbow in both of its sleeves. Su-tsung rewarded him by appointing him a Remembrancer in the Imperial Chancellery.

The Chancellery's personnel comprised, in order of seniority, two Presidents, two Vice-Presidents, two Grand Counsellors, four Administrators, four Grand Secretaries, six Omissioners, and six Remembrancers. Tu Fu's position in it was therefore a fairly minor one.

In November 757, with the assistance of its Uighur allies, the Imperial army recaptured Ch'ang-an, and when the Emperor made his triumphal entry into the capital in early December amidst scenes of hysterical rejoicing, Tu Fu was a member of the entourage which accompanied him.

Theoretically a Remembrancer's functions were advisory: he was to *remind* the Emperor of the administrative duties he had overlooked; but by Tu Fu's time they were largely clerical and ceremonial. Tu Fu, however, took them very seriously, addressing frequent memoranda to the Emperor on matters of state, and no doubt getting himself thought of as an infernal nuisance.

The morning levée of the imperial court began at five or six in the morning, and the hundreds of officials who participated had to be dressed in their court robes and ready to take up their places long before it was daylight. In this poem Tu Fu shows himself spending the whole night in his office in order to make sure of presenting a memorial the next morning.

The poem begins in the lengthening shadows of evening, continues with the coming out of the stars and rising of the moon, and proceeds, in the short space of its eight lines, through the long watches of a sleepless night.

FORM

This is a pentasyllabic poem in Regulated Verse, like No. 4 and No. 6. Notice the parallelism in the two central couplets: 'stars' with 'moon', 'myriad' with 'nine', 'bronze' with 'jade', and so on. The point of the whole poem is revealed in the final couplet, a device commonly employed in Regulated Verse.

EXEGESIS

1. *Huā yīn yì-yuán mù*
   Blossom shaded inner-walls becomes-evening

2. *Jiū-jiū xī niǎo guò*
   Chirrup-chirruping roosting-birds pass

3. *Xīng lín wàn-hù dòng*
   Stars looking-down-on myriad-doors move

4. *Yuè pàng jiǔ-xiāo duō*
   Moon coming-beside ninefold-sky becomes-much

5. *Bù-qǐn tīng jīn-yuè*
   Not-sleep hear bronze-traceries

6. *Yīn fēng xiǎng yù-kē*
   Along wind imagine jade-bells

Jīn-yuè: decorative reinforcements of the palace doors, like the wrought-iron traceries which used to embellish the doors of churches and great houses in Europe; used here by metonymy for the doors themselves. Tu Fu imagines that he hears the opening of the great doors which separated the inner palace into which only the eunuchs might enter from the outer part in which were the halls of audience and the offices of the various secretariats. The ceremony of the morning levée began with their opening.

Yù-kē are the jade bridle-bells of officials arriving and dismounting on their way to the morning audience. Tu Fu imagines that he can hear this noise borne on the wind. What he really heard was doubtless the tinkling of the little bells which hung beneath the eaves of the palace roofs.

7. *Míng-zhāo yǒu fēng-shì*
   Tomorrow-morning have sealed-business

8. *Shuò wèn yè rú-hé*
   Frequently ask night like-what

Fēng-shì: Omissioners and Remembrancers could, if they had some very important or urgent matter to bring to the attention of the Emperor, step out of the ranks and make an oral submission at the audience. For less grave affairs they submitted written memoranda under a sealed cover. These were alluded to as *fēng-shì*— 'sealed affairs'.

TRANSLATION

'Spring Night in the Imperial Chancellery'

Evening falls on palace walls shaded by flowering trees, with cry of birds flying past on their way to roost. The stars quiver as they look down on the myriad doors of the palace, and the moon's light increases as she moves into the ninefold sky. Unable to sleep, I seem to hear the sound of the bronze-clad doors opening for the audience, or imagine the sound of bridle-bells borne upon the wind. Having a sealed memorial to submit at tomorrow's levée, I make frequent inquiries about the progress of the night.

9

至德二載甫自金光門出，間道
Zhì-dé èr-zǎi Fǔ zì Jīn-guāng-mén chū, jiàn-dào

歸鳳翔。乾元初從左拾遺移華州
guī Fèng-xiáng. Qián-yuán chū cóng zuǒ-shí-yí yí Huá-zhōu

掾。與親故別，因出此門。
yuàn. Yǔ qīn-gù bié, yīn chū cǐ mén.

有悲往事。
Yǒu bēi wǎng-shì.

此道昔歸順
1. *Cǐ dào xī guī-shùn,*

西郊胡正繁
2. *Xī-jiāo hú zhèng fán.*

至今猶破膽
3. *Zhì-jīn yóu pò dǎn,*

應有未招魂
4. *Yīng yǒu wèi zhāo hún.*

近侍歸京邑
5. *Jìn-shì guī jīng-yì,*

移官豈至尊
6. *Yí guān qǐ zhì-zūn?*

無才日衰老
7. *Wú-cái rì shuāi-lǎo,*

駐馬望千門
8. *Zhù-mǎ wàng qiān-mén.*

TITLE AND SUBJECT

Zhì-dé èr-zǎi: 'In the second year of the Chih-te period', i.e. 757. Throughout the Imperial period Chinese dates were normally given in terms of year-names which were chosen arbitrarily. Sometimes the same year-name was used for the whole of a reign, and this became the regular practice at the beginning of the Ming dynasty, with the consequence that the Ming and Ch'ing emperors are usually called by the year-names of their reigns. Thus the second and fourth Ch'ing emperors are called respectively K'ang-hsi and Ch'ien-lung, although in reality these are the names not of persons but of periods. Su-tsung changed the year-name four times during his reign. The first time was in 756 on his proclamation as Emperor in Ling-wu, when he changed the fifteenth year of the period T'ien-pao, which occupies the second half of his father Hsüan-tsung's reign, to the first year of Chih-te. T'ien-pao and Chih-te mean respectively 'Heavenly Treasure' and 'Supreme Virtue'; but it is customary to leave year-names untranslated because in a great many cases it is impossible to discover what their inventors meant by them.

Fú zì Jīn-guāng-mén chū: 'Fu from Golden-light-gate went-out.'
Fú: Tu Fu refers to himself by his own name, as was the Chinese custom. We should say 'I'.
Jīn-guāng-mén: the Gate of Golden Light was the centre of the three western gates in the outer walls of Ch'ang-an. Tu Fu would naturally pass through one of them on his way to Feng-hsiang.
jiàn-dào guī Fèng-xiáng: 'unfrequented-routes made-way-to Feng-hsiang.'
guī here means not 'return' as it often does, but 'betake oneself to' in the sense of going where one ought to go. The reader will probably have grasped by now that the cardinal rule of Chinese

grammar enunciated earlier, that the modifier always precedes the thing it modifies, applies to verbs as well as nouns. *Jiàn-dào guī* therefore means 'betake oneself *by way of* unfrequented routes'.

Qián-yuán chū: 'Ch'ien-yüan beginning'; i.e. in 758.

cóng zuǒ-shí-yí: 'from Left-Remembrancer'.

'Left Remembrancer' or 'Remembrancer of the Left' means Remembrancer in the Imperial Chancellery which, it will be remembered, was referred to as the 'Department of the Left'. The six Remembrancers who worked in the Chancellery were so designated in order to distinguish them from other 'Remembrancers' who worked in the Grand Secretariat.

yí Huá-zhōu yuán: 'was-transferred-to Hua-chou subordinate-official'.

Whether from pride or tact, Tu Fu's use of the word *yí* 'transfer' conceals the fact that this was a demotion. He was sent to Hua-chou in disgrace. *Yuán* was a general term used for the subordinates of prefects and provincial governors. The post Tu Fu was given in Hua-chou was actually that of Education Officer.

Yǔ qīn-gù bié, yīn chū cǐ mén: 'from relatives-friends take-leave, therefore went-out this gate.'

You would not normally leave Ch'ang-an by the Gate of Golden Light if you were going to Hua-chou, since Hua-chou was *east* of the city. The point is that Tu Fu had friends and relations in the western suburbs whom he wanted to say goodbye to before he left.

Yǒu bēi wǎng-shì: 'had grieving-for past-affairs', i.e. he was reminded of the very different circumstances in which he had left by that same gate a year or so before.

This poem was probably written in the summer of 758. Tu Fu's demotion was no doubt partly due to the fact that he had gained for himself a reputation as a troublemaker; but principally it was because he was a protégé of an elderly statesman called Fang Kuan who was also banished about this time.

Fang Kuan was Hsüan-tsung's most trusted minister during and after his flight into Szechwan, and when news of the Crown Prince's enthronement at Ling-wu reached Ch'eng-tu, he was one of the two high-ranking officials sent by Hsüan-tsung to bear the Instrument of Abdication and the Great Seal to the new Emperor. Su-tsung kept Fang Kuan with him and at first made much of him;

but the suspicions he soon began to entertain about him were aggravated by the calumnies of other courtiers and strengthened by Fang Kuan's disastrous failure as a general. The fall and disgrace of so important a person invariably involved the demotion or banishment of scores of friends and protégés in the administration.

FORM

This poem is always classified as a pentasyllabic poem in Regulated Verse, in spite of the fact that there is no close parallelism in the central couplets. If we contrast it with No. 1, an eight-line poem which *has* got close parallelism in its central couplets but which is classified as an Old Style poem because it does not obey the Rules of Euphony, we must conclude that to the Chinese critic tonal pattern was of pre-eminent importance in classifying different types of verse.

EXEGESIS

1. *Cǐ dào xī guī-shùn*
   This way formerly returned-to-obedience

2. *Xī-jiāo hú zhèng fán*
   West-suburbs barbarians just-then numerous

Guī-shùn: expression used of one leaving enemy-occupied territory for territory held by the Emperor.

3. *Zhì-jīn yóu pò dǎn*
   Till-now still broken courage

4. *Yīng yǒu wèi zhāo hún*
   Must have not-yet summoned souls

Dǎn: literally 'gall-bladder'—the seat of courage. To have a broken gall-bladder means to have lost one's nerve.

Zhāo hún: illness or shock may cause a person's soul to leave his body, in which case the proper rituals must be performed for recalling it. Actually we ought to say 'souls' rather than 'soul', though; because according to popular theory a person had not one but ten souls: three spiritual souls (*hún*) and seven animal souls (*pò*). Tu Fu means, I think, that he did perform or have performed for him the prescribed rituals for summoning back his souls, but perhaps one or two of them are still at large.

5. *Jin-shì guī jīng-yì*
   Close-attendance returned-to capital-town
6. *Yí guān qǐ zhì-zūn*
   Transferring appointment surely-not supremely-honoured-one

Jin-shì 'in close attendance', i.e. in the Emperor's entourage. As an official who served the Emperor during his exile and was with him when he re-entered the capital, Tu Fu feels entitled to special consideration.

Zhì-zūn refers to the Emperor. Tu Fu refuses to believe that his demotion can have been the Emperor's personal wish. It must have been the work of the evil counsellors who surround him.

7. *Wú-cái rì shuāi-lǎo*
   Without-talent daily-more old-and-decrepit
8. *Zhù-mǎ wàng qiān-mén*
   Stop-horse gaze-at thousand-doors

The place of the 'thousand doors' is the imperial palace in which the Emperor lives, towards whom Tu Fu feels a mixture of sorrow, regret, and deep disappointment. He feels that the chance of fulfilling his political ambitions has now finally eluded him: he is too old and undistinguished for a second opportunity ever to come his way.

TRANSLATION

In the second year of Chih-te (757), I left the capital by the Gate of Golden Light and made my way secretly to the court at Feng-hsiang. At the beginning of Ch'ien-yüan (758), I was transferred from the post of Remembrancer in the Imperial Chancellery to that of a subordinate official in the prefectural government of Hua-chou. In order to take leave of friends and relations, I left the city by this same gate, a circumstance which brought back sad memories of past events.

When last year I made my way to grace by this same road, the western outskirts of the city were full of barbarian soldiers. To this day my nerves remain shattered, and I think some of my souls must still be in need of recall. I returned to the capital in the entourage of the Emperor. I am sure my present removal was not the doing of his Sacred Majesty. Lacking in ability, growing increasingly old and useless, I rein in my horse and gaze sadly towards the Imperial palace.

贈衛八處士

Zèng Wèi Bā chǔ-shì

人生不相見

1. *Rén-shēng bù xiāng-jiàn,*

動如參與商

2. *Dòng rú shēn yǔ shāng;*

今夕復何夕

3. *Jīn-xī fù hé xī,*

共此燈燭光

4. *Gòng cǐ dēng-zhú guāng?*

少壯能幾時

5. *Shào-zhuàng néng jǐ-shí?*

鬢髮各已蒼

6. *Bìn-fà gè yǐ cāng.*

訪舊半爲鬼

7. *Fǎng jiù bàn wéi guǐ,*

驚呼熱中腸

8. *Jīng-hū rè zhōng-cháng.*

馬知二十載
9. *Yān zhī èr-shí zǎi*

重上君子堂
10. *Chóng shàng jūn-zǐ táng!*

昔別君未婚
11. *Xī bié jūn wèi hūn,*

兒女忽成行
12. *Ér-nǔ hū chéng háng!*

怡然敬父執
13. *Yí-rán jing fù-zhí,*

問我來何方
14. *Wèn wǒ lái hé-fāng.*

問答乃未已
15. *Wèn-dá nǎi wèi yǐ,*

驅兒羅酒漿
16. *Qū ér luó jiǔ-jiāng.*

夜雨剪春韭
17. *Yè yǔ jiǎn chūn jiǔ,*

新炊間黃粱
18. *Xīn chuī jiàn huáng-liáng.*

10. *To the Recluse Wei Pa*

主稱會面難
19. *Zhǔ chēng huì-miàn nán,*

一舉累十觴
20. *Yì-jǔ léi shí shāng;*

十觴亦不醉
21. *Shí shāng yì bú zuì,*

感子故意長
22. *Gǎn zǐ gù-yì cháng.*

明日隔山岳
23. *Míng-rì gé shān-yuè,*

世事兩茫茫
24. *Shì-shì liǎng máng-máng.*

TITLE AND SUBJECT

Zèng means 'present to'.

Wèi is a surname.

Bā means 'the Eighth'; that is, eighth in the family. This type of appellation was extremely common in the T'ang period. It has remained so in vulgar and familiar language until modern times.

Chŭ-shì is often translated 'hermit' or 'recluse'. It does have this sense sometimes; but, as can be seen from the poem which follows, Eighth Brother Wei is no anchorite living in a lonely cell, but a country gentleman with a sizeable family. Basically a *chŭ-shì* is an educated man who opts out of the usual curriculum of examination and office, preferring to lead a life of quiet retirement in the countryside. Persons of such temperament and inclinations would naturally tend to select places of scenic interest to live in; but they did not necessarily inhabit caves.

Hua-chou, the prefecture to which Tu Fu was sent as Education Officer, took its name from Hua-shan, the westernmost of the Five Great Peaks referred to in the introduction to the first poem in this book. It seems to be Hua-shan that Tu Fu is referring to in line 23.

This poem was written in the spring of 759. Early in this year Tu Fu was sent on official business to Loyang, the Eastern Capital, as it was called, and it seems likely that he visited this old friend while on the journey there or back.

FORM

This is a pentasyllabic Old Style poem. It has the same rhyme (*-ang*) throughout: twelve instances in all.

EXEGESIS

1. *Rén-shēng bù xiāng-jiàn*
   Man's-life not see-one-another

2. *Dòng rú shēn yǔ shāng*
   Often like Shen and Shang

Shen and Shang are the names of two constellations. Shen is made up of the stars Rigel, Betelgeuse, and Bellatrix in Orion, and

Shang of the stars σ, α (Antares), and τ in Scorpio. One of these constellations is always setting as the other is rising, so they never see each other.

3. *Jīn-xī fù hé xī*
   This-evening then what evening

4. *Gòng cǐ dēng-zhú guāng*
   Share this lamp light

   Line 3 echoes an ancient song, supposed to be already a thousand years old in Tu Fu's day, which would be familiar to his readers.

5. *Shào-zhuàng néng jǐ-shí*
   Youth-vigour can how-long

6. *Bìn-fà gè yǐ cāng*
   Temple-hair each already grey

7. *Fǎng jiù bàn wéi guǐ*
   Inquire old-acquaintances half are ghosts

8. *Jīng-hū rè zhōng-cháng*
   Startled-cries heat inside-bowels

9. *Yān zhī èr-shí zǎi*
   How know twenty years

10. *Chóng shàng jūn-zǐ táng*
    Again ascend gentleman's hall

    Shàng 'ascend' is polite language for 'enter' or 'visit'. The notion underlying this usage is that everything about the person one is speaking to is lofty and above oneself.
    Jūn-zǐ: i.e. 'your'.

11. *Xī bié jūn wèi hūn*
    Former parting you not-yet married

12. *Ér-nǚ hū chéng háng*
    Sons-daughters suddenly form row

13. *Yí-rán jìng fù-zhí*
    Gladly honour father's-friend

14. *Wèn wǒ lái hé-fāng*
    Ask me come-from what-direction

Fù-zhí ('father's friend') is an archaic term which occurs in one
of the ancient handbooks on ritual and etiquette which form part
of the Confucian canon. 'The dutiful child on meeting one of his
father's friends should neither approach nor retire without being
bidden to do so, nor should he speak unless first spoken to.' Perhaps
Tu Fu is quizzically contrasting the jolly clamour of the children
with the stuffy behaviour which Confucian etiquette dictated.

15. *Wèn-dá nǎi wèi yǐ*
    Questions-answers being not-yet finished

16. *Qū ér luó jiǔ-jiāng*
    Chase children arrange wine-liquor

17. *Yè yǔ jiǎn chūn jiǔ*
    Night rain cut spring chives

18. *Xīn chuī jiàn huáng-liáng*
    Fresh-cooked-rice mix-with yellow-millet

19. *Zhǔ chēng huì-miàn nán*
    Host mentioning meeting's difficulty

20. *Yì-jǔ léi shí shāng*
    At-one-go successively-pours ten cups

21. *Shí shāng yì bú zuì*
    Ten cups still not inebriated

22. *Gǎn zǐ gù-yì cháng*
    Moved-by your-friendship's lastingness

23. *Míng-rì gé shān-yuè*
    Tomorrow separated-by mountain-peak

24. *Shì-shì liǎng máng-máng*
    World's affairs on-both-sides lost-to-sight

TRANSLATION

'To the Recluse, Wei Pa'

Often in this life of ours we resemble, in our failure to meet, the Shen and Shang constellations, one of which rises as the other one sets. What lucky chance is it, then, that brings us together this evening under the light of this same lamp? Youth and vigour last but a little time.—Each of us now has greying temples. Half of the friends we ask each other about are dead, and our shocked cries sear the heart. Who could have guessed that it would be twenty years before I sat once more beneath your roof? Last time we parted you were still unmarried, but now here suddenly is a row of boys and girls who smilingly pay their respects to their father's old friend. They ask me where I have come from; but before I have finished dealing with their questions, the children are hurried off to fetch us wine. Spring chives are cut in the rainy dark, and there is freshly steamed rice mixed with yellow millet. 'Come, we don't meet often!' you hospitably urge, pouring out ten cupfuls in rapid succession. That I am still not drunk after ten cups of wine is due to the strength of the emotion which your unchanging friendship inspires. Tomorrow the Peak will lie between us, and each will be lost to the other, swallowed up in the world's affairs.

11

月夜憶舍弟

Yuè-yè yì shè-dì

戍鼓斷人行
1. *Shù gǔ duàn rén xíng,*

邊秋一雁聲
2. *Biān qiū yí yàn shēng.*

露從今夜白
3. *Lù cóng jīn-yè bái,*

月是故鄉明
4. *Yuè shì gù-xiāng míng.*

有弟皆分散
5. *Yǒu dì jiē fēn-sàn,*

無家問死生
6. *Wú jiā wèn sǐ-shēng.*

寄書長不達
7. *Jì shū cháng bù dá,*

況乃未休兵
8. *Kuàng nǎi wèi xiū bīng.*

TITLE AND SUBJECT

Yuè-yè: 'moonlit night', which is the title of No. 4.

Yì: 'think of', 'remember', 'call to mind'.

Shè-dì. Chinese kinship terms are extremely complicated. For example, there are five words for 'aunt' depending on whether you mean mother's sister, father's sister, mother's brother's wife, wife of father's elder brother, or wife of father's younger brother. Matters used to be further complicated by the exigencies of polite language. Thus 'your father' was *yán-fù* (literally 'strict father'), whilst 'my father' was *jiā-fù* (literally 'family father'). 'My elder brother' was *jiā-xiōng* with the same *jiā*; but 'my younger brother' was *shè-dì* (literally 'house younger brother'), *shè* being the term used in conjunction with younger relatives: nephews and so forth.

Tu Fu's mother died when he was an infant, but he had three half-brothers and a half-sister who were children of his father's second marriage. He was deeply attached to all four of them, and expressed affectionate concern for them in many of his poems.

In this title *yuè-yè* modifies the verb *yì* which follows it: 'think of *on* a moonlit night'. The whole title therefore means, 'Thinking of My Brothers on a Moonlit Night'.

The fighting whose overtones darken this poem is that same bloody and protracted civil war which began with the rebellion of An Lu-shan in December 755. In spite of the murder of An Lu-shan by his own son and the recovery of Ch'ang-an in 757, it dragged on for a further six years, depopulating and impoverishing Northern China and inflicting such grievous damage on the economic and political fabric of the T'ang state that it never afterwards properly recovered.

Some commentators think this poem was written at the end of October 759 after the fall of Loyang to Shih Ssu-ming, a former general of An Lu-shan who had surrendered to the T'ang court in February 758, but rebelled again a few months later and subsequently murdered An Lu-shan's parricidal son and set himself up as Emperor of Yen in the East. I think it must have been written a little before that, however, because it refers to White Dew, the Chinese name for the chilly part of autumn which follows the Mid-Autumn Festival, which in 759 fell in early September. I strongly suspect that this poem, like No. 4, may have been written on the occasion of that festival.

Tu Fu, for reasons which are still in dispute, threw up his job in Hua-chou at the beginning of autumn, 759, and journeyed with his wife and children to the frontier town of Ch'in-chou, three hundred miles west of Ch'ang-an, near the western end of the Great Wall. He was in Ch'in-chou no more than six or seven weeks before setting off once more on his travels; but it was a highly productive period. More than sixty of his poems are attributed to it.

FORM

This is a formally perfect pentasyllabic poem in Regulated Verse. An unusual feature which appears in the first of the two central antithetical couplets (i.e. in lines 3–4) is worth remarking on. Before Tu Fu's time the caesura between the second and third syllables in pentasyllabic Regulated Verse (as in lines 5 and 6 here) and between the fourth and fifth syllables in heptasyllabic Regulated Verse was virtually invariable; but Tu Fu, who was a great technical innovator, frequently experimented with different rhythms. In these two lines the caesura comes after the *first* syllable, which has the effect of concentrating a very heavy emphasis on the initial words *lù* and *yuè*.

EXEGESIS

1. *Shù gǔ duàn rén xíng*
   Garrison drums cut-off people's travel

2. *Biān qiū yí yàn shēng*
   Frontier autumn one goose sound

One distinguished scholar thinks Tu Fu wrote this poem while still on his way to Ch'in-chou; but I think he must be there already, complaining that he feels cut off: no postal services and no visitors. Otherwise I find the first line hard to understand.

Yí yàn shēng is an ambivalent image. The migratory wild goose is a symbol of autumn; but a well-known literary convention also associates it with an exile's letter from home. The sound of the wild goose sets in motion the train of thought which begins with a feeling of beleaguerment and a melancholy awareness of winter's approach and ends with anxiety about his absent brothers.

3. *Lù cóng jīn-yè bái*
   Dew from this-night white

4. *Yuè shì gù-xiāng míng*
   Moon is old-home bright

Gù-xiàng: perhaps 'homeland' or 'homestead' would be a more accurate rendering. We tend to say 'home' both for the place (*gù-xiàng*) and the people (*jiā*: 'family'). Unfortunately Tu Fu talks about his *gù-xiàng* in this line and then goes on to complain that he hasn't got a *jiā* in line 6. But this is quite deliberate. The goose reminds him that this is the mid-autumn moon, and the mid-autumn moon makes him think of his old homestead; but the family who should occupy the homestead is all scattered and has no headquarters to which he can apply for information about its separate members. Everyone has a *gù-xiàng*, since everyone must have been born and brought up somewhere or other, but a person in Tu Fu's position could reasonably say that he had no *jiā* since the *jiā* had been broken up.

5. *Yǒu dì jiē fēn-sàn*
   Have brothers all are-scattered

6. *Wú jiā wèn sǐ-shēng*
   Haven't family ask dead-alive

7. *Jì-shū cháng bù dá*
   Sent letters always not arrive

8. *Kuàng nǎi wèi xiū bīng*
   Especially as not-yet end fighting

Jì-shū: it isn't clear whether these are the letters which Tu Fu writes to his brothers or those which they write to him. If the former, it could be objected that Tu Fu couldn't know whether his letters had reached them or not; if the latter, it could equally well be objected that he had no means of knowing that they had written any. Common sense suggests that this should be understood as a general statement about the breakdown of mails due to the deplorable situation.

TRANSLATION

'Thinking of My Brothers on a Moonlit Night'

Travel is interrupted by the war-drums of the garrisons. The sound of a solitary wild goose announces the coming of autumn to the frontier. From tonight onwards the dew will be white. The moon is that same moon which shines down on my birthplace. My brothers are scattered in different places. I have no home to tell me whether they are alive or dead. The letters we write never seem to reach their destination; and it will be worse now that we are at war once more.

12

佳人
Jiā-rén

絕代有佳人
1. Jué-dài yǒu jiā-rén,

幽居在空谷
2. Yōu-jū zài kōng gǔ.

自云良家子
3. Zì yún liáng-jiā-zǐ,

零落依草木
4. Líng-luò yī cǎo-mù.

關中昔喪亂
5. Guān-zhōng xī sāng-luàn,

兄弟遭殺戮
6. Xiōng-dì zāo shā-lù.

官高何足論
7. Guān gāo hé zú lún,

不得收骨肉
8. Bù-dé shōu gǔ-ròu.

世情惡衰歇
9. Shì-qíng wù shuāi-xiē,

萬事隨轉燭
10. Wàn-shì suí zhuǎn zhú.

夫壻輕薄兒
11. Fū-xū qīng-bó-ér,

新人美如玉
12. Xīn-rén měi rú yù.

合昏尚知時
13. Hé-hūn shàng zhī shí,

鴛鴦不獨宿
14. Yuān-yāng bù dú sù.

但見新人笑
15. Dàn jiàn xīn-rén xiào,

那聞舊人哭
16. Nǎ wén jiù-rén kū!

在山泉水清
17. Zài shān quán-shuǐ qīng,

出山泉水濁
18. Chū shān quán-shuǐ zhuó.

12. A Fine Lady

侍婢賣珠廻

19. *Shì-bēi mài zhū huí,*

牽蘿補茅屋

20. *Qiān luó bǔ máo-wū.*

摘花不揷髮

21. *Zhé huā bù chā fà,*

采柏動盈掬

22. *Cǎi bó dòng yíng jū.*

天寒翠袖薄

23. *Tiān hán cuì xiù bó,*

日暮倚修竹

24. *Rì-mù yǐ xiū zhú.*

TITLE AND SUBJECT

Jiā-rén: a somewhat archaic term for a woman of beauty and breeding. I translate 'fine lady'. It is taken from the opening couplet, which Tu Fu was certainly inspired to write by the beginning of an ancient song attributed to a musician who lived at the court of Emperor Wu of the Han dynasty, Li Yen-nien:

> In the North Country there is a fine lady
> Who without rival stands all alone

This poem records Tu Fu's meeting with a decayed gentlewoman. He comes upon her in a lonely valley near the tumbledown cottage in which she lives. Struck by her beauty and the once expensive but, for the time of year, impracticably thin finery in which she is dressed, he falls into conversation with her and discovers that she lost her family in the Troubles and has been cast off by a philandering husband, encouraged to make an open break with her by the removal of her influential brothers. She now lives with a single faithful servant, far from the society which has rejected her, existing precariously on the sale of her remaining jewellery, and perhaps also of the flowers which she would appear to have been picking when Tu Fu first came upon her 'under the tall bamboos'.

Some Chinese commentators used to understand this poem as an allegory (the lady standing for an out-of-office statesman and the philandering husband for his Emperor), but I find this quite impossible to believe. There is no reason at all why we shouldn't think of it as a faithful record of a real encounter.

Notice that we have no description of what the lady was wearing or doing until we are nearly at the end of the poem. This, it seems to me, is a realistic touch. In real life it is only when we know something about a person's history that the trivialities of his dress and deportment begin to take on significance; so Tu Fu only properly notices the pathetic dress and the spray of flowers and leaves when he is in a position to understand their real meaning.

FORM

This is a 'Five Old' poem, i.e. an Old Style poem in pentasyllabic verse. Its unadorned simplicity and straightforwardness, which make it an ideal 'beginner's piece', conceal a great amount of artistry. A perceptive reader might perhaps feel that this is like the Ballad Style already encountered in Nos. 2, 3, 5, and 7. The two couplets 15–16 and 17–18 are certainly suggestive of that style. But there is a subtle difference. A little study will reveal that this poem is both less diffuse and more reflective than true Ballad Style poems. It is in fact a very successful—and original—imitation of the earliest type of pentasyllabic poetry of which the anonymous Nineteen Old Poems, dating from the second or third century, are the most conspicuous example. These poems owe many of their characteristics to the fact that they represent the moulding of a popular song form by writers whose literary tastes inclined to the philosophical.

What makes this piece so original, although stylistically it is a highly successful imitation of a much earlier sort of poetry, is that the *jiā-rén* emerges from it as thoroughly and convincingly contemporary. There is nothing archaic or 'period' about the poem *as a whole*.

EXEGESIS

1. *Jué-dài yǒu jiā-rén*
   Surpassing-generation is fine-lady

2. *Yōu-jū zài kōng gǔ*
   Obscurely-living in empty valley

Jué-dài: 'surpassing all others in her generation', i.e. 'matchless', 'peerless'. The grammar of the first line is strikingly peculiar. *Jué-dài* of course qualifies *jiā-rén*, and the prose order would be *Yǒu jué-dài zhī jiā-rén*. The fact that nearly everyone who read the poem would recall the lines of Li Yen-nien's song would, I think, carry them over any difficulty they might have felt about this line. The crabbedness of the grammar also imparts an 'antique' look to it and helps to fix the style of the poem from the outset.

3. *Zì yún liáng-jiā-zǐ*
   Self says good-family-daughter

4. *Líng-luò yī cǎo-mù*
   Decayed-in-fortune lives-with grasses-trees

Líng-luò: literally 'withered and falling', like the leaves in late autumn. Here it is used metaphorically of the lady's fortune. *Yī* is ambiguous. It can mean 'fall back on', 'go to live with' (like a disappointed or rejected wife 'going back to mother') and this is, I think, the uppermost meaning here. It can also mean 'follow', 'accord with', a sense which tends to emerge when you start thinking about the literal and more usual meaning of *líng-luò*: i.e. the lady is withering just like the grasses and trees which surround her. A third sense, very close to the first one, is 'rely on'; and there is more than a suggestion in line 21 that she is living partly from her takings as a florist, though Tu Fu is too much of a gentleman to state openly that she is doing anything so vulgar as actually *earning* money. I am afraid I can see no means of perpetuating the ambiguity in English translation. It is one of those touches, however, which make this a much less simple poem than a cursory reading might lead one to suppose.

5. *Guān-zhōng xī sāng-luàn*
   Within-the-passes yester-year fell-to-rebels

6. *Xiōng-dì zāo shā-lù*
   Brothers met-with killing

Her brothers must have been high officials under Yang Kuo-chung who were put to death during the rebel army's occupation of Ch'ang-an.

7. *Guān gāo hé zú lún*
   Office high how sufficient consider

8. *Bù dé shōu gǔ-ròu*
   Not-able collect bones-flesh

Hé zú lún: 'was unavailing'.
Shōu gǔ-ròu: i.e. she was unable to beg back their gibbeted corpses for decent burial.

9. *Shì-qíng wù shuāi-xiē*
   World's-feelings hate decayed-finished

10. *Wàn-shì suí zhuǎn zhú*
    Myriad-affairs follow turning lamp

Zhuǎn zhú: 'turning lamp', sometimes *zhuǎn fēng zhú* 'turning in the wind lamp': i.e. a lamp-flame flickering in the wind. An image of fickleness and inconstancy.

11. *Fū-xū qīng-bó-ér*
    Husband fickle-fellow

12. *Xīn-rén měi rú yù*
    New-woman beautiful as jade

13. *Hé-hūn shàng zhī shí*
    Vetch-tree even knows time

14. *Yuān-yāng bù dú sù*
    Mandarin-ducks not alone sleep

Hé-hūn: the *albizzia julibrissia*, a tree whose vetch-like leaves
fold up at night time: hence the lady's remark about its 'knowing
the time'. Mandarin ducks are a well-known symbol of conjugal
fidelity. The lady contrasts the constancy and affection of Nature's
humbler creatures with the neglect and callousness that she has
been shown by Man.

15. *Dàn jiàn xīn-rén xiào*
    Only sees new-woman's smile

16. *Nǎ wén jiù-rén kū*
    How hear old-woman's weeping

Jiù-rén: i.e. his former wife.

17. *Zài shān quán-shuǐ qīng*
    In mountain spring-water clear

18. *Chū shān quán-shuǐ zhuó*
    Emerge mountain spring-water muddy

Once a woman has left her husband a thousand things will be
said and believed of her, even though she is innocent, and her
reputation is ruined past recovery.

19. *Shì-bēi mài zhū huí*
    Serving-maid selling pearls returns

20. *Qiān luó bǔ máo-wū*
    Drags creeper mend thatch roof

It has been objected that creeper is not a suitable material for
mending thatch with, but I think the objectors have failed to
understand the point of *qiān* ('pull', 'drag') which I think Tu Fu

uses advisedly. What the women do in their efforts to keep out the weather is to rearrange a living vine or creeper which is already growing over the house, so that its foliage covers up some of the holes. This is the sort of amateurish and ineffectual thing one can very well imagine them doing, whereas rethatching the holes, apart from the objection that *qiān* doesn't mean 'pluck' and creeper can't be used as thatch, would be a skilled job wholly outside the capacities of a gentlewoman and a lady's maid.

21. *Zhé huā bù chā fà*
    Picks flowers not stick-in hair

22. *Cǎi bó dòng yíng jū*
    Plucks cypress often fills grasp

Cypress leaves were sometimes chewed to allay the pangs of hunger. I think this is why the lady plucks handfuls of them in line 22: not, as is usually suggested, because cypress is a symbol of bitterness.

23. *Tiān hán cuì xiū bó*
    Weather cold blue sleeves thin

24. *Rì mù yǐ xiū zhú*
    Day evening leans long bamboos

TRANSLATION

'A Fine Lady'

There is a fine lady of matchless beauty who lives obscurely in a lonely valley. She says she is the daughter of a good family, driven by misfortunes into the wilds. When of late the heartlands were convulsed with disorder, her brothers met their deaths at the hands of the rebels. The high rank they had held was all unavailing: she could not entreat their dead bodies for burial.

The way of the world is to hate what has had its day; and fortune is as fickle as a lamp-flame. Her husband is not faithful to her. His new woman is as lovely as a jewel. Even the vetch-tree knows when it is evening; and the mandarin ducks do not sleep alone. Yet he has eyes only for the smiles of the new woman: no ear for the sobbing of the old. In the mountain the waters of the stream are clear, but once they have left the mountain they are muddy.

When her servant-girl gets back from selling her pearls, she has to pull creepers to cover the holes in the thatched roof with. The flowers which the lady picks are not for wearing in her hair; of bitter cypress she plucks many a handful. Her gay blue sleeves are thin against the cold. As evening falls she rests by the tall bamboos.

13

夢李白
Mèng Lǐ Bó (1)

死別已吞聲

1. *Sǐ-bié yǐ tūn-shēng,*

生別常惻惻

2. *Shēng-bié cháng cè-cè.*

江南瘴癘地

3. *Jiāng-nán zhàng-lì dì,*

逐客無消息

4. *Zhú-kè wú xiāo-xī.*

故人入我夢

5. *Gù-rén rù wǒ mèng,*

明我長相憶

6. *Míng wǒ cháng xiāng-yì.*

君今在羅網

7. *Jūn jīn zài luó-wǎng,*

何以有羽翼

8. *Hé-yǐ yǒu yǔ-yì?*

恐非平生魂

9. *Kǒng fēi píng-shēng hún,*

路遠不可測

10. *Lù yuǎn bū kě cè.*

魂來楓林青

11. *Hún lái fēng-lín qīng,*

魂返關塞黑

12. *Hún fǎn guān-sài hè*

落月滿屋梁

13. *Luò yuè mǎn wū-liáng,*

猶疑照顏色

14. *Yóu yí zhào yán-sè!*

水深波浪濶

15. *Shuǐ shēn bō-làng kuò,*

無使蛟龍得

16. *Wú shǐ jiāo-lóng dé!*

TITLE AND SUBJECT

Mèng: 'dream', here a verb, 'dreaming of'.

Lǐ Bó: Li Po and Tu Fu are often looked upon as the greatest of all the T'ang poets and their very different personalities and styles are frequently contrasted.

Li Po (701–62) was considerably senior to Tu Fu, and when Tu Fu first made his acquaintance in Honan in 744 or 745, he was already a famous poet whilst Tu Fu was a comparatively unknown young man. Tu Fu was completely captivated by the older poet's magnetic personality and treasured the memory of their brief association for the rest of his life, addressing a number of poems to him at different times and from different places.

The An Lu-shan rebellion which devastated Northern China and wrought so great an upheaval in Tu Fu's life almost passed Li Po by. During its first year he was leading a fairly carefree existence in the Yangtze Valley near Kiukiang. Early in 757, however, he became involved in the fortunes of Prince Lin, a member of the Imperial family who had been given command of a fleet on the Yangtze for the purpose of conducting operations against the rebels, but who, in anticipation of the imminent break-up of the régime, seems to have decided to set up an independent administration of his own centred on Nanking. At the beginning of 757, when his fleet was anchored at Kiukiang, Prince Lin invited Li Po on board as a sort of civilian adviser or cultural mascot. After a very enjoyable and convivial cruise down the river, Li Po apparently realized what was afoot when the fleet reached Yangchow and deserted, along with many of Prince Lin's officers. Following the defeat and execution of Prince Lin in March 757, Li Po was arrested near Kiukiang and held in prison for several months. He was released on the initiative of a visiting Government Inspector, but rearrested a year later when the Chief Minister who had been the ultimate authority for his release fell from power. He was sentenced to banishment in Yeh-lang, a malarial district in Kwei-chow from which an ageing hedonist like Li Po would have little prospect of returning alive. Fortunately—whether from ineptitude or humanity or a combination of the two—the bureaucratic machine seems not to have hustled him unduly, for when news of an amnesty in which he was included reached him in the early summer of 759, he was little more than half-way to his place of exile.

The exact date of this poem is uncertain. A commonly held view is that it was written while Tu Fu was at Ch'in-chou. Another view is that it must have been written earlier because it seems to imply (in lines 4 and 7) that Li Po is still in trouble, and must therefore belong to a period earlier than the amnesty. The date will probably always remain uncertain; but I do not in any case find the argument for the second view a very compelling one. It overlooks the fact that Tu Fu's news about Li Po may have been, and, indeed, probably was, months out of date. Scholars accustomed to handling dated sources easily forget that information they can obtain in three-quarters of a minute by taking a book off a shelf may have taken weeks or months to reach a contemporary—particularly one living in a remote frontier city in time of war. Whatever the date of the poem, it is clear that when Tu Fu wrote it he thought of Li Po as a condemned man whose banishment would probably cost him his life.

FORM

This is an Old Style pentasyllabic poem. Note that the two 'Dreaming of Li Po' poems are of equal length (sixteen lines in eight couplets).

EXEGESIS

1. *Sǐ-bié yǐ tūn-shēng*
   Death-partings have-end-of sobbing

2. *Shēng-bié cháng cè-cè*
   Life-partings unremitting anguish

3. *Jiāng-nán zhàng-lì dì*
   Chiang-nan pestilential country

4. *Zhú-kè wú xiāo-xī*
   Banished-man not-any news

In Tu Fu's time the name 'Chiang-nan' was used to designate a vast area in which both Kiukiang and Yeh-lang would be included. It does not therefore give us much indication of where Tu Fu imagined Li Po to be at the time he was writing the poem.

5. *Gù-rén rù wŏ mèng*
   Old-friend entered my dream

6. *Míng wŏ cháng xiāng-yì*
   Makes-clear I always think-of-him

7. *Jūn jīn zài luó-wăng*
   You now are-in net

8. *Hé-yǐ yŏu yŭ-yì*
   How have-got feather-wings

Luó-wăng: i.e. the net of the law. This is dream-logic. 'How did you get here? I thought you were supposed to be in prison.'

9. *Kŏng fēi píng-shēng hún*
   Afraid is-not living soul

10. *Lù yuăn bū kě cè*
    Road far cannot-be measured

It is by no means easy to see the connexion between these two lines. I think Tu Fu means that the distance from Chiang-nan to Ch'in-chou is so immense that Li Po's soul would be unable to make the journey there and back while he slept. He has a fearful suspicion that Li Po has died in prison or in exile, and that what he is being visited by is a soul permanently detached from its body. Line 10 is meant to explain line 9. We should perhaps feel the connexion more easily if the lines were the other way round.

11. *Hún lái fēng-lín qīng*
    Soul come maple-woods green

12. *Hún făn guān-sài hè*
    Soul return passes dark

Fēng-lín: the maple-woods are on the banks of the River Yangtze. They are also referred to in the third-century B.C. *Summons of the Soul*. It was still light when Li Po's soul left Chiang-nan, but so great is the distance that the journey back through the passes was made at night.

13. *Luò yuè mǎn wū-liáng*
    Sinking moon fills roof-beams

14. *Yóu yí zhào yán-sè*
    Still doubtful shine-on your-face

These two lines describe Tu Fu's feelings on waking. The dream
had been so vivid, that when he opened his eyes and saw the whole
room bathed in moonlight, he looked around half expecting the
moonlight to reveal Li Po still standing in one of its corners.

15. *Shuǐ shēn bō-làng kuò*
    Water deep waves broad

16. *Wú shǐ jiāo-lóng dé*
    Don't let water-dragons get

TRANSLATION

'Dreaming of Li Po' (1)

After the separation of death one can eventually swallow back one's
grief, but the separation of the living is an endless, unappeasable
anxiety. From pestilent Chiang-nan no news arrives of the poor
exile. That my old friend should come into my dream shows how
constantly he is in my thoughts. I fear that this is not the soul of
the living man: the journey is so immeasurably far. When your
soul left, the maple woods were green: on its return the passes
were black with night. Lying now enmeshed in the net of the law,
how did you find wings with which to fly here? The light of the
sinking moon illumines every beam and rafter of my chamber,
and I half expect it to light up your face. The water is deep, the
waves are wide: don't let the water-dragons get you!

14

夢李白
Mèng Lǐ Bó (2)

浮雲終日行
1. *Fú-yún zhōng-rì xíng,*

遊子久不至
2. *Yóu-zǐ jiǔ bú zhì.*

三夜頻夢君
3. *Sān yè pín mèng jūn,*

情親見君意
4. *Qíng-qīn jiàn jūn yì.*

告歸常齷齪
5. *Gào-guī cháng jú-cù,*

苦道來不易
6. *Kǔ dào 'Lái bú yì:*

江湖多風波
7. *'Jiāng-hú duō fēng-bō,*

舟楫恐失墜
8. *'Zhōu-jí kǒng shī-zhuì!'*

出門搔白首

9. *Chū mén sāo bái shǒu,*

若負平生志

10. *Ruò fù píng-shēng zhì.*

冠蓋滿京華

11. *Guān-gài mǎn jīng-huá,*

斯人獨憔悴

12. *Sī-rén dú qiáo-cuì!*

孰云網恢恢

13. *Shú yún wǎng huī-huī?*

將老身反累

14. *Jiāng-lǎo shēn fǎn léi!*

千秋萬歲名

15. *Qiān-qiū wàn-suì míng,*

寂寞身後事

16. *Jì-mò shēn-hòu shì!*

TITLE AND SUBJECT

In these two 'Dreaming of Li Po' poems Tu Fu ranges over three distinct and incompatible theories of dream interpretation without apparently being aware that he is doing so. In No. 13 lines 5–6 he says that the dream apparition shows that Li Po has been on his mind a lot: a perfectly rational, psychological explanation which would pass muster in modern scientific circles today. He immediately follows this, however, by expressing the view that it is Li Po's soul which has visited him, and he continues to assume this throughout the rest of the poem. In the second couplet of this second poem Tu Fu says in effect, 'The fact that I am seeing so much of you lately in my dreams proves that *you* have been thinking a lot about *me*', which seems to imply a sort of telepathic relationship between the dreamer and the person dreamed of. No doubt we could discover similar inconsistencies in our own views on such matters if we could examine them sufficiently objectively, since it is perfectly possible, outside the realm of theology, to believe or half-believe several quite incompatible things simultaneously.

FORM

It is only a coincidence that the rhyme used throughout this poem appears in the modern pronunciation to be the same as the rhyme used throughout No. 13.

EXEGESIS

1. *Fú-yún zhōng-rì xíng*
   Floating-clouds all-day move

2. *Yóu-zǐ jiǔ bú zhì*
   Wanderer long not arrive

Floating clouds are a symbol of restless wanderings and put Tu Fu in mind of Li Po. So much is clear and not in dispute. But which destination is the wanderer so long in reaching? Since we are uncertain when the poem was written and do not in any case know how much out of date Tu Fu's information about Li Po's movements was, it is virtually impossible to answer this question, though one could hazard a number of guesses. For example, Tu Fu may have learned of Li Po's pardon and have received news from an informant in Yo-chou or some such place that Li Po had been expected back for several weeks but had still not arrived. Or he may have thought that Li Po was still on his way to banishment and have received word from an informant at Yeh-lang, or a place on the route to it, that Li Po had still not turned up, though months had gone by since his sentence. Either explanation would account for Tu Fu's half-expressed fear that Li Po had been drowned. Or conceivably Tu Fu had received a long-delayed letter from Li Po and been informed of some project of which we know nothing. It seems pointless to speculate, since we have no means of knowing.

3. *Sān yè pín mèng jūn*
   Three nights repeatedly dream-of you

4. *Qíng-qīn jiàn jūn yì*
   Kindly-concern see your mind

Qíng-qīn: i.e. 'your kindness in visiting me so often'. Just as a hospital patient might say, 'How kind of you to come so regularly! I can see that you are a real friend!'

5. *Gào-guī cháng jú-cù*
   Take-leave always flurried

6. *Kǔ dào Lái bú yì*
   Ruefully say Come not easy

7. *Jiāng-hú duō fēng-bō*
   River-lakes much wind-waves

8. *Zhōu-jí kǒng shī-zhuì*
   Boat-oars fear lose-sink

9. *Chū mén sāo bái shǒu*
   Go-out door scratch white head

10. *Ruò fù píng-shēng zhì*
    As-if disappointed-in life-time ambition

11. *Guān-gài mǎn jīng-huá*
    Official fill capital-city

12. *Sī-rén dú qiáo-cuì*
    This-man alone is-wretched

Guān-gài: literally 'carriage-awnings and caps of office', the symbols of official rank. From line 11 onwards are Tu Fu's reflections on waking from his dream.

13. *Shú yún wǎng huī-huī*
    Who says net wide-meshed

14. *Jiāng-lǎo shēn fǎn léi*
    Growing-old body yet in-trouble

Wǎng huī-huī: a quotation from the ancient Taoist text *Tao te ching*: 'Heaven's net has a broad mesh, yet nothing escapes from it.' The net here is not the net of the law as in No. 13, line 7, but the net with which the Emperor, as a fisher of men, gathers up men of talent to put in positions of responsibility in his administration. Li Po, one of the biggest fish of all, if we are talking about men of talent, has somehow managed to elude the imperial fisherman. This is not strictly true, since Li Po was once summoned to court by Hsüan-tsung, but failed to make use of his opportunities there through his inability to stay sober for any length of time.

Fǎn as a verb means 'return', 'go back', but it is used here adverbially: 'contrariwise', 'contrary to what one might reasonably have expected'. It is often impossible to render it in English except by the use of an adversative conjunction.

15. *Qiān qiū wàn-suì míng*
    Thousand-autumn myriad-year name

16. *Jì-mò shēn-hòu shì*
    Forlorn post-mortem affair

Line 16 is the predicate of line 15: 'Imperishable renown is a chilly, post-mortem thing', i.e. better a few home-comforts now than a name that will last through the centuries.

TRANSLATION

'Dreaming of Li Po' (2)

All day long the floating clouds drift by, and still the wanderer has
not arrived! For three nights running I have repeatedly dreamed of
you. Such affectionate concern on your part shows your feelings
for me! Each time you said goodbye you seemed so uneasy. 'It
isn't easy to come', you would say bitterly; 'The waters are so
rough. I am afraid the boat will capsize!' Going out of my door you
scratched your white head as if your whole life's ambition had been
frustrated.

The capital is full of new officials, yet a man like this is so
wretched! Who is going to tell me that the 'net is wide' when this
ageing man remains in difficulties? Imperishable renown is cold
comfort when you can only enjoy it in the tomb!

15

天末懷李白
Tiān-mò huái Lǐ Bó

涼風起天末

1. Liáng fēng qǐ tiān-mò,

君子意如何

2. Jūn-zǐ yì rú-hé?

鴻雁幾時到

3. Hóng-yàn jǐ-shí dào?

江湖秋水多

4. Jiāng-hú qiū-shuǐ duō!

文章憎命達

5. Wén-zhāng zèng mìng-dá,

魑魅喜人過

6. Chī-mèi xǐ rén guò.

應共冤魂語

7. Yīng gòng yuān-hún yǔ,

投詩贈汨羅

8. Tóu shī zèng Mì-luó.

TITLE AND SUBJECT

Tiān-mò, literally 'sky's end', is the Chinese equivalent of 'the world's end', 'the ends of the earth'.

Huái: 'yearn for', 'think longingly of', 'have on one's mind'.

Tiān-mò modifies the verb *huái* in the same way that *yuè-yè* modifies the verb *yì* in the title of No. 11. The whole title therefore means 'Longing for Li Po *at* the world's end'.

The two 'Dreaming of Li Po' poems are thought to have been composed in the autumn of 759 at Ch'in-chou in Kansu, but without much certainty. This poem was almost certainly written at that time and place. Ch'in-chou, one of the frontier towns of the north-west, would seem like 'the end of the earth' to a metropolitan Chinese. The bitter north-west wind from the Gobi is proverbial in North China for its coldness and meanness, and it would begin to get under way in late autumn. And Tu Fu refers in this poem to the rain-swollen rivers of autumn.

In the autumn of 759 Li Po would have been at Yo-chou near Lake Tung-t'ing, having arrived there several months previously on the way back from his uncompleted journey into exile. There is a suggestion in this poem that Tu Fu knows Li Po is in Yo-chou, since he refers to the river Mi-lo which is in the Tung-t'ing area; yet he does not appear to be aware that Li Po has been pardoned. As in the case of the last two poems, we can only guess at the extent of Tu Fu's information about Li Po at the time he wrote the poem.

FORM

This is a pentasyllabic poem in Regulated Verse. A stylistic purist might object that *jǐ-shí dào* in line 3 does not properly parallel *qiū-shuǐ duō* in line 4; but as I explained earlier, the great poets of this age were less hidebound about the forms of Regulated Verse than later generations came to be. A more serious stylistic criticism could be levelled against the monotony of the repeated substantival openings of lines 1–6: *liáng-fēng, jūn-zǐ, hóng-yàn, jiāng-hú, wén-zhāng, chī-mèi*: though this is partially offset by the syntactical variety which these lines show in the three syllables after the caesura.

EXEGESIS

1. *Liáng-fēng qǐ tiān-mò*
   Cold wind rises world's end

2. *Jūn-zǐ yì rú-hé*
   Gentleman's ideas like-what

Qǐ tiān-mò: the grammar of this may seem surprising after the *tiān-mò huái* . . . of the title. Expressions of place and direction can, however, be placed after the verb, particularly if there is no other verbal complement (like the *Lǐ Bó* of the title). In prose it is usual to find a prepositional particle between the verb and the post-verbal locative, but with very few exceptions it is omitted in syllabic verse.

Jūn-zǐ: i.e. 'your'. Cf. No. 10, l. 10.

3. *Hóng-yàn jǐ-shí dào*
   Wild-goose what-time arrive

4. *Jiāng-hú qiū-shuǐ duō*
   Rivers-lakes autumn-water much

Hóng-yàn: The wild goose, as I have explained in the note on No. 11, line 2, is regularly used in Chinese verse to symbolize letters from (or to) a person far away. This is the sense in which the 'goose' of this line has almost invariably been interpreted. But *hóng-yàn*, the particular word for 'goose' which is used here, also symbolizes a traveller in difficulties; and surely this is the sense which line 4, the other half of this couplet, demands? Comparison with lines 2 and 6 of No. 14 seems to my mind to clinch this interpretation.

5. *Wén-zhāng zèng mìng-dá*
   Literature hates destiny-successful

6. *Chī-mèi xǐ rén guò*
   Mountain-demons rejoice people passing

Chī-mèi are goblins who lurk in the hills and devour the unwary traveller. I think a double meaning is intended by this line. *Guò* means 'pass', 'come by', 'visit'; but it also has the quite distinct sense of 'error', 'fault' (compare our word 'transgression' which derives from a Latin word meaning 'crossing' or 'passage'). The surface sense of this line is, 'In the wild places where your journey is leading you the goblins are waiting in eager anticipation to pounce on the wayfarer who chances their way; so do be careful'; but I think it is not too fanciful to read into it the second meaning 'The philistines are delighted when a person like you slips up': i.e. A lot of people were secretly pleased when Li Po compromised himself with Prince Lin.

7. *Yīng gòng yuān-hún yǔ*
    Ought with wronged-ghost talk

8. *Tóu shī zèng Mì-luó*
    Drop poem present Mi-lo

The 'wronged ghost' is the spirit of the fourth-century B.C. poet Ch'ü Yüan, who was banished by the king of Ch'u as a result of false allegations made against him by his enemies and finally drowned himself in the river Mi-lo. A century after his death a young Han poet called Chia I dropped a set of verses into the river as an offering to his wronged ghost while on his way to exile in Ch'ang-sha. Tu Fu suggests that Li Po, whose misfortunes, he thinks, are due to others' malice, should compare notes, while he is in the area, with the ghost of that other wronged poet, Ch'ü Yüan, and should enlist his support by dropping a set of verses into the river just as that other exile Chia I did many centuries before.

In view of the obsessive preoccupation with water and drowning found in all of these three poems about Li Po, it seems to me very likely that a rumour had reached Tu Fu in Ch'in-chou that Li Po had been drowned while on his way to exile.

TRANSLATION

'Thoughts of Li Po from the World's End'

Here at the world's end the cold winds are beginning to blow. What message have you for me, my master? When will the poor wandering goose arrive? The rivers and lakes are swollen with autumn's waters. Art detests a too successful life; and the hungry goblins await you with welcoming jaws. You had better have a word with the ghost of that other wronged poet. Drop some verses into the Mi-lo as an offering to him!

16

蜀相

Shǔ xiàng

丞相祠堂何處尋
1. Chéng-xiàng cí-táng hé-chù xún?

錦官城外柏森森
2. Jǐn-guān-chéng-wài bó sēn-sēn.

映堦碧草自春色
3. Yìng jiē bì cǎo zì chūn-sè,

隔葉黃鸝空好音
4. Gé yè huáng-lí kōng hǎo-yīn.

三顧頻煩天下計
5. Sān gù pín-fán tiān-xià jì,

兩朝開濟老臣心
6. Liǎng cháo kāi-jì lǎo-chén xīn.

出師未捷身先死
7. Chū-shī wèi jié shēn xiān sǐ,

長使英雄淚滿襟
8. Cháng shǐ yīng-xióng lèi mǎn jīn.

TITLE AND SUBJECT

Shǔ is a place-name. Anciently it was the name of a state which occupied part of what is now the province of Szechwan. In the third century A.D. it was the name of a much larger state: one of the Three Kingdoms which emerged after the break-up of the Han empire.

Xiàng means 'minister' or 'chancellor'. The 'minister of Shu' referred to here is the famous Three Kingdoms statesman, Chu-ko Liang (181–234), whose proverbial loyalty and astuteness still delight audiences of the Chinese opera.

In the restless, wandering life that Tu Fu led following his resignation from the post at Hua-chou, he came nearest to settling permanently at Ch'eng-tu, the administrative capital of Szechwan, or Shu as it was sometimes still called in his day. Tu Fu's 'thatched hall'—or what purports to be a remote descendant of it—is still to be seen in that city.

Tu Fu left Ch'in-chou in November 759 and moved to a place called T'ung-ku, near the Kansu–Szechwan border. This move proved unsatisfactory and he left T'ung-ku for Ch'eng-tu in late December.

Poets could no more make a living from their poems in Tu Fu's day than they can today; they could, however, earn a certain amount of money by writing obituaries, epitaphs, and the like, and they could, particularly if they had held office in the past, rely to some extent on patronage and on the freemasonry which existed among members of the official class. Repeatedly shuttled from one side of the empire to the other, members of this class tended to cling to the contacts they had established in the course of their official careers. In Ch'eng-tu there were officials whom Tu Fu had known at Su-tsung's court, and in 762 a former member of the Chancellery, in which he had served, became Governor over the whole province with his headquarters at Ch'eng-tu. Tu Fu therefore found Ch'eng-tu congenial and spent three and a half out of the next five years in the little retreat which he had built for himself outside the city.

A newcomer to Ch'eng-tu would naturally want to visit the famous historical sites of the city during the weeks following his

arrival. I therefore place this visit to the shrine of Chu-ko Liang
in the spring of 760. Tu Fu arrived at Ch'eng-tu in mid-winter
when the weather would not have been very suitable for out-of-
town excursions.

FORM

A heptasyllabic poem in Regulated Verse—the first example of this
metre we have so far encountered. In the longer line the parallelism
of the central couplets requires greater skill to achieve. In this poem
the parallelism of these lines is technically perfect. Notice the
colours 'emerald' and 'yellow' in lines 3 and 4 and the numbers
'three' and 'two' in lines 5 and 6. 'Colour' and 'sound' in lines 3
and 4 would also be considered a 'good' antithesis.

EXEGESIS

1. *Chéng-xiàng cí-táng hé-chù xún*
   Chancellor's shrine-hall what-place seek

2. *Jǐn-guān-chéng-wài bó sēn-sēn*
   Brocade-intendant-city-outside cypresses thick

Jǐn-guān-chéng: Ch'eng-tu was called the City of the Brocade
Officer because it had once been the centre of a brocade industry
and had sent a tribute of brocade to the court under the supervision
of a 'Brocade Intendant'.
Bó sēn-sēn: We should say in English, '*Where* the cypresses grow
thick'. The cypresses were popularly supposed to have been
planted by Chu-ko Liang himself.

3. *Yìng jiē bì cǎo zì chūn-sè*
   Shining-on steps emerald grass by-itself spring-colour

4. *Gé yè huáng-lí kōng hǎo-yīn*
   Screened-by leaves yellow oriole in-vain lovely-sound

Yìng can mean 'cast a shadow', 'make a reflection', or 'shine on'
these three functions being not very precisely distinguished in
Chinese usage. I am not at all sure what Tu Fu means by *yìng jiē*.

However we explain it, it is clear that the grass is growing *on* the steps, because the main point of this couplet is to convey an impression of utter stillness and ruinous neglect. This is a place where people scarcely ever come. If *yìng* means 'casts its shadow on', then I suppose he is referring to the dappled light and shade made by the spring sunlight shining on the grass growing between the stone slabs of the steps. But I suspect that it means simply 'shines against', 'is offset by', 'stands out against'—because the spring green is so vivid. If he were talking about the *shadows* made by the grass, the 'emerald' would sink to the level of a stock epithet, which seems unlikely since its antithetical contrast with 'yellow' in the next line lends it a certain amount of weight. It could be argued that the 'yellow' isn't functional either, because the oriole is said to be screened by the leaves. But probably flashes of yellow would be visible through the leaves from time to time, in which case 'yellow' is highly functional.

Zì and *kōng* are both used here as adverbs. The oriole 'has a lovely voice' (i.e. sings beautifully) 'in vain' (literally 'emptily') because there is no one there to hear it. The grass wears its spring colours 'for itself' because there is no one there to look at it. Tu Fu uses these two colourless little adverbs with marvellous dexterity to suggest the stillness and remoteness of the shrine. This is rather a good example of the way in which every word in Tu Fu's poems is made to carry the maximum amount of weight.

5. *Sān gù pín-fán tiān-xià jì*
   Three visits insisting-troubling whole-world plan

6. *Liǎng cháo kāi-jì lǎo-chén xīn*
   Two reigns founding-aiding old-servant heart

Chu-ko Liang's two eve-of-campaign proclamations, composed for the Shu expeditions of 227 and 228 against the hostile kingdom of Wei, rank amongst the best-known pieces of Chinese prose literature. Tu Fu echoes the language of the first of them in the *sān gù* of line 5. In this first proclamation Chu-ko Liang recalls his first meeting with Liu Pei, who subsequently became First Ruler of Shu. At the time Chu-ko Liang was living in retirement in a cottage on Sleeping Dragon Hill in Honan, and the soldier-adventurer Liu Pei, who had come to call on him and ask him to be his adviser, was subjected to a series of deliberate snubs designed to test his seriousness of purpose. Liu Pei countered with such humility and persistence that Chu-ko Liang finally gave him his wholehearted support and helped him to carve out an empire for himself in the south-west. 'His late Majesty', says Chu-ko Liang in the proclamation, 'utterly disregarding my humble status, thrice called on me in my thatched abode to consult me about the state of the empire' (. . . *sān gù chén yú cǎo-lù zhī zhōng, zì chén yǐ dāng-shì zhī shì*). *Sān gù* is a sufficiently unusual phrase for it to be quite clear that the *sān gù* of this couplet is a deliberate quotation.

Liǎng cháo: literally 'two courts', i.e. that of the First Ruler, Liu Pei, and that of his weakling son Liu Ch'an, the Second Ruler. Chu-ko Liang's devoted service of the latter was particularly meritorious in that Liu Pei, who had no illusions about his own son, as he lay dying urged Chu-ko Liang to set aside Liu Ch'an and become emperor himself if he wished to do so.

Kāi-jì: *kāi* 'opening' has here the sense of 'initiating' or 'founding' and refers to the part Chu-ko Liang played in the foundation of the kingdom of Shu. *Jì* 'assisting' here has the sense of 'maintaining': i.e. maintaining and defending Liu Ch'an's patrimony. The *kāi* belongs to the first reign and the *jì* to the second.

The grammar of these two lines may seem more than a little puzzling. They are examples of the sort of 'pregnant construction' which is fairly common in Chinese syntax, where predication includes a much wider range of relationships than it does in European languages. By analysis, *sān gù pín-fán* is the subject of a sentence whose predicate is *tiān-xià jì*, and *liǎng cháo kāi-jì* is the subject of a sentence whose predicate is *lǎo-chén xīn*. Let us express it in this way:

Three visits insisting-troubling   *equals*   whole-world plan
Two reigns founding-aiding   *equals*   old-servant heart

The first 'equals' stands for a relationship which could be paraphrased 'was a meritorious action which bore fruit in', whilst the second could be paraphrased 'was visible proof, if proof were needed, of'. Even in Modern Chinese, simple predication can be used to express a causal relationship. For example, you can say: 'His doing this *is* he doesn't love her any more' where in English we should have to say 'is because he doesn't love her any more', or 'shows that he doesn't love her any more'.

7. *Chū-shī wèi jié shēn xiān sǐ*
   Lead-out-army not-yet victorious body first die

8. *Cháng shǐ yīng-xióng lèi mǎn jīn*
   Always cause heroic-men tears cover bosom

Chū-shī: Chu-ko Liang's famous proclamations are called *chū-shī-biǎo* 'leading-out-army proclamations'.

Chu-ko Liang was personally commanding the expeditionary force against Wei when he died, before anything decisive had been achieved by it.

Jīn: The Chinese word means that part of the dress which covers the chest. I think 'bosom' is the best we can do with it in English, though in fact it means part of the clothing, not part of the body.

TRANSLATION

'The Chancellor of Shu'

Where is the shrine of the Chancellor to be found?—Beyond the walls of the City of Brocade, amidst densely growing cypresses. Vivid against the steps, the emerald grass celebrates its own spring unseen. Beyond the trees a yellow oriole sings its glad song unheard.

The importunate humility of those three visits resulted in the grand strategy which shaped the world for a generation; his services under two reigns, both as founder and as maintainer, revealed the true loyalty of the old courtier's heart. That he should have died before victory could crown his expedition will always draw a sympathetic tear from men of heroic stamp.

17

客至

Kè zhì

舍南舍北皆春水
1. *Shè-nán shè-běi jiē chūn shuǐ,*

但見羣鷗日日來
2. *Dàn jiàn qún-ōu rì-rì lái.*

花徑不曾緣客掃
3. *Huā-jìng bù-céng yuán kè sǎo,*

蓬門今始為君開
4. *Péng-mén jīn shǐ wèi jūn kāi.*

盤飱市遠無兼味
5. *Pán sūn shì yuǎn wú jiān-wèi,*

樽酒家貧只舊醅
6. *Zūn jiǔ jiā pín zhǐ jiù pēi.*

肯與鄰翁相對飲
7. *Kěn yǔ lín-wēng xiāng-duì yǐn,*

隔籬呼取盡餘杯
8. *Gé lí hū-qǔ jìn yú bēi.*

TITLE AND SUBJECT

Kè means 'guest', 'visitor'.

Zhì means 'arrives'.

This poem was written in Ch'eng-tu, probably in the spring of 760. Thanks to a financial grant from the Governor, Tu Fu had now completed the building of his 'thatched house' outside the city and was living a life of quiet rural retirement, happier, perhaps, than he had been for a number of years. The occasion of this poem, we learn from a note supplied by the poet himself, was the visit of a 'Prefect Ts'ui'. It is thought that this Prefect Ts'ui may have been a maternal uncle of Tu Fu's. His mother had been a Miss Ts'ui. In spite of his elevated position, Uncle Ts'ui was clearly a good sport, prepared to drink his impoverished nephew's abominable wine with a brave smile and to make himself agreeable to the rustic neighbours.

FORM

Heptasyllabic Regulated Verse, like the last poem, which was probably written within a few weeks of it. In T'ang Chinese *lái*, *kāi*, *pēi*, *bēi* become true rhymes.

EXEGESIS

1. *Shè-nán shè-běi jiē chūn shuǐ*
   House-south house-north both springtime water

2. *Dàn jiàn qún-ōu rì-rì lái*
   Only see flock-gulls every-day come

Some Chinese critics think that Tu Fu is complaining of neglect when he says that only the seagulls visit him. But in ancient Chinese tradition to be a friend of the gulls is to be innocent and simple—a child of nature. I think Tu Fu, far from complaining, is boasting about how remote and secluded his country retreat is, and how close to nature he is living.

3. *Huā-jìng bù-céng yuán kè sǎo*
Flower-path not-have because-of guest swept

4. *Péng-mén jīn shǐ wèi jūn kāi*
Wicker-gate now first-time for you open

Line 3 doesn't mean 'I haven't bothered to sweep the path for you' but 'I haven't had occasion to sweep the path up to now because no one has been to see me.'

Huā-jìng because it is lined with fruit-trees and therefore, in late spring, thick with fallen petals.

5. *Pán sūn shì yuǎn wú jiān wèi*
Dish-repast market far no double flavour

6. *Zūn jiǔ jiā pín zhǐ jiù pēi*
Jar-wine household poor only old brewing

Pán sūn, zūn jiǔ: i.e. the food *in* the dish, the wine *in* the jar.

Shì yuǎn, jiā pín are in hypotactic relationship to the clauses which follow: '*because* the market is far', '*since* we are so poor'.

It would not occur to a European host to apologize because the wine was old, but the Chinese of Tu Fu's time liked it fresh.

7. *Kěn yǔ lín-wēng xiāng-duì yǐn*
Willing with neighbour-gaffer opposite drink

8. *Gé lí hū-qǔ jìn yú bēi*
Intervening fence call-take finish remaining cups

Kěn: i.e. 'If you are willing . . . I will call over the fence to him.'

Qǔ used by itself is a verb meaning 'take', 'get'. In T'ang colloquial it was frequently used as a verbal suffix. We might say that *hū-qǔ* means 'call over', 'call to' in contrast to *hū* 'call'.

TRANSLATION

'The Guest'

The waters of springtime flow north and south of my dwelling. Only the flocks of gulls come daily to call on me. I have not swept my flower-strewn path for a visitor, and my wicker-gate opens the first time today for you. Because the market is far away, the dishes I serve you offer little variety; and because this is a poor household, the only wine in my jars comes from an old brewing. If you are willing to sit and drink with my old neighbour, I shall call to him over the fence to come and finish off the remaining cupfuls with us.

18

奉濟驛重送嚴公四韻
Fèng-jì yì chóng sòng Yán gōng sì yùn

~~~~~~

遠送從此別

1. Yuǎn sòng cóng cǐ bié,

青山空復情

2. Qīng shān kōng fù qíng!

幾時杯重把

3. Jǐ-shí bēi chóng bǎ,

昨夜月同行

4. Zuó-yè yuè tóng xíng?

列郡謳歌惜

5. Liè-jùn ōu-gē xī;

三朝出入榮

6. Sān cháo chū-rù róng.

江村獨歸去

7. Jiāng-cūn dú guī-qù,

寂寞養殘生

8. Jì-mò yǎng cán-shēng.

TITLE AND SUBJECT

Fèng-jì: a place about one hundred miles north-east of Ch'eng-tu.

Yì: 'post-station'. In former times these stations were maintained by the Imperial government along all the main lines of communication to supply lodgings or a change of mount to couriers and mandarins travelling on official business.

Chóng: 'again', 'a second time'.

Sòng: 'see off'.

Chóng sòng is therefore to see off for a second time: i.e., having already gone for some distance with a person, then changed your mind and gone on for a further part of the journey.

Yán: a surname.

Gōng: 'duke'.

The person referred to in this way is Yen Wu, a friend of Tu Fu who had become Governor over both parts of what is now the province of Szechwan early in 762. Tu Fu calls him 'duke' because he had lately been created Duke of Cheng as a reward for his victories over the Tibetans. He was summoned to court in July 762 for consultations, and Tu Fu went with him as far as Feng-chi to see him off.

Sì yùn: 'four rhymes'. T'ang poets often referred to their poems deprecatingly as so many 'rhymes', much in the way that English poets were once in the habit of referring to the 'lines' they had written.

On seeing off the patron and friend on whom he so much depended, Tu Fu felt a mixture of apprehension and hope. There was a faint hope that Yen Wu might be able to arrange a court appointment for him, and there were apprehensions as to what would sustain him if Yen Wu's supporting hand were to be permanently removed. By the time he came to write this poem (the last of several which he addressed to Yen Wu during the farewell journey) he seems to have convinced himself that any aspirations he might have entertained were futile. He ends it by stating, somewhat bleakly, that he is going back to bury himself in a life of retirement.

The departure of a Governor would invariably be the occasion for scores of adulatory odes by his clients and subordinates. In this poem Tu Fu successfully breathes into a lifeless stereotype some of the affection which he genuinely feels for the recipient.

FORM

Pentasyllabic Regulated Verse. The 'four rhymes' of the title refers to the four instances of the same rhyme occurring at the ends of the four couplets which make up the poem. In T'ang phonology the approximate sounds of *qíng*, *xíng*, *róng*, and *shēng* would have been *zyēng*, *gēng*, *yuēng*, and *shēng*.

EXEGESIS

1. *Yuǎn-sòng cóng cǐ bié*
   Far-send-off from here part

2. *Qīng shān kōng fù qíng*
   Green hills vainly repeat emotion

Kōng fù qíng: I think Tu Fu means that the grief he had felt at the prospect of parting and which he thought he had mastered is reawakened by the sight of the green hills which are soon to swallow up his friend; but it is all of no avail, for this time he really *must* take final leave of him: there is nothing he can do to prevent Yen Wu's departure.

3. *Jǐ-shí bēi chóng bǎ*
   What time cups again hold

4. *Zuó-yè yuè tóng xíng*
   Last-night's moon together walk

i.e. 'When shall we once more walk together under the moon, as we did during last night's party?' This was July, and they would have been drinking out-of-doors.

5. *Liè-jùn ōu-gē xī*
    Adjoining-departments ballad-songs regret

6. *Sān cháo chū-rù róng*
    Three reigns going-out-entering glorious

Jùn is, I think, used here in its ancient, Han sense to designate an administrative unit smaller than, though comparable with, a province: a department. Yen Wu was Governor over both the eastern and western divisions of Szechwan.

Sān cháo: Hsüan-tsung and Su-tsung both died in May 762 within a fortnight of each other, and both tragically: Hsüan-tsung in the virtual imprisonment imposed on him by the Goneril-like behaviour of his son; Su-tsung abandoned on his sickbed while a war to the death was waged between his hateful Empress and his still more hateful Chief Eunuch. The new Emperor who had summoned Yen Wu to court was Su-tsung's son, Tai-tsung. Yen Wu had already held high office under Hsüan-tsung before the outbreak of the An Lu-shan rebellion. Tai-tsung was therefore the third emperor he had served.

Chū-rù: i.e. both in the provincial administration (*chū*) and at court (*rù*).

7. *Jiāng-cūn dú guī-qù*
    River-village alone go-back

8. *Ji-mò yǎng cán-shēng*
    Solitary support remaining-life

Line 7 is, of course, an instance of inversion: 'To my river-village I now return alone.'

TRANSLATION

'A Second Farewell at the Feng-chi Post-station to His Grace the Duke of Cheng'

The long farewell journey must at last end here. In vain do the green hills renew my emotion. How long will it be before we again hold the winecups in our hands and walk together under last night's moon? The songs of two provinces regret your parting. Three reigns have seen you distinguished at court and in the field. Now I must return alone to my village by the river, to support my remaining days in quiet solitude.

19

聞官軍收河南河北

Wén guān-jūn shōu Hé-nán Hé-běi

劍外忽傳收薊北

1. *Jiàn-wài hū chuán shōu Jì-běi,*

初聞涕淚滿衣裳

2. *Chū wén tì-lèi mǎn yī-shāng.*

却看妻子愁何在

3. *Què kàn qī-zǐ chóu hé zài?*

漫卷詩書喜欲狂

4. *Màn juǎn shī-shū xǐ yù kuáng!*

白日放歌須縱酒

5. *Bái-rì fàng-gē xū zòng-jiǔ,*

青春作伴好還鄉

6. *Qīng-chūn zuò-bàn hǎo huán-xiāng.*

即從巴峽穿巫峽

7. *Jí cóng Bā-xiá chuān Wū-xiá,*

便下襄陽向洛陽

8. *Biàn xià Xiāng-yáng xiàng Luò-yáng.*

TITLE AND SUBJECT

Wén: 'hear'.

Guān-jūn: literally 'official army', i.e. the government troops, the Imperial army.

Shōu: 'recover'.

Hé-nán, Hé-běi: These do not quite correspond to the 'Honan', 'Hopei' of the modern atlas. 'Hopei' included, besides the present province of Hopei, all the land of Shantung and Honan north of the Yellow River, whilst 'Honan' included most of the present-day province of Shantung as well as most of modern Honan. This area had been the scene of rebel activity since An Lu-shan raised the standard of revolt at his headquarters near present-day Peking in 755.

Tu Fu wrote this poem in the early spring of 763 at Tzu-chou, thirty miles south-east of the post-station which had been the scene of his parting from Yen Wu in No. 18. He had been forced to go there instead of returning to his 'river village' by the outbreak of disorders in Ch'eng-tu which followed Yen Wu's departure.

In November 762 Loyang fell to the Imperial forces. It was a costly victory, since the city was mercilessly pillaged by the Uighur allies with whose assistance it had been recovered; nevertheless it signalled the final demoralization of the rebel forces, whose commanders now surrendered one after another as the Imperial armies marched east. Shih Ch'ao-i, the rebel 'emperor', hanged himself in February 763, and his decapitated head, surrendered along with what remained of rebel-held territory by his chief lieutenant, was dispatched to Ch'ang-an for the Emperor's inspection. So ended, after seven years, the futile war which had devastated and depopulated the greater part of North China. Tu Fu's jubilant excitement on hearing the news still rings across the centuries.

FORM

Heptasyllabic Regulated Verse. Tu Fu was an important innovator in this form, which before his time was little used above the level of polite versification. Nos. 16 and 17 were already well above that level. The amount of emotion which the form is made to carry in this poem would have been unthinkable in the works of an earlier poet.

EXEGESIS

1. *Jiàn-wài hū chuán shōu Jì-běi*
   Chien-beyond suddenly is-reported recovering Chi-pei
2. *Chū wén tì-lèi mǎn yī-shāng*
   First hear tears cover clothing

Jiàn-wài: abbreviation of *Jiàn-gé-wài* 'beyond the Chien-ko pass', i.e. Szechwan, to which the Chien-ko pass is a door if you approach it from the direction of Ch'ang-an. Compare the reference to Hsüan-tsung's flight into Szechwan in line 15 of No. 7.

Jì-běi: Chi-pei is used here as a more literary and 'poetic' name for Hopei.

Tì-lèi: strictly speaking *tì* is the moisture which runs from one's nose when one weeps. Although undeniably a part of the phenomenon, it is considered by Western authors too indecorous to be mentioned in a serious context. Indeed, I know of no English word for it other than 'snivel', which is rarely used except as a verb and usually metaphorically. In Chinese no such taboo exists, and it is possible to refer to the 'jade *tì*' of a weeping woman without making her in any way vulgar or ridiculous.

3. *Què kàn qī-zǐ chóu hé zài*
   Turn-back look-at wife-children sorrow where is
4. *Màn juǎn shī-shū xǐ yù kuáng*
   Carelessly roll poems-writings glad about-to-become crazy

Màn juǎn shī-shū: with trembling hands, Tu Fu begins packing straight away.

5. *Bái-rì fàng-gē xū zòng-jiǔ*
   White-sun let-go-singing must give-way-to-wine
6. *Qīng-chūn zuò-bàn hǎo huán-xiāng*
   Green-spring act-as companion good-to return-home

Huán-xiāng: 'home' for Tu Fu is the district near Loyang where his half-brothers lived. In his own note on this poem Tu Fu says that he has some farm-land at the Eastern Capital (Loyang).

7. *Jí cóng Bā-xiá chuān Wū-xiá*
   Immediately from Pa-gorge traverse Wu-gorge

8. *Biàn xià Xiāng-yáng xiàng Luò-yáng*
   Then down-to Hsiang-yang on-to Lo-yang

Bā-xiá, *Wū-xiá*: two of the famous 'Yangtze gorges'. What is nowadays called the Pa Gorge is sixty or seventy miles *east* of the Wu Gorge, which would make nonsense of Tu Fu's itinerary. It has been suggested that the *Bā-xiá* of this couplet refers to the Yangtze at Chungking which was called Pa in Tu Fu's day.

The trip Tu Fu is so light-heartedly proposing is approximately as far as the motoring distance from Lyons to Stockholm.

TRANSLATION

'On Learning of the Recovery of Honan and Hopei by the Imperial Army'

To the land south of Chien-ko news is suddenly brought of the recovery of Chi-pei. When I first hear it, my gown is all wet with tears. I turn and look round at my wife and children, and have not a sorrow in the world. Carelessly I roll together the volumes of verse I have been reading, almost delirious with joy. There must be singing out loud in full daylight: we must drink and drink! I must go back home: the green spring shall be my companion. I shall go at once, by way of the Pa Gorge, through the Wu Gorge, then to Hsiang-yang, and so, from there, on towards Loyang!

20

别房太尉墓

Bié Fáng-tài-wèi mù

他鄉復行役
1. *Tā-xiāng fù xíng-yì,*

駐馬別孤墳
2. *Zhù-mǎ bié gū fén.*

近淚無乾土
3. *Jìn lèi wú gān tǔ,*

低空有斷雲
4. *Dī kōng yǒu duàn yún.*

對碁陪謝傅
5. *Duì qí péi Xiè fù,*

把劍覓徐君
6. *Bǎ jiàn mì Xú jūn.*

惟見林花落
7. *Wéi jiàn lín huā luò,*

鶯啼送客聞
8. *Yīng tí sòng kè wén.*

TITLE AND SUBJECT

Bié: 'part from', 'take leave of'.

Fáng: a surname, here that of Fang Kuan, the elder statesman in whose fall from grace in 758 Tu Fu had been involved.

Tài-wèi: a title, 'Grand Marshal', which at this time was purely honorary. The court bestowed it on Fang Kuan posthumously on learning of his death.

Mù: 'tomb'. It helps to know that the Chinese used to bury their dead in the open countryside outside the towns, and that they invariably raised an earth mound over the grave.

Tai-tsung's new government recalled Fang Kuan from his sojourn 'in the wilderness' as a provincial administrator by offering him a distinguished post at court in May 763. Broken in health, however, he fell ill and died a few months later at a monastery in Lang-chou while on his way to take up the new appointment. The occasion of this poem seems to have been a visit Tu Fu made to Lang-chou to pay his respects to the tomb of his late friend and patron before setting off on the journey to Ch'eng-tu. His friend Yen Wu, whom we last encountered on the way to Ch'ang-an, had now, in the spring of 764, after a brief but ambitious career at court, been reappointed to his former post of Governor over the two departments of Szechwan, and Tu Fu had resolved to return with his family to the 'river village' outside Ch'eng-tu and resume occupation of his thatched house.

FORM

Pentasyllabic Regulated Verse.

EXEGESIS

1. *Tā-xiāng fù xíng-yì*
   Other-district again travelling-journey

2. *Zhù-mǎ bié gū fén*
   Halt-horse part-from lonely grave

Tā-xiāng: the opposite of *gù-xiāng*: 'other' in the sense of other than the one you come from, hence 'away from home', 'far from home', 'in a strange land', etc.

3. *Jīn lèi wú gān tǔ*
   Recent tears no dry soil

4. *Dī kōng yǒu duàn yún*
   Low sky has broken clouds

Jīn lèi: a poetic conceit. The 'low sky' and ragged clouds of the next line show that it has been raining. A little more subtle than saying 'The sky weeps for you.' Not so very much more, one would have thought; yet some commentators have found this line baffling.

5. *Duì qí péi Xiè fù*
   Face *wei-ch'i* keep-company Hsieh Tutor

6. *Bǎ jiàn mì Xú jūn*
   Grasp sword seek Hsü lord

Qí: some people will know this game better by its Japanese name, *go*. It is played with little black and white counters on a large board, the object being to surround as many as possible of one's opponent's 'men'.

Xiè fù: 'Grand Tutor Hsieh' is Hsieh An (320–85) of the Eastern Chin dynasty who was posthumously awarded the honorary title of *T'ai-fu* or 'Grand Tutor'. In the Eastern Chin period most of China north of the Yangtze was in barbarian hands, and when the barbarian emperor Fu Chien launched a massive invasion designed to extend his control over the Chinese-held south, Hsieh An was in control of the Chinese government and most of the commanders on the Chinese side were members of his family. At the Battle of the River Fei in 383 the Chin army completely routed the barbarian hordes. It is said that news of this famous victory was brought to Hsieh An as he sat playing *wei-ch'i*, but that he received it with no trace of emotion and continued playing the game.

I think Tu Fu means by this allusion: 'I was privileged to accompany the great man in his hours of leisure, and was sometimes present when matters of great moment were brought to his notice.'

Bǎ jiàn mì Xú jūn is another historical allusion. It refers to the story of Chi Cha, prince of Wu, a contemporary of Confucius famous for his wisdom and for his extensive travels in pursuit of culture. (Wu was a very backward and undeveloped country in his day.) While visiting the little state of Hsü, Chi Cha noticed that the

Lord of Hsü was interested in a sword he was wearing. He decided to give it to him as a present; but as no suitable occasion presented itself he resolved to offer it to him when he returned on a second visit. When he visited Hsü again, however, he was distressed to learn that the Lord of Hsü was now dead. He therefore hung the sword on a tree beside his grave and departed.

The point of the allusion is something like this: 'I owe you so much and I should so like to have seen you before you died. But I was too late; and so I can only offer this gesture at your tomb as a token of what I should like to have said and done.'

7. *Wéi jiàn lín huā luò*
   Only see woods blossom fall

8. *Yīng tí sòng kè wén*
   Oriole's song speeds visitor's hearing

Sòng kè wén: i.e. its sound follows him on his way until he is out of earshot.

TRANSLATION

'Leave-taking at the Grave of Grand Marshal Fang'

In a place far from home, and about to embark once more on my travels, I stop to take leave of the lonely grave. The earth is all wet with recent tears: broken clouds drift in a lowering sky. I who once sat at play with Grand Tutor Hsieh, now come sword in hand to seek the Lord of Hsü. But I see only the blossoms falling in the woods and hear the cry of the oriole speeding me on my way.

21

登樓
Dēng lóu

花近高樓傷客心
1. *Huā jìn gāo lóu shāng kè xīn:*

萬方多難此登臨
2. *Wàn-fāng duō nán cǐ dēng-lín!*

錦江春色來天地
3. *Jǐn-jiāng chūn-sè lái tiān-dì,*

玉壘浮雲變古今
4. *Yù-léi fú-yún biàn gǔ-jīn.*

北極朝庭終不改
5. *Běi-jí cháo-tíng zhōng bù gǎi,*

西山寇盜莫相侵
6. *Xī-shān kòu dào mò xiāng-qīn!*

可憐後主還祠廟
7. *Kě-lián Hòu-zhǔ huán cí-miào,*

日暮聊爲梁父吟
8. *Rì-mù liáo wéi Liáng-fù-yín.*

TITLE AND SUBJECT

Dēng means 'climb'.

Lóu means 'upper story', 'building with upper story', here 'tower'.

In Chinese literature poems composed on top of high buildings practically form a genre of their own. Even in this short selection of Tu Fu there are two others (No. 33 and No. 34, with which this one should be compared).

The tower of this poem's title may have been one of the western gate-towers of Ch'eng-tu. At all events, it was a tower in Ch'eng-tu from which Tu Fu could see the Brocade River and the Western Mountains in the distance.

The date of this poem is probably a month or two later than that of the preceding one: i.e. late spring, 764. It contains references to recent events. Towards the end of the previous year Ch'ang-an had fallen into the hands of the Tibetans, and for a brief fortnight the empire was ruled by a member of the Imperial clan whom they installed as their puppet. Tai-tsung returned to the capital, from which he had fled some time before its fall, at the beginning of 764, but in the spring of that year the Tibetans still occupied parts of Western Szechwan and the North-West. Hence the gay spring scene revealed to Tu Fu as he gazes down from his tower fills him not with elation but with gloomy apprehensions.

FORM

Regulated Verse in heptasyllabics.

EXEGESIS

1. *Huā jìn gāo lóu shāng kè xīn*
   Flowers near high tower hurt visitor's heart

2. *Wàn-fāng duō nàn cǐ dēng-lín*
   Myriad-directions many troubles this climb-look-down

   Wàn-fāng: i.e. 'everywhere'.

The grammar of line 2 is perhaps a little puzzling. *Dēng-lín* is the main verb and *cǐ* an adverb of manner: 'I mount like this', i.e. 'I make this ascent.' *Wàn-fāng duō nàn* is a subordinate clause modifying the main one (the relationship—a temporal one—as is so often the case in Chinese grammar, is unexpressed): 'I make this ascent *at a time when* everywhere there are many difficulties.'

3. *Jǐn-jiāng chūn-sè lái tiān-dì*
   Brocade-river spring-colours bring heaven-earth
4. *Yù-léi fú-yún biàn gǔ-jīn*
   Jade-fort floating-clouds change ancient-modern

Jǐn-jiāng: an affluent of the river Min flowing south of the old city of Ch'eng-tu, so-called supposedly because the weavers used to wash their brocades in it.

Chūn-sè: 'the spring scene'.

Yù-léi: a mountain north-west of the city.

In this couplet the poet describes a quasi-mystical vision of all nature and all time. Tu Fu often approaches closely to a mystical experience when contemplating the grandeurs of nature; but as a rule he is rapidly twitched out of his vision by some domestic or political consideration, or by the importunity of some bodily infirmity.

5. *Běi-jí cháo-tíng zhōng bù gǎi*
   North-pole court in-the-end not change
6. *Xī-shān kòu-dào mò xiāng-qīn*
   West-mountains raiding-brigands do-not invade

Běi-jí: the Pole Star keeps to a fixed place in the sky whilst all the other stars revolve around it and do it homage, hence it symbolizes the Emperor or the Imperial government—which is, incidentally, in the far north in relation to Ch'eng-tu. Tu Fu says of the Imperial government that 'in the end it didn't change' because in spite of the brief interregnum when the Tibetans set up a puppet emperor of their own in Ch'ang-an, the metropolis is now once more in Chinese hands and Tai-tsung restored to his throne.

Kòu-dào: the Tibetans, who still held parts of Szechwan.

7. *Kě-lián Hòu-zhǔ huán cí-miào*
   Pitiable Second-Ruler still-has temple
8. *Rì-mù liáo wéi Liáng-fù-yín*
   Day's-eve want make Liang-fu-song

Line 7 is thought to contain a veiled criticism of Tai-tsung, whose misplaced confidence in eunuch advisers was held responsible for

many of the Empire's current difficulties. Even the effete Second
Ruler of Shu is still honoured, says Tu Fu, thanks to the greatness
of his predecessor and the brilliance of his famous minister, Chu-ko
Liang. So there is some hope for Tai-tsung yet.

Liáng-fù-yín: Liang-fu is the name of a small mountain among
the foothills of T'ai-shan. The *Liang-fu-yin* was a dirge-like folk-
song which Chu-ko Liang was fond of singing when he was still
living in retirement in Shantung. Line 8 therefore has a double
meaning: (1) As evening falls I should like to make a poem about
my musings on top of the tower. (2) I wish that in this dark and
difficult hour I could be given a position of trust like that held by
Chu-ko Liang, save the state, and make myself and my ruler
famous for all time.

TRANSLATION

'On the Tower'

Flowers near the high tower sadden the heart of the visitor. It is
at a time when the Empire is everywhere beset by troubles that he
has climbed up to see this view. The Brocade River scene, dressed
in spring's colours, brings a whole universe before his eyes, whilst
the floating clouds above Marble Fort Mountain seem to unfold
all time in their mutating shapes. The Court of the Northern Star
remains unchanged. Let the marauders from the Western Mountains cease their raiding! Even the poor Second Ruler still has his
shrine. As evening falls I shall sing a song of Liang-fu.

22

宿府
Sù fú

清秋幕府井梧寒
1. *Qīng qiū mù-fú jǐng wú hán,*

獨宿江城蠟炬殘
2. *Dú sù jiāng-chéng là-jù cán.*

永夜角聲悲自語
3. *Yǒng yè jué shēng bēi zì-yǔ,*

中天月色好誰看
4. *Zhōng tiān yuè-sè hǎo shuí kān?*

風塵荏苒音書絕
5. *Fēng-chén rěn-rǎn yīn-shū jué,*

關塞蕭條行路難
6. *Guān-sài xiāo-tiáo xíng-lù nán.*

已忍伶俜十年事
7. *Yǐ rěn líng-píng shí nián shì,*

強移棲息一枝安
8. *Qiǎng yí xī-xī yì zhī ān.*

TITLE AND SUBJECT

Sù: 'to lodge', 'to pass the night (at)'.

Fŭ: 'prefecture', 'headquarters', 'office', 'residency'.

Compare this title with the title of No. 8.

In the summer of 764, Yen Wu appointed Tu Fu to an advisory post at his headquarters in Ch'eng-tu and obtained for him the nominal court position which would enable him to assume once more, after five years' unemployment, the uniform and insignia of official rank. Presumably Tu Fu commuted between his 'river village' and the city, sleeping at the office when pressure of business left him insufficient time for returning in the daylight.

FORM

Regulated Verse in heptasyllabics (like the previous poem).

Parallelism in the final couplet is rather unusual.

Notice the bisyllabic alliterative or homoioteleutic descriptive terms which occur at the same point in each of the lines 5–8: *rĕn-răn, xiāo-tiáo, líng-píng, xī-xí*—deliberately employed, no doubt, in order to emphasize by their dinning, incantatory effect the great weariness that the poet feels.

A formal innovation occurs in the second couplet, in both lines of which the caesura occurs between the fifth and sixth (instead of between the fourth and fifth) syllables. The same device is used in a later poem (No. 29) and in a strikingly similar couplet—a fact which may be of considerable psychological significance.

EXEGESIS

1. *Qīng qiū mù-fŭ jĭng wú hán*
   Clear autumn general-headquarters well wu-t'ung-trees cold

2. *Dú sù jiāng-chéng là-jù cán*
   Alone spend-night river-city wax-candles consumed

Mù-fŭ: literally 'tent-office', since military headquarters had once been under canvas.

3. *Yǒng yè jué shēng bēi zì-yǔ*
   Long night bugle sounds sad self-talk

4. *Zhōng tiān yuè-sè hǎo shuí kān*
   Mid sky moon-colour good who looks

Shuí kàn: i.e. no one looks: rhetorical question for negative, as often.

The device which Tu Fu uses in this couplet to suggest the sadness and loneliness of the night is somewhat similar to the one employed in lines 3 and 4 of No. 16: the bugles talk to themselves and the moon shines unseen just as in No. 16 the grasses bloom unseen and the oriole sings unheard in the deserted temple.

5. *Fēng-chén rěn-rǎn yīn-shū jué*
   Wind-dust interminable news-letters cut

6. *Guān-sài xiāo-tiáo xíng-lù nán*
   Passes-frontier desolate travel-roads hard

Fēng-chén has the sense of 'troubles', especially when warfare is involved.

7. *Yǐ rěn líng-píng shí nián shì*
   Already endured tribulations ten years affairs

8. *Qiǎng yí xī-xì yì zhī ān*
   Forcibly move roost-rest one branch peace

Shí nián: a round number. Actually it was eight and a half years since the outbreak of the An Lu-shan rebellion.

The 'single peaceful branch' on which Tu Fu so reluctantly perches is, of course, his post under Yen Wu.

TRANSLATION

'A Night at Headquarters'

In the clear autumn air, the wu-t'ung trees beside the well in the courtyard of the Governor's headquarters have a chilly look. I am staying alone here in the River City. The wax candle is burning low. Through the long night distant bugles talk mournfully to themselves, and there is no one to watch the lovely moon riding in the midst of the sky. Protracted turmoils have cut us off from letters, and travelling is difficult through the desolate frontier passes. Having endured ten years of vexatious trials, I have perforce moved here to roost awhile on this single peaceful bough.

23

丹青引　贈曹將軍霸

Dān-qīng yǐn　　Zèng Cáo jiāng-jūn Bà

將軍魏武之子孫

1. *Jiāng-jūn Wèi-wǔ zhī zǐ-sūn,*

於今為庶為清門

2. *Yú-jīn wéi shù wéi qīng-mén.*

英雄割據雖已矣

3. *Yīng-xióng gē-jù suī yǐ-yǐ,*

文采風流今尚存

4. *Wén-cǎi fēng-liú jīn shàng cún:*

學書初學衛夫人

5. *Xué shū chū xué Wèi-fū-rén,*

但恨無過王右軍

6. *Dàn hèn wú guò Wáng-yòu-jūn.*

丹青不知老將至

7. *Dān-qīng bù zhī lǎo jiāng zhì,*

富貴於我如浮雲

8. *Fù-guì yú wǒ rú fú-yún!*

開元之中常引見

9. *Kāi-yuán zhī zhōng cháng yǐn-jiàn,*

承恩數上南熏殿

10. *Chéng-ēn shuò shàng Nán-xūn-diàn.*

凌煙功臣少顏色

11. *Líng-yān gōng-chén shǎo yán-sè,*

將軍下筆開生面

12. *Jiāng-jūn xià-bǐ kāi shēng-miàn.*

良相頭上進賢冠

13. *Liáng xiàng tóu-shàng jìn-xián-guān,*

猛將腰間大羽箭

14. *Měng jiàng yāo-jiān dà-yǔ-jiàn.*

褒公鄂公毛髮動

15. *Bǎo-gōng È-gōng máo-fà dòng,*

英姿颯爽來酣戰

16. *Yīng zī sà-shuǎng lái hān zhàn.*

先帝御馬玉花驄

17. *Xiān-dì yù-mǎ Yù-huā-cōng,*

畫工如山貌不同

18. *Huà-gōng rú shān mào bù tóng.*

是日牽來赤墀下

19. *Shì-rì qiān-lái chì-chí-xià,*

迥立閶闔生長風

20. *Jiǒng lì chāng-hé shēng cháng fēng.*

詔謂將軍拂絹素

21. *Zhào wèi jiāng-jūn fú juān-sù,*

意匠慘淡經營中

22. *Yì-jiàng cǎn-dàn jīng-yíng-zhōng.*

斯須九重眞龍出

23. *Sī-xū jiǔ-chóng zhēn lóng chū,*

一洗萬古凡馬空

24. *Yì-xǐ wàn-gǔ fán mǎ kōng!*

玉花却在御榻上

25. *Yù-huā què zài yù-tà-shàng,*

榻上庭前屹相向

26. *Tà-shàng tíng-qián yì xiāng-xiàng.*

至尊含笑催賜金

27. *Zhì-zūn hán-xiào cuī sì-jīn,*

圉人太僕皆惆悵

28. *Yǔ-rén tài-pú jiē chóu-chàng.*

弟子韓幹早入室

29. *Dì-zǐ Hán Gān zǎo rù-shì,*

亦能畫馬窮殊相

30. *Yì néng huà mǎ qióng shū xiàng.*

幹惟畫肉不畫骨

31. *Gān wéi huà ròu bú huà gǔ,*

忍使驊騮氣凋喪

32. *Rěn shǐ Huá-liú qì diāo-sāng!*

將軍善畫蓋有神

33. *Jiāng-jūn shàn huà gài yǒu shén,*

必逢佳士亦寫眞

34. *Bì féng jiā-shì yì xiě-zhēn.*

即今漂泊干戈際

35. *Jí-jīn piāo-bó gān-gē jì,*

屢貌尋常行路人

36. *Lǚ mào xún-cháng xíng-lù rén.*

窮塗反遭俗眼白

37. *Qióng-tú fǎn zāo sú yǎn bái,*

世上未有如公貧

38. *Shì-shàng wèi yǒu rú gōng pín.*

但看古來盛名下
39. *Dàn kàn gǔ-lái shèng-míng-xià,*

終日坎壈纏其身
40. *Zhōng-rì kǎn-lǎn chán qí shēn.*

TITLE AND SUBJECT

Dān means 'cinnabar', 'vermilion'.

Qīng means 'blue', 'green'.

Dān-qīng means 'painting'.

Yín is a kind of song or lay. The term, like *xíng*, occurs a good deal in ballad literature.

Zèng: 'present', 'offer'.

Cáo Bà: name of a well-known contemporary painter of horses.

Jiāng-jūn 'general': refers to an honorary title given him by Hsüan-tsung in recognition of his services as a court painter. He was not in fact a military man.

Ts'ao Pa was a very distinguished court painter of Hsüan-tsung's reign who had since fallen on hard times and was now an old man living in poverty at Ch'eng-tu. Tu Fu's sympathy for a fellow artist in trouble and his deep interest in a craft other than his own find expression in three of the poems included in this selection: this one and No. 24 on the painter Ts'ao Pa, and a later poem (No. 31) about a famous dancer.

Tu Fu is not much given to flattery, though living in an age when poetic flattery was a commonplace; yet this poem is loaded with the most obsequious flatteries. If it is constantly borne in mind that they are addressed to an old man who had once been famous but is now living in poverty and obscurity, I think they will be found warm-hearted and touching, and far from repellent.

FORM

The forty lines of this poem are divisible into five eight-line stanzas, each marked by a change of rhyme. As a matter of technical interest, the rhyme scheme uses level and oblique tone rhymes in alternate stanzas. From the point of view of the sense, the poem is similarly divided, with the exception that there is no division of meaning between the third and fourth stanzas:

(1) lines 1–8 praise the general's noble ancestry, nobility of character, etc.

(2) lines 9–16 concern his paintings in the Gallery of Famous Men.

(3) lines 17–24 describe his painting of the Emperor's horse, Jade Flower.

(4) lines 25–32 continue the account of the painting of Jade Flower and compare the general with his pupil Han Kan.

(5) lines 33–40 concern Ts'ao Pa's present poverty and hardship.

Tu Fu's use of the heptasyllabic Ballad Style for this sort of descriptive study (notice the typical 'linking iteration' in lines 25 and 26) was an entirely novel departure, quite different, it should be noted, from the 'dramatic encounter' found in the Ballad of the Army Carts (No. 2), the Ballad of Lovely Women (No. 3), and the Unfortunate Prince (No. 5), which are much closer in style to the ballad of tradition. Tu Fu's motive for adopting so improbable a medium for a poem about a painter can only be guessed at, but is triumphantly justified by its success.

EXEGESIS

1. *Jiāng-jūn Wèi-wǔ zhī zǐ-sūn*
   General Wei-wu's descendant

2. *Yú-jīn wéi shù wéi qīng-mén*
   At-present are commoner are cold-door

Jiāng-jūn: i.e. Ts'ao Pa, to whom this poem is addressed.
Wèi-wǔ: Emperor Wu (the 'Warlike Emperor') of the Wei dynasty, i.e. Ts'ao Ts'ao (A.D. 155–220), great soldier-statesman and adversary of Chu-ko Liang.
The first line is a sentence. *Jiāng-jūn* is its subject and *Wèi-wǔ zhī zǐ-sūn* its predicate: 'You, General, are Wei-wu's descendant.'
Qīng-mén 'cold-door': a poor man.

3. *Yĩng-xióng gē-jù suī yĭ-yĭ*
   Hero's divide-occupy although all-over-with

4. *Wén-cǎi fēng-liú jīn shàng cún*
   Culture-brilliance romantic-style now still survives

Gē-jù refers to the tripartite division of China between Ts'ao Ts'ao, Liu Pei, and Sun Ch'üan resulting in the foundation of the so-called 'Three Kingdoms'.

Fēng-liú, which can be either an adjective or a noun, is always a difficult word to translate: 'stylish', 'romantic', 'glamour', 'panache', 'refinement' are a few of its meanings.

5. *Xué shū chū xué Wèi-fū-rén*
   Study writing first study Wei-Lady

6. *Dàn hèn wú guò Wáng-yòu-jūn*
   Only regret not surpass Wang-Right-general

Wèi-fū-rén: Lady Wei was writing-mistress to China's most famous calligrapher, Wang Hsi-chih (321–79), whose honorary title was General of the Right (*yòu-jūn*), though he was not a military man, any more than Ts'ao Pa.

The notion that Ts'ao Pa learned calligraphy from the fourth-century Lady Wei and all but equalled the great Wang Hsi-chih is, needless to say, a poetic conceit.

7. *Dān-qīng bù zhī lǎo jiāng zhì*
   Painting not know age going-to arrive

8. *Fù-guì yú wǒ rú fú-yún*
   Riches-rank to me like floating-clouds

'To me': in this couplet Tu Fu pretends to be using Ts'ao Pa's own words. The couplet is a highly flattering one, because it likens Ts'ao Pa by implication to the great sage Confucius who, in the *Analects*, claims that in his enthusiasm for learning he is 'unaware of the approach of old age' and says that riches and honours unrighteously acquired 'are to me as floating clouds'.

9. *Kāi-yuán zhī zhōng cháng yĭn-jiàn*
   K'ai-yüan's within often summoned-to-presence

10. *Chéng-ēn shuò shàng Nán-xūn-diàn*
    Receiving-favour frequently ascended Southern-fragrance-hall

Kāi-yuán: the K'ai-yüan period (713–42) occupied the first three-quarters of Hsüan-tsung's reign (712–55).

Nán-xūn-diàn: an audience-hall in the Imperial palace at Ch'ang-an.

11. *Líng-yān gōng-chén shǎo yán-sè*
    Mount-mists meritorious-service-ministers lacked colour

12. *Jiāng-jūn xià-bǐ kāi shēng-miàn*
    General went-to-work-with-brush opened new appearance

Líng-yān gōng-chén: the portraits of twenty-four soldiers and statesmen, distinguished for their services towards the founding of the dynasty, which were painted in the Ling-yen ('Sleeping Above the Mists') Gallery by Imperial command in 643. Eighty years later (*Kāi-yuán zhī zhōng*) they were beginning to look dowdy and in need of repainting.

13. *Liáng xiàng tóu-shàng jìn-xián-guān*
    Good ministers' head-top promoting-worthy-hats

14. *Měng jiàng yāo-jiān dà-yǔ-jiàn*
    Fierce generals' waist-mid great-feather-arrows

Jìn-xián-guān: name of the hat of stiff black gauze worn as part of their court dress by civilian officials.

Dà-yǔ-jiàn: a specially long-shafted arrow with four feathers favoured by the T'ang emperor T'ai-tsung, who was an accomplished bowman.

15. *Bǎo-gōng È-gōng máo-fà dòng*
    Pao-duke O-duke whiskers-hair move

16. *Yīng zī sà-shuǎng lái hān zhàn*
    Heroic looks grim-bold come drunk battles

Bǎo-gōng È-gōng: Tuan Chih-hsüan, duke of Pao, the tenth of the twenty-four portraits, and Wei-ch'ih Ching-te, duke of O, the seventh: both distinguished soldiers.

17. *Xiān-dì yù-mǎ Yù-huā-cōng*
    Late-emperor's imperial-horse Jade-flower-mane

18. *Huà-gōng rú shān mào bù tóng*
    Painters like mountains likenesses not same

Xiān-dì: i.e. Hsüan-tsung.

Yù-mǎ: *yù* is one of the honorifics used in court language when referring to objects belonging to the Emperor. Thus his reading is *yù-lǎn* 'Imperial surveying', his writing *yù-bǐ* 'Imperial brush-work', and his seal *yù-bǎo* 'the Imperial treasure'.

Rú shān: 'numerous (as the hills)'. The English metaphor ('mountains of . . .') is used rather differently.

19. *Shì-rì qiān-lái chì-chí-xià*
    That-day lead-up red-steps-below

20. *Jiǒng lì chāng-hé shēng cháng fēng*
    Remote stand palace-gate produce long wind

The magnificent war-horse seems to bring a wind from the plains with him as he is led through the palace gate into the court-yard below the throne-room.

21. *Zhào wèi jiāng-jūn fú juān-sù*
    Command tells general spread white-silk

22. *Yì-jiàng cǎn-dàn jīng-yíng-zhōng*
    Thought-craftsmanship painfully planning-midst

Fú: smoothing out the silk on a table ready for painting.

23. *Sī-xū jiǔ-chóng zhēn lóng chū*
    In-a-moment nine-fold true dragon emerges

24. *Yì-xǐ wàn-gǔ fán mǎ kōng*
    At-one-wash myriad-ages ordinary horses blank

Jiǔ-chóng here means the sky, which in Chinese mythology is 'ninefold' or nine-segmented.

Note that this is a perfectly antithetical couplet.

25. *Yù-huā què zài yù-tà-shàng*
    Jade-flower withdrawn at Imperial-couch-above

26. *Tà-shàng tíng-qián yì xiāng-xiàng*
    Couch-above court-before high each-other-face

Xiāng-xiàng: they look at each other, the Jade Flower in the painting now hung up behind the Emperor's throne, and the Jade Flower in the courtyard below. The adverb *yì* 'on high' strictly speaking should belong only to the painted horse; but the real Jade Flower has a high, proud look, so it can be used of him too.

27. *Zhì-zūn hán-xiào cuī sì-jīn*
    Supremely-honoured-one with-smile hastens present-money

28. *Yŭ-rén tài-pú jiē chóu-chàng*
    Stable-boys chief-grooms all melancholy

Zhì-zūn: i.e. the Emperor.

Chóu-chàng: I suspect that the grooms look glum because they are green with envy, not, as one commentator believes, because they are so full of admiration that they don't know what to do.

29. *Dì-zǐ Hán Gān zǎo rù-shì*
    Pupil Han Kan long-since entered-room

30. *Yì néng huà mǎ qióng shū xiàng*
    Also can paint horses exhaust different shapes

Rù-shì: in the *Analects* Confucius says of one of his disciples that he has 'gone up into the hall, but not yet entered the chamber': i.e. he had mastered the general principles of his teaching but not yet penetrated its inner meaning. Tu Fu means that Ts'ao Pa long ago admitted Han Kan to all his secrets.

Han Kan was, in point of fact, the most famous horse painter of the T'ang era. Copies of a few of his paintings still survive.

31. *Gān wéi huà ròu bú huà gǔ*
    Kan only paints flesh not paint bone

32. *Rěn shǐ Huá-liú qì diāo-sāng*
    Endure make Hua-liu spirit withered-lost

'Flesh' and 'bone' are terms constantly used by Chinese critics of painting and calligraphy. A 'fleshy' style is soft, weak, or flabby; a 'bony' style is dynamic, strong, and spare.

Huá-liú: a legendary horse, one of the eight coursers of king Mu of Chou. Here it symbolizes any superlatively good horse.

This seemingly malicious slur on a good painter must be understood in the light of Ts'ao Pa's circumstances. He is an impoverished and neglected old man, whilst his pupil Han Kan is, we may suppose, still a fashionable and prosperous painter. Tu Fu is doing his best to cheer the old man up.

33. *Jiāng-jūn shàn huà gài yǒu shén*
General good-at painting is-because has divinity

34. *Bì féng jiā-shì yì xiě-zhēn*
Must meet exceptional-man also paint-portrait

35. *Jí-jīn piāo-bó gān-gē jì*
At-present vagrant warfare juncture

36. *Lǚ mào xún-cháng xíng-lù rén*
Often paint ordinary walk-road people

37. *Qióng-tú fǎn zāo sú yǎn bái*
Desperate-straits instead meet vulgar eye white

38. *Shì-shàng wèi yǒu rú gōng pín*
In-the-world never was like you poor

Yǎn bái refers to Juan Chi (A.D. 210–63), an eccentric of whom it was said that when he was in the company of 'vulgar' persons (he placed Confucian scholars and courtiers in this category) he showed only the whites of his eyes. The adverb *fǎn* means 'opposite to what you would expect, or to what is proper': i.e. Ts'ao Pa, fallen on hard times, far from being able to snub vulgar persons must often submit to being snubbed by them himself.

Gōng 'duke' could be used for 'you' when speaking to old gentlemen.

39. *Dàn kàn gǔ-lái shèng-míng-xià*
Only look from-of-old famous-names-below

40. *Zhōng-rì kǎn-lǎn chán qí shēn*
All-day frustrations entangled their bodies

TRANSLATION

'A Song of Painting. To General Ts'ao Pa'

You, General, are a descendant of Emperor Wu of Wei, but now, a commoner, live in humble circumstances. Though the heroic empire-building of your ancestor is long past, his brilliant culture and elegant style live on in you. In calligraphy you first studied under the Lady Wei, your only regret being that you could not excel Wang Hsi-chih. Painting, you forget the advance of old age: to you wealth and rank are as insubstantial as floating clouds.

During the K'ai-yüan period (713–42) you were often summoned to court. Frequently you were favoured with invitations to the Hall of Southern Fragrance. When the colours in the portraits of distinguished statesmen and soldiers in the Rising Above the Mists Gallery had become faded, you, with your brush, gave them a new, fresh look. On the heads of good ministers you painted 'Promotion of the Worthy' hats; at the belts of fierce generals you painted 'Big Feather' arrows. The Duke of Pao and the Duke of O, their beards and hair bristling, appeared, from their heroic and forbidding expressions, to be drunk with many battles.

Our late Emperor's horse Jade Flower was painted by artists as numerous as the hills, but the paintings were not good likenesses. One day he was led out below the Red Terrace. As he stood far off there in the gates, a great wind seemed to have entered the palace. An order was given commanding you to prepare your silk for a painting. With deep intensity your artist's mind pondered and planned a while, and then, quite suddenly, the veritable dragon emerged from the pregnant sky, annihilating in a trice a myriad ordinary horses painted from old times up to now.

When the portrait was taken up and hung behind the throne, the Jade Flower above the throne and the one in the forecourt faced each other proudly. His Imperial Majesty with a smile hurried those who were to fetch the reward. And how out of countenance all the grooms and stable-boys looked! Your disciple Han Kan long ago graduated to the 'inner sanctum'; but he paints only the outward flesh: he does not know how to suggest the bone within, and is quite capable of allowing a Hua-liu to lose all its life and spirit.

Your excellence as a painter is divinely inspired. You used also to paint portraits, though only if you met an unusual person. Today, drifting about in an age of violence, you often make likenesses of quite ordinary people, and in your present dire straits have to endure sour looks from vulgar eyes. Surely there can be no one in the world quite as poor as you! However, if one but examines those who have been famous from ancient times to the present, one finds that they were constantly enmeshed in hardships and difficulties.

24

韋諷錄事宅觀曹將軍畫馬圖

Wéi Fèng lù-shì zhái guān Cáo jiāng-jūn huà mǎ-tú

國初以來畫鞍馬

1. *Guó-chū yǐ-lái huà ān-mǎ*

神妙獨數江都王

2. *Shén-miào dú shǔ Jiāng-dū-wáng.*

將軍得名三十載

3. *Jiāng-jūn dé míng sān-shí zǎi,*

人間又見真乘黃

4. *Rén-jiān yòu jiàn zhēn Chéng-huáng.*

曾貌先帝照夜白

5. *Céng mào xiān-dì Zhào-yè-bái,*

龍池十日飛霹靂

6. *Lóng-chí shí rì fēi pī-lì.*

內府殷紅瑪瑙盤

7. *Nèi-fǔ yān-hóng mǎ-nǎo pán*

婕妤傳詔才人索

8. *Jié-yú chuán zhào cái-rén suǒ.*

盤賜將軍拜舞歸

9. *Pán sì jiāng-jūn bài-wǔ guī,*

輕紈細綺相追飛

10. *Qīng wán xì qǐ xiāng-zhuī fēi.*

貴戚權門得筆跡

11. *Guì-qī quán-mén dé bǐ-jì,*

始覺屏障生光輝

12. *Shǐ jué píng-zhàng shēng guāng-huī.*

昔日太宗卷毛騧

13. *Xī-rì Tài-zōng Juǎn-máo-guā,*

近時郭家獅子花

14. *Jìn-shí Guō-jiā Shī-zǐ-huā:*

今之新圖有二馬

15. *Jīn zhī xīn tú yǒu èr mǎ,*

復令識者久歎嗟

16. *Fù lìng shì-zhě jiǔ tàn-jiē.*

此皆騎戰一敵萬

17. *Cǐ jiē qí-zhàn yī dí wàn,*

縞素漠漠開風沙

18. *Gǎo sù mò-mò kāi fēng-shā.*

其餘七匹亦殊絕

19. *Qí-yú qī pǐ yì shū-jué,*

迥若寒空雜霞雪

20. *Jiǒng ruò hán kōng zá xiá xuě.*

霜蹄蹴踏長楸間

21. *Shuāng tí cù-tà cháng qiū jiān,*

馬官廝養森成列

22. *Mǎ-guān sī-yǎng sēn chéng liè.*

可憐九馬爭神駿

23. *Kě-lián jiǔ mǎ zhēng shén-jùn,*

顧視清高氣深穩

24. *Gù-shì qīng-gāo qì shēn-wěn.*

借問苦心愛者誰

25. *Jiè-wèn kǔ-xīn ài-zhě shuí?*

後有韋諷前支盾

26. *Hòu yǒu Wéi Fèng qián Zhī Dùn.*

憶昔巡幸新豐宮

27. *Yì xī xún-xìng Xīn-fēng-gōng,*

翠花拂天來向東

28. *Cuì-huā fú tiān lái xiàng dōng;*

騰驤磊落三萬匹

29. *Téng-xiāng lěi-luò sān-wàn pǐ,*

皆與此圖筋骨同

30. *Jiē yǔ cǐ tú jīn-gǔ tóng.*

自從獻寶朝河宗

31. *Zì-cóng xiàn bǎo cháo Hé-zōng,*

無復射蛟江水中

32. *Wú fù shè jiāo jiāng-shuǐ-zhōng.*

君不見金粟堆前松柏裏

33. *Jūn bú jiàn Jīn-sù-duī-qián sōng bó lǐ*

龍媒去盡鳥呼風

34. *Lóng-méi qù jìn niǎo hū fēng!*

TITLE AND SUBJECT

Wéi Fèng: name of an official with whom Tu Fu became acquainted while staying in Ch'eng-tu.

Lù-shì: his title, 'recorder'.

Z hái: 'house', 'residence'.

Guān: 'see', 'look at'.

Cáo jiāng-jūn 'General Ts'ao' is our friend Ts'ao Pa, to whom the last poem was addressed.

Huà: here a verb: 'painted by'.

Mǎ-tú: 'horse-painting'.

The painting which Tu Fu saw at Wei Feng's house in Ch'eng-tu was Ts'ao Pa's 'Nine Horses' (*Chiu ma t'u*). It was still extant three centuries later, when the Sung poet Su Tung-p'o (1036–1101) saw it at the house of a collector called Hsüeh Shao-p'eng in Ch'ang-an and wrote a poem in praise of it. Su Tung-p'o mentions T'ai-tsung's horse 'Curly' and Kuo Tzu-i's horse 'Lion' (cf. lines 13 and 14 of this poem) as being amongst the nine horses in the painting.

It is interesting to compare this poem with the previous one. Each contains a somewhat similar panegyric of Ts'ao Pa's earlier achievements as a court painter; but whereas No. 23, being addressed to Ts'ao Pa in person, is concerned throughout with the fortunes of the painter, this poem, centred on the painting rather than on the artist, allows the poet's associations to range more freely, ending in the magnificent lament of lines 31–34.

FORM

This poem, like the last, is in Ballad Style (note the unmetrical *jūn bū jiàn* of the penultimate line which may be compared with lines 16 and 32 of No. 2). There are six changes of rhyme, but the poem divides naturally into five sections over which the rhymes are distributed as follows:

(1) lines 1–4   x a x a
(2) lines 5–12   b b x b c c x c
(3) lines 13–22 d d x d x d e e x e
(4) lines 23–26 f f x f
(5) lines 27–34 g g x g x g x g

The first section is about horse-painters generally; the second describes an occasion similar to the one which forms the central part of the previous poem—the old painter's brilliant début at court (Night Shiner in line 5 of this section, like Jade Flower in the previous poem, was one of Hsüan-tsung's greys: the pair of them are several times mentioned together in contemporary literature); the third section describes the Nine Horses painting which is the subject of this poem; the fourth section pays brief tribute to Wei Feng, who owns the painting; and the final section, whose nostalgic *Yì xí* ('I remember . . .') has already been encountered in No. 7, is a moving lament for Hsüan-tsung and the departed splendour of his reign.

EXEGESIS

1. *Guó-chū yǐ-lái huà ān-mǎ*
   State beginning-since paint saddle-horses

2. *Shén-miào dú shǔ Jiāng-dū-wáng*
   Divinely-inspired only reckon Chiang-tu-prince

   Jiāng-dū-wáng: Li Hsü, Prince of Chiang-tu, a nephew of Emperor T'ai-tsung (reg. 627–49)

3. *Jiāng-jūn dé míng sān-shí zǎi*
   General get name thirty years

4. *Rén-jiān yòu jiàn zhēn Chéng-huáng*
   Among-men again see true *Ch'eng-huang*

   A T'ang treatise on painting says that Ts'ao Pa first became known as a painter in the mid K'ai-yüan period (i.e. *circa* 725) and that he was commissioned by the Emperor to paint meritorious officials and horses from the imperial stables at the end of the T'ien-pao period (before 755). Hence the 'thirty years' of line 3.

   Chéng-huáng: name of a divine horse miraculously born from the earth in the reign of the legendary sage-king Shun.

5. *Céng mào xiān-dì Zhào-yè-bái*
   Once painted Late Emperor's Shining-in-the-Night-grey

6. *Lóng-chí shí rì fēi pī-lì*
   Dragon Pool ten days flew-with thunderings

The Dragon Pool was in the palace grounds north of the Hall of Southern Fragrance (see line 10 in the preceding poem). It formed naturally in 689 after a period of heavy rainfall and was so called because someone claimed to have seen a dragon emerging from it.

7. *Nèi-fǔ yān-hóng mǎ-nǎo pán*
   Inner-treasury dark-red agate dish

8. *Jié-yú chuán zhào cái-rén suǒ*
   Ladies-in-waiting pass order maids-of-honour search

9. *Pán sì jiāng-jūn bài-wǔ guī*
   Dish presented general obeisance-danced returned

10. *Qīng wán xì qǐ xiāng-zhuī fēi*
    Light satins fine damasks each-other-pursuing flew

Bài-wǔ: T'ang court etiquette prescribed, for very ceremonious occasions, a dance of obeisance which combined a quite complicated series of balletic movements.

11. *Guì-qī quán-mén dé bǐ-jì*
    Imperial-relations in-power-households get brush-traces

12. *Shǐ jué píng-zhàng shēng guāng-huī*
    Begin feel screens producing radiance

Lines 9–12 must be taken closely together. Following Ts'ao Pa's commissioning by the Emperor, all the 'best people' are anxious to obtain specimens of his work. The showers of silks with which they pursue him are not, I suspect, gifts, as is often stated, but the raw materials for making into screens, etc., after they have been embellished with his art. The payments would come later.

13. *Xī-rì Tài-zōng Juǎn-máo-guā*
    Former-days T'ai-tsung's Curly-hair-dun

14. *Jìn-shí Guō-jiā Shī-zǐ-huā*
    Near-time Kuo-family Lion-dapple

Juǎn-máo-guā: one of the six war-horses of T'ai-tsung (597–649) whose likenesses have been preserved for all time in stone bas-reliefs, of which there are many rubbings and reproductions. He is the fifth of the six horses and is represented bearing in his body the nine arrows with which he was wounded in the campaign against Liu Hei-t'a.

Guō-jiā: Kuo Tzu-i (697–781) was one of the loyal T'ang generals responsible for putting down the rebellion of An Lu-shan and his heirs. In January 764 he emerged from semi-retirement and recovered Ch'ang-an from the Tibetans. The horse 'Lion' is thought to have been one of the gifts bestowed on him by Tai-tsung after his return to the capital. If this identification is correct, the painting must have been made only a very short time before Tu Fu saw it.

15. *Jīn zhī xīn tú yǒu èr mǎ*
    Present new picture has two horses

16. *Fù lìng shì-zhě jiǔ tàn-jiē*
    Again cause connoisseurs long sigh-exclaim

17. *Cǐ jiē qí-zhàn yī dí wàn*
    These both mounted-battle one oppose ten-thousand

18. *Gǎo-sù mò-mò kāi fēng-shā*
    White-silk vast-vast opens wind-sand

19. *Qí-yú qī pǐ yì shū-jué*
    Remaining seven ones also outstanding-excellent

20. *Jiǒng ruò hán kōng zá xiá xuě*
    Distance like cold void mix sunset snow

The arrangement of lines 17–20 seems at first sight odd. Two statements, p_1 and p_2, about the horses, and two statements, q_1 and q_2, about the background, are expressed in the order p_1 q_1 p_2 q_2. 'Interweaving' some Chinese critic has called this. I suspect, however, that this is no mere rhetorical device. If the picture, as is extremely likely, was a long horizontal scroll which had to be examined by unrolling with the left hand and rolling with the right, you might in fact have looked at Curly and Lion with their background and then the other seven horses and their background as virtually separate pictures. And anyone who has looked through one of these long scroll-paintings will know that scenes of high interest—the focal parts of the painting—are frequently separated from each other by lengths of misty emptiness. The fact that Su Tung-p'o, who saw this painting in the eleventh century, mentions the horses Curly and Lion in the introduction to his verses about it seems to increase the probability that the painting began with these two horses and portrayed the other seven further along the scroll.

21. *Shuāng tí cù-tà cháng qiū jiān*
    Frosty hooves trample tall catalpas amidst

22. *Mǎ-guān sī-yǎng sēn chéng liè*
    Horse-officials ostlers forestlike form ranks

23. *Kě-lián jiǔ mǎ zhēng shén-jùn*
    Lovable nine horses vie-in godlike-mettlesomeness

24. *Gù-shì qīng-gāo qì shēn-wěn*
    Glance-looks pure-high spirits deep-firm

Shén-jùn is almost certainly a deliberate reference to a famous remark of the Buddhist monk Chih Tun (314–66) when he was twitted for his unmonkish love of horseflesh (he kept a stable of several horses): 'I can't resist their *shén-jùn*.' Chih Tun is mentioned by name three lines further on in the poem.

25. *Jiè-wèn kǔ-xīn ài-zhě shuí*
    Pray-tell-me earnest-heart lover who

26. *Hòu yǒu Wéi Fèng qián Zhī Dùn*
    Latterly is Wei Feng previously Chih Tun

27. *Yì xī xún-xing Xīn-fēng-gōng*
    Remember once imperial-progress Hsin-feng-palace

28. *Cuì-huā fú tiān lái xiàng dōng*
    Kingfisher-flower brushing sky came towards east

Xīn-fēng-gōng: Hsin-feng was the name of a district east of the capital at the foot of Li-shan in which was situated the Hua-ch'ing Palace and its hot springs. Hsüan-tsung was in the habit of spending the winter there.

Cuì-huā: the Imperial banner, elsewhere referred to as the 'rainbow banner'. Cf. No. 7, line 5.

29. *Téng-xiāng lěi-luò sān-wàn pǐ*
    Leaping-cantering crowd-on-crowd three-myriad horses

30. *Jiē yǔ cǐ tú jīn-gǔ tóng*
    All with this picture sinews-bones same

31. *Zì-cóng xiàn bǎo cháo Hé-zōng*
    Since presented treasure paid-court-to River-god

32. *Wú fù shè jiāo jiāng shuǐ zhōng*
    Not again shoot dragon river waters in

Each of these lines contains an allusion: the first to the legend of king Mu of Chou who is supposed to have journeyed many hundreds of miles to the west and seen many marvels. His meeting with the god of the Yellow River and offering to him of jade treasures came at the end of his journeying, and symbolizes Hsüan-tsung's death. The second allusion is to the story that Emperor Wu of the Han dynasty in 106 B.C. while sailing on the Yangtze shot and captured a water-dragon. This I think is meant to symbolize the sort of kingly triumphs which, since the passing of the glorious K'ai-yüan, T'ien-pao era, will never be seen again.

33. *Jūn bú jiàn Jīn-sù-duī-qián sōng bó lǐ*
    My-lord not see Gold-grain-hill-before pines cypresses in

34. *Lóng-méi qù jìn niǎo hū fēng*
    Dragon's-harbingers gone entirely birds cry wind

Jīn-sù-duī: the Hill of Golden Grain, where Hsüan-tsung's tomb was. He was buried there in 763.

Lóng-méi: in one of the hymns used in the Imperial sacrifices of the Han dynasty the Heavenly Horse is called 'dragon-harbinger'.

TRANSLATION

'On Seeing a Horse-painting by Ts'ao Pa in the House of the Recorder Wei Feng'

Among painters of saddle-horses who have won recognition since the beginning of our dynasty, the Prince of Chiang-tu was for long the only one who could be reckoned an inspired painter. Then, thirty years after General Ts'ao first won a name for himself, the world once more beheld a true *Ch'eng-huang* in its midst.

On one occasion, when he painted our late Imperial Majesty's grey, Night Shiner, thunders rolled for ten days over the face of the Dragon Pool. Ladies-in-waiting conveyed an Imperial Command and maids-of-honour made search for a certain dish of dark red agate in the Inner Treasury.

The dish bestowed, our grateful General performed his dance of obeisance and returned home, soon followed by a rain of fine silks and satins from the households of the Imperial kinsmen and all the most powerful in the land, who felt that their screens would acquire no lustre until graced with some sample of his handiwork.

Two famous horses, one, T'ai-tsung's dun horse Curly, of former times, the other, Kuo Tzu-i's dappled grey Lion, of more recent date, are now to be seen in this new painting of the General's, drawing cries of admiration from the connoisseur and looking, both of them, a match for ten thousand in mounted combat. The white silk ground behind them seems to open out into a vast expanse of wind-blown sand.

The other seven horses in the painting are also magnificent specimens. Remote above them, sunset and snow commingle in a wintry sky. Their frosty hooves paw and trample a road lined with tall catalpa trees. By them, in rows, stand their grooms and stable-boys.

Nine splendid horses, close-matched in godlike mettle, their glances proud and free, their spirits firm and deep-seated! And who have been the most devoted lovers of these creatures? Wei Feng in latter times; in earlier days, Chih Tun.

I remember the Imperial progress to the palace at Hsin-feng in the old days, the halcyon banner brushing the sky on its eastward journey and the undulating throng on throng of the thirty thousand trotting horses, each bone for bone and sinew for sinew a peer of the horses in this painting. But since the state visit to the River Lord and the offering of precious things, there has been no more shooting of dragons in the waters. Have you not seen? The Dragon's Messengers have all departed from amidst the pines and cypresses that stand in front of the Hill of Golden Grain. Only the birds are left, crying on the wind.

25

古柏行

Gǔ bó xíng

❧❧❧❧❧❧❧❧

孔明廟前有老柏

1. *Kǒng-míng miào-qián yǒu lǎo bó,*

柯如青銅根如石

2. *Kē rú qīng-tóng gēn rú shí.*

霜皮溜雨四十圍

3. *Shuāng pí liù yǔ sì-shí wéi,*

黛色參天二千尺

4. *Dài sè cān tiān èr-qiān chǐ.*

君臣已與時際會

5. *Jūn-chén yǐ yǔ shí jì-huì,*

樹木猶為人愛惜

6. *Shù-mù yóu wéi rén ài-xī.*

雲來氣接巫峽長

7. *Yún lái qì jiē Wū-xiá cháng,*

月出寒通雪山白

8. *Yuè chū hán tōng Xuě-shān bái.*

憶昨路繞錦亭東

9. *Yì zuó lù rào Jǐn-tíng dōng,*

先主武侯同閟宮

10. *Xiān-zhǔ Wǔ-hóu tóng bì-gōng.*

崔嵬枝幹郊原古

11. *Cuī-wéi zhī-gàn jiāo-yuán gǔ,*

窈窕丹青戶牖空

12. *Yáo-tiáo dān-qīng hù-yǒu kōng.*

落落盤據雖得地

13. *Luò-luò pán-jù suī dé-dì,*

冥冥孤高多烈風

14. *Míng-míng gū-gāo duō liè-fēng.*

扶持自是神明力

15. *Fú-chí zì shì shén-míng lì,*

正直元因造化工

16. *Zhèng-zhí yuán yīn zào-huà gōng.*

大厦如傾要梁棟

17. *Dà shà rú qīng yào liáng-dòng,*

萬牛迴首邱山重

18. *Wàn niú huí shǒu qiū-shān zhòng.*

不露文章世已驚

19. *Bú lù wén-zhāng shì yǐ jīng,*

未辭剪伐誰能送

20. *Wèi cí jiǎn-fá shuí néng sòng?*

苦心豈免容螻蟻

21. *Kǔ xīn qǐ miǎn róng lóu-yǐ,*

香葉終經宿鸞鳳

22. *Xiāng yè zhōng jīng sù luán-fèng.*

志士幽人莫怨嗟

23. *Zhì-shì yōu-rén mò yuàn-jiē:*

古來材大難為用

24. *Gǔ-lái cái dà nán wéi yòng.*

TITLE AND SUBJECT

Gǔ: 'old', 'ancient'.

Bó: 'cypress'.

In May 765 Tu Fu's patron Yen Wu died in Ch'eng-tu and Tu Fu and his family once more embarked on their travels. Journeying mostly by river, and with stops which in one case lasted for several months, they arrived at K'uei-chou, overlooking the Yangtze gorges, in the spring of 766. After lodging for a brief period in the city, they found a cottage in a hill-village a few miles outside it.

K'uei-chou had been part of the old kingdom of Shu and contained a temple to the great Shu statesman Chu-ko Liang, who was one of Tu Fu's heroes. The ancient tree of the title, supposed to have been planted by Chu-ko Liang's own hand, stood in the precincts of this temple. At the end of the ninth century it was thought to be completely dead, but it suddenly started sprouting again in the spring of 967. Under Tu Fu's contemplative gaze the old cypress becomes first a cosmic tree of supernatural size, and then a symbol of afflicted genius—its heart riddled with ants, but with phoenixes in its upper branches—and of neglected greatness: real greatness, whether in tree or man, makes its possessor too big for use in this world of little men.

It is interesting to compare this poem with No. 7, also inspired by a visit to one of Chu-ko Liang's shrines, but written four years earlier. To my mind this later poem has a grandeur which the earlier one lacks.

FORM

Although Tu Fu calls it a 'ballad' (*xíng*), there is little in this poem that formally identifies it as Ballad Style verse.

There is a single change of rhyme, occurring at line 9. Structurally this poem therefore bears a strong resemblance to No. 7 (*Āi jiāng-tóu*), a heptasyllabic Ballad Style poem in which the rhyme changes at 'I remember . . .' (*Yì xí . . .*) in the fifth line. Here, too, the rhyme changes at 'I remember . . .'.

This poem contains four instances of what looks like inversion of a noun and its qualifying adjective, but is in fact the rhetorical figure whereby an adjective is replaced by an abstract noun. In lines 7, 8, 11, 12 the literal meaning is 'the length of Wu Gorge', 'the whiteness of the Snowy Mountains', 'the antiquity of the plain outside the city', 'the emptiness of doors and windows', though the sense is, of course, 'long Wu Gorge', 'white Snowy Mountains', 'ancient plain' and 'empty doors and windows'. The same figure of speech is found in Greek, Latin, and English. It makes for ambiguity in Chinese because the adjective so placed is in the predicative position. In prose the particle *zhī* placed between the two would make the meaning quite clear. The omission of particles in order to meet the requirements of the prosody accounts for a considerable amount of the difficulty of Chinese poetry.

EXEGESIS

1. *Kǒng-míng miào-qián yǒu lǎo bó*
   K'ung-ming temple-before is old cypress

2. *Kē rú qīng-tóng gēn rú shí*
   Boughs are-like bronze roots are-like rock

   Kǒng-míng: the courtesy-name or 'style' of Chu-ko Liang.

3. *Shuāng pí liù yǔ sì-shí wéi*
   Frosty-bark washed-with-rain forty spans

4. *Dài sè cān tiān èr-qiān chǐ*
   Jet-colour greets-sky two-thousand feet

   'Frosty bark' is of course metaphorical. *Liù yǔ* is also as a rule explained as a metaphor; though it is by no means clear how the tree can look frost-rimed and rain-washed simultaneously.

5. *Jūn-chén yǐ yǔ shí jì-huì*
   Ruler-minister already with time have-met

6. *Shù-mù yóu wéi rén ài-xī*
   Tree still is-by people cherished

   Yǔ shí jì-huì: the usual interpretation makes this a reference to the felicitous meeting of Liu Pei and Chu-ko Liang with each other; but the antithesis with the next line makes it seem much likelier that it refers to their death.

7. *Yún lái qì jiē Wū-xiá cháng*
   Clouds come exhalations join Wu gorge's length

8. *Yuè chū hán tōng Xuě-shān bái*
   Moon emerges cold communicates-with Snowy-mountains
   whiteness

It seems most unlikely that you could actually see the peaks of
north-west Szechwan from K'uei-chou, especially at night-time.
In Tu Fu's mind the huge tree is already becoming a cosmic tree.
This is not to be explained as simple hyperbole; it is another
instance of the 'vision' which sometimes comes upon Tu Fu when
he contemplates views or objects, like the momentary glimpse of
eternity in No. 21.

9. *Yì zuó lù rào Jǐn-tíng dōng*
   Remember yesteryear road wound Brocade-pavilion east

10. *Xiān-zhǔ Wǔ-hóu tóng bì-gōng*
    First Ruler Martial Marquis same shrine-temple

Brocade pavilion: a little pavilion which Tu Fu constructed
beside the Brocade River near his 'thatched house' in the countryside outside Ch'eng-tu.
Wǔ-hóu: Chu-ko Liang's posthumous title.

11. *Cuī-wéi zhī-gàn jiāo-yuán gǔ*
    Lofty-towering branches-trunk suburban-plain ancient

12. *Yáo-tiáo dān-qīng hù-yǒu kōng*
    Gloomy-secluded paintwork doors-windows empty

Tu Fu momentarily compares the cypresses of the temple at
Ch'eng-tu with the old cypress at K'uei-chou. Cf. No. 16, line 2.
The plain outside Ch'eng-tu is 'ancient' because full of ancient
associations and remains.

13. *Luò-luò pán-jù suī dé-dì*
    Wide-spreading coil-grasping though hold-position

14. *Míng-míng gū-gāo duō liè-fēng*
    Sky-depths lonely-high much fierce-wind

15. *Fú-chí zì shì shén-míng lì*
    Upholding-maintaining of-course is divine-spirit's power

16. *Zhèng-zhí yuán yīn zào-huà gōng*
    Straight-uprightness actually due-to creator's labour

These two lines follow closely on the sense of lines 13–14. The fact that the tree has grown so straight and firm, although so wind-beaten and exposed, must be due to divine intervention.

17. *Dà shà rú qīng yào liáng-dòng*
    Great hall if collapse want beams-rafters

18. *Wàn niú huí shǒu qiū-shān zhòng*
    Myriad oxen turn-round heads hill-mountain weight

The oxen, harnessed to the great tree which has been felled—in imagination—to make beams and rafters, turn their heads round questioningly to see what the huge weight is that they are supposed to haul but cannot shift.

19. *Bú lù wén-zhāng shì yǐ jīng*
    Not reveal design-embellishment world already marvels

20. *Wèi cí jiǎn-fá shuí néng sòng*
    Never decline cutting-chopping who can carry-off

Actually, says Tu Fu, it doesn't need a carpenter working on it to make it a thing of wonder. Just as it is, in its natural state, it is that already.

21. *Kǔ xīn qǐ miǎn róng lóu-yǐ*
    Bitter heart how avoid harbouring ants

22. *Xiāng yè zhōng jīng sù luán-fèng*
    Aromatic leaves always sustain roosting phoenixes

The tree whose timber is riddled by termites, but with the Bird of Paradise roosting in its topmost branches, is a wonderful image of the creative artist. 'Bitter heart' is, of course, a play on words: it is both the bitter core of the cypress wood and the anguished, careworn heart of the poet. As a matter of interest, Tu Fu's very first childish attempt at verse was a little poem about a phoenix, and in the course of his life he frequently used the phoenix as his own symbol.

23. *Zhì-shì yōu-rén mò yuàn-jiē*
   Aspiration-gentlemen hidden-people don't resentfully-sigh

24. *Gǔ-lái cái dà nán wéi yòng*
   From-of-old material great hard to-be used

Cái dà contains another word-play. *Cái* can mean both 'timber' and 'talent'. Just as a tree can be too big to use (you could chop it down, but *shuí néng sòng?* 'who could cart it away?'), so a man's talent can be too great to use if no one is 'big' enough to employ him. The *zhì-shì*, *yōu-rén* are men with high ideals and aspirations who live in obscurity because they have not been 'discovered'.

TRANSLATION

'Ballad of the Old Cypress'

In front of the temple of Chu-ko Liang there is an old cypress. Its branches are like green bronze; its roots like rocks. Around its great girth of forty spans its rimy bark withstands the washing of the rain. Its jet-coloured top rises two thousand feet to greet the sky. Prince and statesman have long since paid their debt to time; but the tree continues to be cherished among men. When the clouds come, continuous vapours link it with the mists of the long Wu Gorge; and when the moon appears, the cypress tree shares the chill of the Snowy Mountains' whiteness.

   I remember a year or so ago, where the road wound east round my Brocade River pavilion, the First Ruler and Chu-ko Liang shared the same shrine. There, too, were towering cypresses, on the ancient plain outside the city. The paintwork of the temple's dark interior gleamed dully through derelict doors and windows. But this cypress here, though it holds its ground well, clinging with wide-encompassing, snake-like hold, yet, because of its lonely height rising into the gloom of the sky, meets much of the wind's fierce blast. Nothing but the power of Divine Providence could have kept it standing for so long; its straightness must be the work of the Creator himself! If a great hall had collapsed and beams for it were needed, ten thousand oxen might turn their heads inquiringly to look at such a mountain of a load. But it is already marvel enough to astonish the world, without any need to undergo a craftsman's embellishing. It has never refused the axe: there is simply no one who could carry it away if it were felled. Its bitter heart has not escaped the ants; but there are always phoenixes roosting in its scented leaves. Men of ambition, and you who dwell unseen, do not cry out in despair! From of old the really great has never been found a use for.

26

寄韓諫議注
Jì Hán Jiàn-yì Zhù

今我不樂思岳陽
1. *Jīn wǒ bū lè sì Yuè-yáng,*

身欲奮飛病在牀
2. *Shēn yù fèn-fēi bìng zài chuáng.*

美人娟娟隔秋水
3. *Měi-rén juān-juān gé qiū-shuǐ,*

濯足洞庭望八荒
4. *Zhuó zú Dòng-tíng wàng bā-huāng.*

鴻飛冥冥日月白
5. *Hóng fēi míng-míng rì yuè-bái.*

青楓葉赤天雨霜
6. *Qīng fēng yè chì tiān yǔ shuāng.*

玉京羣帝集北斗
7. *Yù-jīng qún-dì jí běi-dǒu,*

或騎麒麟翳鳳凰
8. *Huò qí qí-lín yì fèng-huáng.*

芙蓉旌旗煙霧落

9. *Fú-róng jīng-qí yān-wù luò,*

影動倒景搖瀟湘

10. *Yǐng dòng dào-yǐng yáo Xiāo Xiāng.*

星宮之君醉瓊漿

11. *Xīng-gōng zhī jūn zuì qióng-jiāng,*

羽人稀少不在旁

12. *Yǔ-rén xī-shǎo bú zài páng.*

似聞昨者赤松子

13. *Sì wén zuó-zhě Chì-sōng-zǐ,*

恐是漢代韓張良

14. *Kǒng shì Hàn-dài Hán Zhāng Liáng.*

昔隨劉氏定長安

15. *Xī suí Liú-shì dìng Cháng-ān,*

帷幄未改神慘傷

16. *Wéi-wò wèi gǎi shén cǎn-shāng.*

國家成敗吾豈敢

17. *Guó-jiā chéng-bài wú qǐ gǎn!*

色難腥腐餐楓香

18. *Sè-nán xīng-fǔ cān fēng-xiāng.*

周南留滯古所惜

19. *Zhōu-nán liú-zhì gǔ suǒ xī,*

南極老人應壽昌

20. *Nán-jí lǎo-rén yīng shòu-chāng.*

美人胡為隔秋水

21. *Měi-rén hú-wèi gé qiū-shuǐ?*

馬得置之貢玉堂

22. *Yān dé zhì zhī gòng yù-táng?*

TITLE AND SUBJECT

Jì: 'send to', 'address'. Poems entitled '*Zèng* . . .' (e.g. No. 23) were usually presented personally, whilst those entitled '*Jì* . . .' were usually sent by post.

Hán: a surname.

Jiàn-yì: official title, 'admonisher'.

Zhù: name.

The man's full name is *Hán Zhù*. For the order surname, title, name, compare '*Cáo jiāng-jūn Bà*' in the title of No. 23.

Nothing is known about Han Chu beyond what can be deduced from this poem. He appears to have been someone who had held office at the time when Su-tsung re-entered Ch'ang-an in 757 but had subsequently resigned and was now living in retirement at Yo-chou, passing his time in the pursuit of Taoist studies. Tu Fu seems to be urging him to come out of retirement and take an active part in public life once more. The poem was probably written in 766 at Tu Fu's cottage outside K'uei-chou. It tells us that the time of year was autumn and that he was ill in bed when he wrote it.

The imagery of this poem is strongly reminiscent of the 'spirit journeys' which are so familiar a feature of the third century B.C. poetry of Ch'u. Tu Fu even addresses his friend as *měi-rén* 'the Fair One'—the title which the Ch'u poet Ch'ü Yüan used allegorically of his king. Yo-chou at the end of Lake Tung-t'ing is in the heart of Ch'ü Yüan country, a fact which may have suggested to Tu Fu this treatment of his subject.

FORM

Heptasyllabic Old Style verse. The same rhyme is used throughout (thirteen times). From the point of view of the sense, the poem divides into three six-line stanzas followed by a two-line coda, one line of which echoes line 3 at the beginning of the poem.

EXEGESIS

1. *Jīn wǒ bū lè sì Yuè-yáng*
   Now I not happy think-of Yo-yang

2. *Shēn yù fèn-fēi bìng zài chuáng*
   Body want rouse-fly sick in bed

3. *Měi-rén juān-juān gé qiū-shuǐ*
   Beautiful-person lovely-lovely separated-by autumn-water

4. *Zhuó zú Dòng-tíng wàng bā-huāng*
   Washes feet Tung-t'ing gazes eight-wilds

   Zhuó-zú: an allusion to the song which the old fisherman sang
   to Ch'ü Yüan:

   > When the Ts'ang-lang's waters are clear
   > You can wash your hat-strings in them
   > When the Ts'ang-lang's waters are muddy
   > You can wash your feet in them

   meaning, when order prevails in the world you can seek official
   employment (and wear an official's hat with ornamental strings);
   but when society is in disorder you should retire and live like a
   commoner. The implication is that Han Chu withdrew from public
   life in a period of 'turbidity' and is living in retirement on the
   shores of Lake Tung-t'ing.

   Bā-huāng means the ends of the earth, all the points of the
   compass.

5. *Hóng fēi míng-míng rì yuè-bái*
   Swan flies remote-gloom sun moon-white

6. *Qīng fēng yè chì tiān yǔ shuāng*
   Green maples leaves red sky rains frost

   Tu Fu mentions 'green maple woods' in a poem written in 759
   (No. 13) addressed to Li Po, who was believed to be in this area.

7. *Yù-jīng qún-dì jí běi-dǒu*
   Jade-city troops-of-sky-gods assemble north-dipper

8. *Huò qí qí-lín yì fèng-huáng*
   Some riding unicorns others phoenixes

   Qún-dì: *qún* has the force of a plural prefix.

The Celestial City (*yù-jīng*) allegorically represents the court at Ch'ang-an and the lords of the sky the courtiers arriving there.

9. *Fú-róng jīng-qí yān-wù luò*
   Lotus banners mist-fog fall

10. *Yǐng dòng dào-yǐng yáo Xiāo Xiāng*
    Shadows move inverted-reflections stir Hsiao Hsiang

Xiāo Xiāng: two rivers: the Hsiang flows northwards and discharges its waters into Lake Tung-t'ing; the Hsiao is one of its affluents.

I think line 10 means that the shadows of the aerial cavalcade passing overhead disturb the reflections on the calm surface of the rivers.

The lotus banners drooping in the mists of autumn refer, at one level of meaning, to the actual Tung-t'ing scenery: the dying lotus-leaves above the misty waters of the lake. At another level they are the banners of the immortal host riding through the air on its way to banquet in the Celestial City. At yet another level Tu Fu seems to be giving allegorical expression to the idea that impressions of happenings at court reach Han Chu in his Tung-t'ing retreat.

11. *Xīng-gōng zhī jūn zuì qióng-jiāng*
    Star palace's lords drunk-with jasper-liquor

12. *Yú-rén xī-shǎo bú zài páng*
    Feathered-men few not are-at side

Line 12 is often interpreted to mean 'One of the winged Immortals (viz. Han Chu) is missing and not at the Emperor's side'; but I do not see how the words can carry this meaning. I think it means 'Nearly all of the Immortals are there.' The *next* passage (lines 13 *seq.*) goes on to state the exception: Han Chu.

13. *Sì wén zuó-zhě Chì-sōng-zǐ*
    As-if heard-of while-ago Red-pine-master

14. *Kǒng shì Hàn-dài Hán Zhāng Liáng*
    Suspect is Han-era Han Chang Liang

The first Han in line 14 is the name of the dynasty which ruled the Chinese empire from 206 B.C. until A.D. 220. The second is the name of a state, the kingdom of Han, which, during the fourth and third centuries B.C. occupied what are now the areas of central Honan and southern Shansi. Chang Liang of this state became one of the most trusted advisers of Liu Pang, founder of the Han dynasty. In his old age he expressed a determination to retire from public life and become a 'follower of the Master of the Red Pine'. The latter was a legendary Immortal or Taoist Master.

Applying the usual rule of conversion ('Han' = 'T'ang') we get 'Chang Liang of the Han dynasty' = 'Han Chu of the T'ang dynasty'. The fact that the name of the state *Hán* is also Han Chu's surname provides a clue. The sense then is this: 'The Emperor and his courtiers are drinking and feasting in the Celestial City. Nearly all the best and wisest men in the empire are there. Who are the exceptions? Well, one of them is a certain Taoist recluse, one "Master of the Red Pine" whom some identify with Han Chu, a person who has in the past done the court distinguished service but is now living in retirement.'

15. *Xī suí Liú-shì dìng Cháng-ān*
Formerly followed Liu-clansman settled Ch'ang-an

16. *Wéi-wò wèi gǎi shén cǎn-shāng*
Army-tent not changed spirit cruelly-harmed

Liú-shì: i.e. Liu Pang, founder of the Han dynasty. Line 15 is thought to imply that Han Chu (like Tu Fu himself) held a court appointment at the time of Su-tsung's re-entry into Ch'ang-an.

Wéi-wò: the tent in which a general and his staff sat working out the strategy of a campaign. Hence 'strategy', or, by extension, any kind of planning or policy.

17. *Guó-jiā chéng-bài wú qǐ gǎn*
Country's success-failure I how presume

18. *Sè-nán xīng-fǔ cān fēng-xiāng*
Nauseated-by stink-corruption feed-on liquidambar

Line 17 pretends to quote Han Chu's own words. The gist of this couplet is: 'It isn't because I have ideas about the success of government policy (i.e. it isn't for political reasons) that I resigned. It's because I was revolted by official life and hankered for the life of a Taoist ascetic.'

Sè-nán xīng-fǔ is not quite as rude as it sounds, because it could have the sense 'be revolted by ordinary foods'. (Taoists aspired to attain bodily immortality by confining their diet to herbs, drugs, dew, and vapours.) Of course, the other sense—that official life stinks—is also intended; but its ambiguity makes the expression slightly less offensive.

Liquidambar was used by Taoist alchemists as a base for mixing drugs.

19. *Zhōu-nán liú-zhì gǔ suǒ xī*
    Chou-nan delay-stuck ancients that-which deplored

20. *Nán-jí lao-rén yīng shòu-chāng*
    South-pole old-man corresponds longevity-glory

Zhōu-nán liú-zhì refers to the Grand Historiographer, Ssu-ma T'an, father of the great Han historian Ssu-ma Ch'ien (145–86 B.C.). When Emperor Wu inaugurated the much-debated sacrifices on T'ai-shan and other magical rites and ceremonies designed to confirm the power of his dynasty over the spirit world, Ssu-ma T'an, who was deeply interested in these matters, was left behind in Chou-nan. His chagrin at not being invited to accompany the court brought on a sickness from which he never recovered.

The Old Man of the South Pole was the name of a star which is seen low in the night sky during autumn. In Chinese astrology it controlled the peace and good order of society and the longevity and fame of individuals. Readers will perhaps know the Old Man of the South Pole better as the God of Longevity (another of his names), frequently represented in paintings and carvings as a little old man with an enormous bald head.

In this couplet Tu Fu is saying that it would be a pity for Han Chu to be out of things like Ssu-ma T'an. Everything is propitious for his return to public life.

21. *Měi-rén hú-wèi gé qiū-shuǐ*
    Beautiful-person why-for separated-by autumn-water

22. *Yān dé zhì zhī gòng yù-táng*
    How get set him offer jade-hall

Gòng: literally 'tribute', here a verb, 'offer as tribute'. In former times successful examination candidates and other meritorious or distinguished persons sent up to the capital by the provincial governments for employment at court were considered as part of the 'tribute' of the area from which they came.

The 'jade hall' refers to the Imperial palace.

TRANSLATION

'For the Admonisher, Han Chu'

Today I am downcast and my thoughts turn to Yo-yang. My body wants to rouse up and fly there, but illness holds me to my bed. There stands the Beloved One of the radiant looks, beyond the waters of autumn, washing his feet in Tung-t'ing's shallows and gazing towards the world's eight ends. A wild swan flies in the dark depths of heaven; the sun is moon-white; frost descends on the reddening leaves of the green maples.

In the City of Jade the rulers of the sky are assembling about the Pole Star, some riding on unicorns and some on phoenixes, their lotus banners drooping in the mists. The movement of their fleeting forms casts an inverted image in the waters and makes a commotion on the still surface of the Hsiao and Hsiang. The lords of the starry palace are drunk with immortal wine. Few of the Winged Ones are missing from that company.

Yet I seem to have heard a while past of one Master of the Red Pine, whom I guess to be none other than Chang Liang of Han of our own dynasty. Once he followed Liu Pang in the settlement of Ch'ang-an. Now his great plan remains unchanged, but the spirit that informed it has been crushed. He did not presume to prognosticate concerning the fortunes of our state; he left, revolted by the stink of corruption, to sweeten his mouth with a diet of liquidambar.

Yet the delay in Chou-nan has been deplored throughout the ages; and the Old Man of the Southern Sky promises long and glorious years. So why should the Beloved One tarry beyond the waters of autumn? How can we have him placed, a meet and acceptable offering, in the Hall of Jade?

27

詠懷古跡

Yǒng huái gǔ-jì (1)

丩山萬壑赴荆門

1. *Qún-shān wàn-huò fù Jīng-mén,*

生長明妃尚有村

2. *Shēng-zhǎng Míng-fēi shàng yǒu cūn.*

一去紫臺連朔漠

3. *Yí qù zǐ-tái lián shuò-mò,*

獨留青冢向黃昏

4. *Dú liú Qīng-zhǒng xiàng huáng-hūn.*

畫圖省識春風面

5. *Huà-tú shěng zhì chūn-fēng miàn,*

環珮空歸月夜魂

6. *Huán-pèi kōng guī yuè-yè hún.*

千載琵琶作胡語

7. *Qiān zǎi pí-pá zuò hú yǔ,*

分明怨恨曲中論

8. *Fēn-míng yuàn-hèn qǔ-zhōng lún.*

TITLE AND SUBJECT

Yŏng: 'sing'.

Huái: 'thoughts'.

Gŭ-jì: 'ancient site'.

This poem and the one which follows are two of a series of five (this one is the third) each inspired by Tu Fu's visit as a sightseer to some place of interest associated with a famous historical personage. The visit which inspired this poem was to the birthplace of Wang Ch'iang (variously known as Wang Chao-chün, Chao-chün, or Ming-fei), the unfortunate court lady who in 33 B.C. was married to the king of the Huns as a Chinese 'princess'. It may be of some interest to examine the various stages by which the legend grew up which now surrounds her name. According to the earliest version of the story, which is probably the true one, she had a son who succeeded the king after his father's death and, in accordance with the Hunnish custom, married her along with his father's other wives and had sons by her. A later version of the story says that she poisoned herself rather than conform to this incestuous custom. Yet another refinement is that she had failed to find favour with the Emperor Yüan because she had refused to bribe the court painter Ma Yen-shou, with the result that he maliciously blemished her portrait. According to this version of the story, it was only when she had already been promised to the Hunnish king that the Emperor saw her and realized with regret what a beautiful woman he was parting with. Finally, in the thirteenth-century play *The Sorrows of Han*, she does not even consummate her marriage with the Hunnish king but jumps into the River Amur [*sic*] on reaching the Chinese border. Her grave-mound, near Kuei-sui in Suiyuan province, is said to be the only patch of green in a waste of brown.

Wang Ch'iang's name was early associated with the Chinese balloon guitar, or *p'i-p'a*, which was in fact a foreign instrument imported into China during the Han era. She is frequently depicted carrying a guitar, and her sad fate was a favourite subject of poets and singers.

A seventeenth-century writer tells us that in his day the girls of Wang Ch'iang's village were still branded on their faces with moxa 'in order that they might escape selection as Imperial concubines'

—no doubt a mistaken rationalization of a local custom which may have existed centuries before Wang Ch'iang was born. So perhaps the story of the blemished portrait contains a tiny shred of fact.

FORM

Regulated Verse in heptasyllabics.

EXEGESIS

1. *Qún-shān wàn-huò fù Jīng-mén*
   Flock-mountains myriad-valleys arrive Ching-men

2. *Shēng-zhǎng Míng-fēi shàng yǒu cūn*
   Bore-bred Ming-fei still there-is village

Jīng-mén: the 'Gate of Ch'u' (Ching was another name for Ch'u, an ancient kingdom in the central valley of the Yangtze) is a mountain that stands at the beginning of the great plain into which the Yangtze debouches at I-chang.

The grammar of these lines may at first seem a little puzzling. In line 1 *qún-shān wàn-huò* modifies the verb *fù*: 'to numerous-mountains-myriad-valleys-sort-of arrive at', i.e. 'to arrive at by way of many a mountain and valley'. In the second line *shēng-zhǎng Míng-fēi* qualifies the noun *cūn*. In prose this would become *shàng yǒu shēng-zhǎng Míng-fēi zhī cūn* or *shēng-zhǎng Míng-fēi zhī cūn shàng zài*: 'the village which bore and bred Ming-fei', or, as we should say, 'the village where Ming-fei was born and bred'.

3. *Yí qù zǐ-tái lián shuò-mò*
   Once depart purple-terrace continuous northern-desert

4. *Dú liú Qīng-zhǒng xiàng huáng-hūn*
   Only leave Green-grave face twilight

Zǐ-tái: the red-walled terraced buildings of the Imperial palace. *Zǐ* is a term used of various shades of dark red, including what we should call 'purple'. Although 'purple' is the equivalent usually given by Chinese–English dictionaries, we should call the colour of Chinese palace walls 'red' rather than 'purple'.

Qīng-zhǒng: the name given to Wang Ch'iang's grave, north of the Great Wall in Suiyuan.

5. *Huà-tú shěng zhì chūn-fēng miàn*
   Portraits have recorded spring-wind face

6. *Huán-pèi kōng guī yuè-yè hún*
   Girdle-jade vainly returns moon-night soul

A modern Chinese lexicographer has conclusively demonstrated that *shěng* in line 5 is used in its long obsolete and widely forgotten sense of *céng*, i.e. as a modifier of verbal aspect having the sense 'at some time or period in the past'.

7. *Qiān zǎi pí-pá zuò hú yǔ*
   Thousand years guitar makes Hunnish talk

8. *Fēn-míng yuàn-hèn qǔ-zhōng lún*
   Just-like resentment tune-in discussed

I suspect that *fēn-míng* means here not 'clearly' but 'like', 'as if' —a sense it often has in medieval colloquial Chinese.

TRANSLATION

'Thoughts on an Ancient Site' (1)

By many a mountain and many a thousand valley I come to the Gate of Ch'u. The village where Ming-fei was born and bred is to be found there still. Once she had left behind the crimson terraces, the northern desert stretched continuously before her eyes. Now only her Green Tomb is left, solitary against the dusk. Paintings have recorded those features that the spring wind caressed. On moonlight nights the sound of tinkling girdle-gems announces the bootless return of her soul. For a thousand years the *p'i-pa* has spoken its foreign tongue, seeming in its music to be discussing all her wrongs and griefs.

28

詠懷古跡
Yǒng huái gǔ-jì (2)

❧❧❧❧❧❧❧❧❧❧

諸葛大名垂宇宙

1. *Zhū-gé dà-míng chuí yǔ-zhòu,*

宗臣遺象肅清高

2. *Zōng-chén yí-xiàng sù qīng-gāo.*

三分割據紆籌策

3. *Sān-fēn gē-jù yū chóu-cè,*

萬古雲霄一羽毛

4. *Wàn-gǔ yún-xiāo yī yǔ-máo.*

伯仲之間見伊呂

5. *Bó-zhòng zhī jiān jiàn Yī Lǚ,*

指揮若定失蕭曹

6. *Zhǐ-huī ruò dìng shī Xiāo Cáo.*

運移漢祚終難復

7. *Yùn yí Hàn zuò zhōng nán fù,*

志決身殲軍務勞

8. *Zhì jué shēn jiān jūn-wù láo.*

TITLE AND SUBJECT

The site which inspired this last of the five poems on ancient sites is believed to have been the temple of Chu-ko Liang at K'uei-chou which we visited in No. 25 (the Ballad of the Old Cypress).

FORM

Regulated Verse in heptasyllabics.

EXEGESIS

1. *Zhū-gé dà-míng chuí yŭ-zhòu*
   Chu-ko's great name overhangs world

2. *Zōng-chén yí-xiàng sù qīng-gāo*
   Revered-statesman's preserved-likeness awes-with sublimity

Yí-xiàng refers to the painted image of Chu-ko Liang in the Wu-hou temple at K'uei-chou.

3. *Sān-fēn gē-jù yū chóu-cè*
   Tripartite divided-empire hampered designs

4. *Wàn-gŭ yún-xiāo yī yŭ-máo*
   Myriad-ages empyrean one-single feather

Tu Fu, as the next couplet shows, rates Chu-ko Liang one of the greatest statesmen of all time. His greatness cannot be measured by his achievements, says Tu Fu, because he was unlucky enough to live at a time when the empire was divided. He therefore had a much smaller field in which to display his talents.

5. *Bó-zhòng zhī jiān jiàn Yī Lŭ*
   Elder-middle-brothers among see I Lü

6. *Zhĭ-huī ruò dìng shī Xiāo Cáo*
   Control if established lose Hsiao Ts'ao

Yī Lŭ: I Yin and Lü Shang, legendary worthies supposed to have assisted the respective founders of the Shang (1766–1122 B.C.) and Chou (1122–249 B.C.) dynasties.

Xiāo Cáo: Hsiao Ho and Ts'ao Shen, two statesmen who helped Liu Pang (247–195 B.C.) to found the Han empire.

The sense of this couplet is that Chu-ko Liang ranks on a level with I Yin and Lü Shang and would, if he had succeeded in obtaining the amount of control they had, have left Hsiao Ho and Ts'ao Shen standing.

7. *Yùn yí Hàn zuò zhōng nán fù*
   Cycle shifted Han fortunes ultimately hard-to restore

8. *Zhì jué shēn jiān jūn-wù láo*
   Ambition blighted body annihilated military efforts in-vain

Liu Pei and his son (the First Ruler and Second Ruler of Shu), whom Chu-ko Liang served with such dedication, considered themselves the legitimate heirs of the Han emperors, and did in fact call their kingdom 'Han'. The projected Han revival, however, was not to be.

TRANSLATION
'Thoughts on an Ancient Site' (2)

Chu-ko Liang's great fame resounds through the ages. The likeness of this revered statesman still impresses with its sublime expression. The tripartite division of empire hampered his great designs; yet he soars through all the ages, a single feather floating high among the clouds. I Yin and Lü Shang could be reckoned among his peers; whilst Hsiao Ho and Ts'ao Shen would have been as nothing beside him had he only been able to establish his dominion. But the cycle had passed on and the fortunes of the House of Han were not to be restored; and so, hopes blighted, he perished, and his strategy was all in vain.

29

閣夜

Gé yè

岁暮陰陽催短景
1. *Suì-mù yīn-yáng cuī duǎn jǐng,*

天涯霜雪霽寒宵
2. *Tiān-yá shuāng-xuě jì hán xiāo.*

五更鼓角聲悲壯
3. *Wǔ-gēng gǔ-jué shēng bēi-zhuàng,*

三峽星河影動搖
4. *Sān-xiá xīng-hé yǐng dòng-yáo.*

野哭千家聞戰伐
5. *Yě kū qiān jiā wén zhàn-fá,*

夷歌幾處起漁樵
6. *Yí gē jǐ chù qǐ yú qiáo.*

臥龍躍馬終黃土
7. *Wò-lóng Yuè-mǎ zhōng huáng-tǔ,*

人事音書漫寂寥
8. *Rén-shì yīn-shū màn jì-liáo.*

TITLE AND SUBJECT

Gé: a large, high building of more than one story and usually open on two or more of its sides; a large pavilion. The *gé* here referred to is the *Xī-gé*, or 'West House', a public building in K'uei-chou, part of which was placed at Tu Fu's disposal in the autumn of 766 when Po Chen-chieh, formerly on the staff of Tu Fu's patron, Yen Wu, became Prefect of K'uei-chou and Military Governor of the surrounding area.

Gé yè: 'Night at West House'. Tu Fu lodged there on his own when he was staying in the city. There are a number of poems besides this one written while staying at his West House apartment.

FORM

Regulated Verse poem in heptasyllabics.

EXEGESIS

1. *Suì-mù yīn-yáng cuī duǎn jǐng*
   Year's-evening yin-yang hurries short light

2. *Tiān-yá shuāng-xuě jì hán xiāo*
   Heaven's-edge frost-snow cleared cold night

As in other of his poems (e.g. No. 18), Tu Fu wishes to give an impression of the length of the night. He does this by remarking how soon it gets dark in line 1 and mentioning that it is nearly morning in line 3.

3. *Wǔ-gēng gǔ-jué shēng bēi-zhuàng*
   Fifth-watch drums-bugles sound sad-strong

4. *Sān-xiá xīng-hé yǐng dòng-yáo*
   Three-gorges star-river's shadow moves-shakes

Wǔ-gēng: the fifth watch was the last watch of the night—roughly from 3 a.m. to 5 a.m. The drums and bugles announcing the beginning of the watch would be those of the garrison. In army encampments dawn and dusk were similarly announced: three drum-rolls of 333 beats, each roll followed by 12 blasts of the bugle.

Sān-xiá: Ch'ü-t'ang, westernmost of the Three Gorges, rose above the river just below the walls of K'uei-chou. The other two, the Wu Gorge and Hsi-ling, are further downstream.

Xīng-hé: the Milky Way. Its 'shadow' is its shape, cast like a luminous shadow across the vault of the sky.

Su Tung-p'o thought this the best heptasyllabic couplet in the language.

5. *Yě kū qiān jiā wén zhàn-fá*
Countryside weeping thousand families hear warfare

6. *Yí gē jǐ chù qǐ yú qiáo*
Foreign songs several places raise fishing wood-gathering

Zhàn-fá: the death of Yen Wu, Military Governor of the Szechwan area, had been followed by nearly a year of mutinies and disorders.

Yí gē: 'barbarian songs' could mean either the songs of local aborigines or foreign songs. Much of the popular music of the T'ang dynasty was of foreign origin.

7. *Wò-lóng Yuè-mǎ zhōng huáng-tǔ*
Sleeping-dragon Leaping-horse finally yellow-dust

8. *Rén-shì yīn-shū màn jì-liáo*
Human-affairs news-letters vainly melancholy

Wò-lóng 'Sleeping Dragon' is Chu-ko Liang, who, before his 'discovery' by Liu Pei, lived on Sleeping Dragon Hill. He had many associations with K'uei-chou, where, as we have seen in Nos. 23 and 28, there was a shrine to him.

Yuè-mǎ: nickname of Kung-sun Shu, the 'White Emperor', a warlord who controlled this area in the first century and held K'uei-chou as his capital. K'uei-chou was often referred to as the 'city of the White Emperor'.

TRANSLATION
'Night at West House'

In the evening of the year nature's forces swiftly hustle out the brief daylight. Night at the world's end is clear and cold after the frost and snow. The drums and bugles of the fifth watch sound, stirring and sad. Over the Three Gorges the luminous shape of the starry river trembles. In the countryside weeping rises from a thousand homes who have learned of the fighting, whilst here and there outlandish songs can be heard, sung by some fisherman or woodcutter about his work. Sleeping Dragon and Horse Leaper ended in the yellow dust. Idle to feel melancholy at the vexations of life and the lack of news from friends and kinsmen!

30

八陣圖

Bā zhèn tú

功蓋三分國
1. *Gōng gài sān-fēn guó,*

名成八陣圖
2. *Míng chéng bā zhèn tú.*

江流石不轉
3. *Jiāng-liú shí bù zhuǎn,*

遺恨失吞吳
4. *Yí hèn shī tūn Wú!*

Bā: 'eight'.

Zhèn: 'dispositions', 'battle array', 'formation'.

Tú: 'plan', 'figure'.

The 'Eight Formations' was the name given to a sort of 'Giants' Dance' of great stones ranged in regular formation beside and partly in the river near K'uei-chou. They were traditionally supposed to have been the handiwork of Chu-ko Liang and to have been one of three such stone mazes constructed by him to demonstrate military formations. From surviving accounts of these formations it seems likely that they were placed in position in a much earlier age and had had some religious or magical significance, like our own megalithic circles.

To the sightseer Tu Fu they recall his great hero Chu-ko Liang, and stand as a lasting memorial of the disastrous attempt to conquer the eastern kingdom of Wu further downstream.

FORM

This type of four-line poem, composed according to the same laws of euphony as are applied in Regulated Verse, is called a *chüeh-chü*: lit. 'snapped-off lines'. Formally a *chüeh-chü* is exactly the same as the second half of an eight-line poem in Regulated Verse. It therefore *begins* with an antithetical couplet. As seems to be the case in other languages too, the shortness of the poem increases the emphasis on the last line. Chinese poets writing a *chüeh-chü* aim to make the last line striking or haunting or even puzzling, so that the mind of the reader will continue to ponder and savour it long after he has finished reading.

EXEGESIS

1. *Gōng gài sān-fēn guó*
   Achievement covered three-divided kingdoms

2. *Míng chéng bā zhèn tú*
   Fame accomplished-in eight formations plan

3. *Jiāng-liú shí bù zhuǎn*
   River-flow stones don't roll

4. *Yí hèn shī tūn Wú*
   Surviving regret fail swallow Wu

There are several different interpretations of this last line. One of them, according to the twelfth-century poet Su Tung-p'o, was revealed to him by Tu Fu himself in a dream.

TRANSLATION

'The Eight Formations'

Of the achievements surpassing those of all others in that divided world of the Three Kingdoms, that which won him greatest renown was the construction of the Eight Formations. The great stones stand unmoved by the river's currents, a lasting memorial to his regret at having failed to swallow Wu.

觀公孫大娘弟子舞劍器行

Guān Gōng-sūn dà-niáng dì-zǐ wǔ jiàn-qì xíng

大曆二年十月十九日夔府別駕

Dà-lì èr nián shí-yuè shí-jiǔ rì Kuí-fǔ bié-jià

元持宅見臨潁李十二娘舞劍器，

Yuán Chí zhái jiàn Lín-yǐng Lǐ shí-èr-niáng wǔ jiàn-qì,

壯其蔚跂。問其所師，曰： 余公孫大

zhuàng qí wèi qì. Wèn qí suǒ shī, yuē: 'Yú Gōng-sūn dà-

娘弟子也。開元五載，余尚童稚，記於郾城觀

niáng dì-zǐ yě.' Kāi-yuán wǔ zǎi, Yú shàng tóng-zhì, jì Yú Yǎn-chéng guān

公孫氏舞劍器渾脫。瀏灕頓挫，獨出

Gōng-sūn-shì wǔ jiàn-qì hún-tuō. Liú-lí dùn-cuò, dú chū

冠時。自高頭宜春梨園二伎坊內人，

guān shí. Zì gāo-tóu Yí-chūn Lí-yuán èr jì-fāng nèi-rén,

洎外供奉舞女，曉是舞者，聖文神

jì wài gòng-fèng wǔ-nǚ, xiǎo shì wǔ zhě, Shèng-wén-shén-

武皇帝初，公孫一人而已。玉貌錦衣，

wǔ-huáng-dì chū, Gōng-sūn yì-rén ér-yǐ. Yù-mào jǐn-yī,

況余白首！今玆弟子亦匪盛顏。既
kuàng yú bái shǒu! Jīn zī dì-zǐ yì féi shèng-yán. Jì

辨其由來，知波瀾莫二。撫事慷慨，聊
biàn qí yóu-lái, zhī bō-làn mò èr. Fǔ shì kāng-kǎi, liáo

爲劍器行。昔者吳人張旭善草書
wéi jiàn-qì xíng. Xī-zhě Wú-rén Zhāng Xù shàn cǎo-shū

書帖，數嘗於鄴縣見公孫大娘舞
shū-tiè, shuò cháng yú Yè-xiàn jiàn Gōng-sūn dà-niáng wǔ

河西劍器，自此草書長進，豪蕩感激。
Hé-xī jiàn-qì, zì-cǐ cǎo-shū cháng-jìn, háo-dàng gǎn-jí.

即公孫可知矣！
Jí Gōng-sūn kě zhī yǐ!

昔有佳人公孫氏
1. *Xī yǒu jiā-rén Gōng-sūn-shì,*

一舞劍器動四方
2. *Yì wǔ jiàn-qì dòng sì-fāng.*

觀者如山色沮喪
3. *Guān-zhě rú shān sè jǔ-sàng,*

天地爲之久低昂
4. *Tiān-dì wèi zhī jiǔ dī-áng.*

爌如羿射九日落

5. *Huò rú Yì shè jiǔ rì luò,*

矯如羣帝驂龍翔

6. *Jiǎo rú qún-dì cān lóng xiáng,*

來如雷霆收震怒

7. *Lái rú léi-tíng shōu zhèn-nù,*

罷如江海凝清光

8. *Bà rú jiāng-hǎi níng qīng guāng.*

絳脣珠袖兩寂寞

9. *Jiàng chún zhū xiù liǎng jì-mò,*

晚有弟子傳芬芳

10. *Wǎn yǒu dì-zǐ chuán fēn-fāng.*

臨潁美人在白帝

11. *Lín-yǐng měi-rén zài Bó-dì,*

妙舞此曲神揚揚

12. *Miào wǔ cǐ qǔ shén yáng-yáng.*

與余問答既有以

13. *Yǔ yú wèn-dá jì yǒu yǐ,*

感時撫事增惋傷

14. *Gǎn shí fǔ shì zēng wǎn-shāng.*

先帝侍女八千人

15. *Xiān-dì shì-nǚ bā qiān rén,*

公孫劍器初第一

16. *Gōng-sūn jiàn-qì chū dì-yī.*

五十年間似反掌

17. *Wǔ-shí nián jiān sì fǎn-zhǎng,*

風塵澒洞昏王室

18. *Fēng-chén hòng-tóng hūn wáng-shì.*

梨園弟子散如煙

19. *Lí-yuán dì-zǐ sàn rú yān,*

女樂餘姿映寒日

20. *Nǚ-yuè yú-zī yìng hán rì.*

金粟堆南木已拱

21. *Jīn-sù-duī-nán mù yǐ gǒng,*

瞿唐石城草蕭瑟

22. *Qú-táng shí chéng cǎo xiāo-sè.*

玳筵急管曲復終

23. *Dài-yán jí guǎn qǔ fù zhōng,*

樂極哀來月東出

24. *Lè jí āi lái yuè dōng chū.*

老夫不知其所往

25. *Lǎo-fū bù zhī qí suǒ wǎng,*

足繭荒山轉愁疾

26. *Zú jiǎn huāng shān zhuǎn chóu jí!*

TITLE AND SUBJECT

Guān: 'watch'.

Gōng-sūn: surname.

Dà-niáng: lit. 'Eldest Miss'. Kung-sun ta-niang was a well-known dancer in the early years of Hsüan-tsung's reign.

Dì-zǐ: 'disciple', 'pupil'.

Wǔ: 'dance', here used as a verb.

Jiàn-qì: the name of a dance, seemingly of barbarian origin. It was danced by a female performer in military costume and seems to have been some kind of war dance involving much violent movement.

The long prose introduction to this poem provided by Tu Fu himself makes further explanation unnecessary.

FORM

Tu Fu's creative achievement in using a long Ballad Style poem as a medium for describing art has already been mentioned in the notes on No. 23. A well-known successor in this genre is Po Chü-i's 'Song of the Guitar' (*P'i-pa hsing*). The traditional medium for this kind of study was the *fu*, a sort of euphuistic essay in mixed prose and verse.

EXEGESIS

Dà-lì èr nián shí-yuè shí-jiǔ rì
Ta-li second year tenth-month nineteenth day

Kuí-fǔ bié-jià Yuán Chí zhái
K'uei-prefecture Lieutenant-Governor Yüan Ch'ih's house

iiàn Lín-yǐng Lǐ shí-èr-niáng wǔ jiàn-qì
saw Lin-ying Li Twelfth-miss dance chien-ch'i

zhuàng qí wèi qì
impressed-by her brilliance elevation

> *Dà-lì èr nián etc.*: this corresponds to 15 November 767.
> *Lín-yǐng*: in central Honan a little south of Hsüchow.

Wèn qí suǒ shī yuē
Asked the one-who trained-under said

Yú Gōng-sūn dà-niáng dì-zǐ yě
I Kung-sun Eldest-miss's pupil am

Kāi-yuán wǔ zǎi
K'ai-yüan fifth year

yú shàng tóng-zhì jì yú Yǎn-chéng guān Gōng-sūn-shì
I still little-boy remember at Yen-ch'eng seeing the-Kung-sun

wǔ jiàn-qì hún-tuō
dance chien-ch'i hun-t'o

Liú-lí dùn-cuò dú chū guān shí
Flowing-style forceful-attack lone outstanding surpassing age

> *Kāi-yuán wǔ zǎi*: i.e. 717.
> This emendation of the received text, which has 'third year', is widely accepted.
>
> *Yǎn-chéng*: in central Honan only a short distance (about 25 miles) south of Lin-ying, where Madame Kung-sun's pupil came from.
>
> *Hún-tuō*: the *hun-t'o* was originally a cap of black kid's wool—probably what we should call astrakhan—which subsequently gave its name to a dance. A cap of this type was affected by Ch'ang-sun Wu-chi, a trusted member of T'ai-tsung's staff when the latter was Prince of Ch'in and fighting the campaigns which led to the foundation of the T'ang dynasty. The *hun-t'o* is therefore likely to have been a dance which mimed the military exploits of Ch'ang-sun Wu-chi.

Zì gāo-tóu Yí-chūn Lí-yuán èr jì-fāng nèi-rén
From high-heads Like-spring Pear-garden two music-school inner-people

jì wài gòng-fèng wǔ-nǚ
down-to outside supply-entertainment dancing-girls

xiǎo shì wǔ zhě
understood this dance ones-who

Shèng-wén-shén-wǔ-huáng-dì chū
Sagely-peaceful-divinely-warlike-emperor beginning

Gōng-sūn yì-rén ér-yǐ
Kung-sun single-person only

The organization of artistes and entertainers in the employment of the musically gifted and pleasure-loving Hsüan-tsung was recorded by a contemporary of Tu Fu called Ts'ui Ling-ch'in, who fled south during the An Lu-shan rebellion. His account exists, however, only in a corrupt and fragmentary state, and continues to baffle scholars. Roughly, it appears that there were two 'centres' or 'academies' for girl entertainers (singers, dancers, instrumentalists, etc.) located in two of the 'wards' of Ch'ang-an adjoining the palace. These were the *jiào-fāng*. Traditionally one specialized in singing and one in dancing. Especially good performers were transferred to centres inside the palace grounds: singers and dancers to the I-ch'un-yüan; instrumentalists to the Li-yüan. Girls who were transferred to the I-ch'un-yüan and who made frequent appearances before the Emperor were, according to Ts'ui Ling-ch'in, called 'nei-jen' ('Insiders') or 'ch'ien-t'ou-jen' ('Royal Performers', lit. 'in front—i.e. in the presence—people'). Tu Fu's *gāo-tóu* appears to be an alternative version of 'ch'ien-t'ou'. *Jì* was the word used of performers or entertainers. *Èr jì-fāng* therefore obviously refers to the two *jiào-fāng*. But the *wài gòng-fèng wǔ-nǚ* 'royal-command dancers outside the palace' should also mean members of the *jiào-fāng*. Something seems to be wrong with Tu Fu's comprehensive list of entertainers. Much ingenuity has been devoted to explaining this passage; but I think myself that Tu Fu's own recollection of the organization and the terms used was a little hazy by the time he wrote this poem, and that in his mind the I-ch'un-yüan and Li-yüan had become identified with the two *jiào-fāng*, so that you could talk about 'the two *jiào-fāng*, I-ch'un-yüan and Li-yüan'. He is, in any case, showing off a bit in using the terms *gāo-tóu* and *nèi-rén*, which were presumably only used by the *cognoscenti*, and it is precisely when showing off in this way that one is most likely to make a slip.

Shèng-wén-shén-wǔ 'sage-like in peace and godlike in war'. Hsüan-tsung, who had a weakness for titles, assumed this one in

739. In the light of the fiascos which ended his reign, the title has a hollow ring, and is probably used by Tu Fu with deliberate irony.

Yù-mào jǐn-yī, kuàng yú bái shǒu
Jade-face brocade-dress what's-more I'm white-headed

It is usual to treat this as a violent aposiopesis: 'Her jadelike face and her brocade robes—And I am an old, white-headed man now!' Emendations have been suggested to make this read more smoothly, but I prefer the text as it stands.

Jīn zī dì-zǐ yì fěi shèng-yán
Now this pupil also not prime-looks

Jì biàn qí yóu-lái zhī bō-làn mò èr
Having discerned her antecedents know every-nuance not two

Bō-làn: lit. 'big waves and little waves': i.e. every movement and gesture.

Fǔ shì kāng-kǎi liǎo wéi jiàn-qì xíng
Ponder events moved-excited wanted make *chien-ch'i* ballad

Xī-zhě Wú-rén Zhāng Xù shàn cǎo-shū shū-tiè
Formerly Wu-native-of Chang Hsü good-at grass-writing calligraphy.

Zhāng Xù: a famous calligrapher noted for his drunkenness and eccentricity whom Tu Fu celebrated elsewhere in his 'Song of the Eight Immortals'. Contemporaries called him 'Crazy Chang'.

shuò cháng yú Yè-xiàn jiàn Gōng-sūn dà-niáng wǔ Xī-hé jiàn-qì
frequently did at Yeh-hsien see Kung-sun ta-niang dance west river chien-ch'i

Yè-xiàn: like Lin-ying and Yen-ch'eng, this is in Honan province, which must have been the centre of Madame Kung-sun's activities.

Xī-hé jiàn-qì: it has been suggested that *Xī-hé* is here used for the more usual *Hé-xī*, which would mean Chinese Turkestan. Since the *chien-ch'i* was almost certainly a foreign dance, this explanation is, though arbitrary, quite a likely one.

Zì-cǐ cǎo-shū cháng-jìn háo-dàng gǎn-jí
From-this grass-writing greatly-improved enormously grateful

Jí Gōng-sūn kě zhī yǐ
Then Kung-sun can-be known

1. *Xī yǒu jiā-rén Gōng-sūn-shì*
   Once was lovely-lady Kung-sun-clan

2. *Yì wǔ jiàn-qì dòng sì-fāng*
   One dance *chien-ch'i* moved four-quarters

3. *Guān-zhě rú shān sè jǔ-sàng*
   Beholders like hills appearance bewildered

4. *Tiān-dì wèi zhī jiǔ dī-áng*
   Heaven-earth because-of-it long undulated

   Rú shān: like mountains, i.e. very numerous.
   Jiǔ dī-áng: to the dizzy spectators everything seemed to go on moving up and down long after the dance had finished.

5. *Huò rú Yì shè jiǔ rì luò*
   Flashing like Yi shoots nine suns fall

6. *Jiǎo rú qún-dì cān lóng xiáng*
   Superb like sky-lords harnessed dragons soar

   Yì: mythical archer who, when the ten suns of heaven once all came out together and burned up the earth, shot nine of them down with his arrows.

7. *Lái rú léi-tíng shōu zhèn-nù*
   Coming like thunder gathering-in rage

8. *Bà rú jiāng-hǎi níng qīng guāng*
   Stopping like rivers-seas freezing cold light

   It has been suggested that Kung-sun's entry was preceded by a roll of drums which decreased in volume as she glided forward and stopped altogether as she reached the front of the audience and froze into her opening stance. This 'freezing' in the midst of violent action is familiar to anyone who has watched battle scenes in Chinese opera.

9. *Jiàng chún zhū xiù liǎng jì-mò*
   Scarlet lips pearly sleeves both at-rest

10. *Wǎn yǒu dì-zǐ chuán fēn-fāng*
    Latterly was pupil to-pass-on fragrance

11. *Lín-yǐng měi-rén zài Bó-dì*
    Lin-ying beautiful-person at White Emperor

12. *Miào wǔ cǐ qǔ shén yáng-yáng*
    Excellently dances this piece spirits animated

    Bó-dì: the White Emperor city, i.e. K'uei-chou.

13. *Yǔ yú wèn-dá jì yǒu yǐ*
    With me ask-reply already have-reason

14. *Gǎn shí fǔ shì zēng wǎn-shāng*
    Moved-by-time pondering-events increases regret-hurt

15. *Xiān-dì shì-nǚ bā qiān rén*
    Late-Emperor's serving-women eight thousand persons

16. *Gōng-sūn jiàn-qì chū dì-yī*
    Kung-sun's chien-ch'i beginning number-one

17. *Wǔ-shí nián jiān sì fǎn-zhǎng*
    Fifty years-during like turn-over-palm

18. *Fēng-chén hòng-tóng hūn wáng-shì*
    Wind-dust continually darken kingly-house

At the time of writing this poem Tu Fu was in his fifty-fifth year. The fifth year of K'ai-yüan (717) to the second year of Ta-li (767) is in fact fifty years. Tu Fu would have been a little boy of four when he saw the great dancer.

19. *Lí-yuán dì-zǐ sàn rú yān*
    Pear-garden pupils scattered like mist

20. *Nǚ-yuè yú-zì yìng hán rì*
    Female-performer's remaining-looks shine cold sun

21. *Jīn-sù-duī-nán mù yǐ gǒng*
    Golden-grain-mound-south-of trees already join-hands

22. *Qú-táng shí chéng cǎo xiāo-sè*
    Ch'ü-t'ang rock wall grass withered-sad

Royal tombs, like other royal buildings, face the south. The trees south of Hsüan-tsung's tomb are therefore the ones which form the avenue leading up to the entrance of the tomb. The branches of the trees on either side of this avenue have grown until they now meet in the middle.

23. *Dài-yán jí guǎn qǔ fù zhōng*
Tortoiseshell-mat urgent pipe tune again concludes

24. *Lè jí āi lái yuè dōng chū*
Pleasure extreme sorrow comes moon in-east rises

Dài-yán: Chinese of the T'ang period still sat on the floor on mats, like the Japanese. A very expensive mat might have a border of tortoiseshell, a commodity which to Chinese of this period symbolized the height of luxury. *Dài-yán* therefore has the sense of 'luxurious feast' in this context.

25. *Lǎo-fū bù zhī qí suǒ wǎng*
Old-fellow not know his where going

26. *Zú jiǎn huāng shān zhuǎn chóu jí*
Feet calloused wild mountains increasingly sad-at hurry

TRANSLATION

'On Seeing a Pupil of Kung-sun Dance the *Chien-ch'i*— A Ballad'

On the nineteenth day of the tenth month of the second year of Ta-li (15 November 767), in the residence of Yüan Ch'ih, Lieutenant-Governor of K'uei-chou, I saw Li Shih-er-niang of Lin-ying dance the *chien-ch'i*. Impressed by the brilliance and thrust of her style, I asked her whom she had studied under. 'I am a pupil of Kung-sun', was the reply.

I remember in the fifth year of K'ai-yüan (717) when I was still a little lad seeing Kung-sun dance the *chien-ch'i* and the *hun-t'o* at Yen-ch'eng. For purity of technique and self-confident attack she was unrivalled in her day. From the 'royal command performers' and the 'insiders' of the Spring Garden and Pear Garden schools in the palace down to the 'official call' dancers outside, there was no one during the early years of His Sagely Pacific and Divinely Martial Majesty who understood this dance as she did. Where now is that lovely figure in its gorgeous costume? Now even I am an old, white-haired man; and this pupil of hers is well past her prime.

Having found out about the pupil's antecedents, I now realized that what I had been watching was a faithful reproduction of the great dancer's interpretation. The train of reflections set off by this discovery so moved me that I felt inspired to compose a ballad on the *chien-ch'i*.

Some years ago, Chang Hsü, the great master of the 'grass writing' style of calligraphy, having several times seen Kung-sun dance the West River *chien-ch'i* at Yeh-hsien, afterwards discovered, to his immense gratification, that his calligraphy had greatly improved. This gives one some idea of the sort of person Kung-sun was.

In time past there was a lovely woman called Kung-sun, whose *chien-ch'i* astonished the whole world. Audiences numerous as the hills watched awestruck as she danced, and, to their reeling senses, the world seemed to go on rising and falling, long after she had finished dancing. Her flashing swoop was like the nine suns falling, transfixed by the Mighty Archer's arrows; her soaring flight like the lords of the sky driving their dragon teams aloft; her advance like the thunder gathering up its dreadful rage; her stoppings like seas and rivers locked in the cold glint of ice.

The crimson lips, the pearl-encrusted sleeves are now at rest. But in her latter years there had been a pupil to whom she transmitted the fragrance of her art. And now in the city of the White Emperor the handsome woman from Lin-ying performs this dance with superb spirit. Her answers to my questions having revealed that there was good reason to admire, my ensuing reflections fill me with painful emotion.

Of the eight thousand women who served our late Emperor, Kung-sun was from the first the leading performer of the *chien-ch'i*. Fifty years have now gone by like a flick of the hand—fifty years in which rebellions and disorders darkened the royal house. The pupils of the Pear Garden have vanished like the mist. And now here is this dancer, with the cold winter sun shining on her fading features.

South of the Hill of Golden Grain the boughs of the trees already interlace. On the rocky walls of Ch'ü-t'ang the dead grasses blow forlornly. At the glittering feast the shrill flutes have once more concluded. When pleasure is at its height, sorrow follows. The moon rises in the east; and I depart, an old man who does not know where he is going, but whose feet, calloused from much walking in the wild mountains, make him wearier and wearier of the pace.

32

旅夜書懷
Lǚ yè shū huái

細草微風岸

1. *Xì cǎo wéi fēng àn,*

危檣獨夜舟

2. *Wéi qiáng dú yè zhōu:*

星垂平野闊

3. *Xīng chuí píng yě kuò,*

月湧大江流

4. *Yuè yǒng dà-jiāng liú.*

名豈文章著

5. *Míng qǐ wén-zhāng zhù?*

官應老病休

6. *Guān yīng lǎo bìng xiū.*

飄飄何所似

7. *Piāo-piāo hé-suǒ sì?*

天地一沙鷗

8. *Tiān-dì yì shā-ōu!*

TITLE AND SUBJECT

Lǚ: 'travelling'.

   Yè: 'night'.

   Shū: 'write'.

   Huái: 'thoughts'.

This is usually dated 765 and supposed to have been written on the two hundred and fifty mile journey down the Yangtze from Jung-chou to Chung-chou during June or July of that year, following Yen Wu's death in Ch'eng-tu. I prefer the dating of William Hung, who places it in the spring of 767 when the poet was travelling between K'uei-chou and Chiang-ling. The fine grass and the great expanse of level plain surely sound more like the central plain of the Yangtze in spring than the Yangtze gorges in July. The mood of resigned despair also belongs to the later period.

FORM

Regulated Verse poem in pentasyllabics. The first couplet as well as the middle ones is in parallel arrangement.

EXEGESIS

1. *Xì cǎo wéi fēng àn*
   Fine grass slight wind bank

2. *Wéi qiáng dú yè zhōu*
   Tall mast lonely night boat

3. *Xīng chuí píng yě kuò*
   Stars hang-down level plain vastness

4. *Yuè yǒng dà-jiāng liú*
   Moon bobs-from great-river's flow

5. *Míng qǐ wén-zhāng zhù*
   Name how literature famous

6. *Guān yīng lǎo-bìng xiū*
   Office due-to age-sickness resigned

Critics who cannot believe that Tu Fu ever thought of himself as a failure interpret this couplet to mean, 'It isn't true that I only got to be known by the authorities because of my writings. I was a very promising civil servant. It was because of ill health that I have had to give up my official career'; but I do not for a moment think the words support so jejune an interpretation. What Tu Fu is saying here, it seems to me, is that his life has achieved nothing, neither literary fame nor a successful career. From this moment of despair is born the magnificent simile of the last couplet.

7. *Piāo-piāo hé-suŏ sì*
   Drifting-drifting what-am like

8. *Tiān-dì yì shā-oū*
   Sky-earth one sand-gull

TRANSLATION

'Thoughts Written While Travelling at Night'

By the bank where the fine grass bends in a gentle wind, my boat's tall mast stands in the solitary night. The stars hang down over the great emptiness of the level plain, and the moon bobs on the running waters of the Great River. Literature will bring me no fame. A career is denied me by my age and sickness. What do I most resemble in my aimless wanderings? A seagull drifting between earth and sky!

33

登高

Dēng gāo

風急天高猿嘯哀

1. *Fēng jí tiān gāo yuán xiào āi,*

渚清沙白鳥飛迴

2. *Zhǔ qīng shā bái niǎo fēi huí.*

無邊落木蕭蕭下

3. *Wú biān luò mù xiāo-xiāo xià,*

不盡長江滾滾來

4. *Bú jìn cháng jiāng gǔn-gǔn lái.*

萬里悲秋常作客

5. *Wàn-lǐ bēi qiū cháng zuò kè,*

百年多病獨登臺

6. *Bǎi-nián duō bìng dú dēng tái.*

艱難苦恨繁霜鬢

7. *Jiān-nán kǔ-hèn fán shuāng-bìn,*

潦倒新停濁酒杯

8. *Liáo-dǎo xīn tíng zhuó jiǔ bēi!*

TITLE AND SUBJECT

Dēng: 'climb'.

Gāo: 'high'.

The magnificent sorrow of this threnody for dying nature ends with Tu Fu's remark that he has had to give up drinking. Whether the tone intended is fretful or, as I suspect, humorous (cf. the gentle self-mockery at the end of No. 6, which also begins on a note of tragic sorrow), it is hard not to find this ending uncomfortable. Yet Tu Fu does this sort of thing so often that one must look for something other than mere neurotic self-pity if one is to reach any sort of understanding with him at all.

My own view is that Tu Fu's famous compassion in fact includes himself, viewed quite objectively and almost as an afterthought. We can perhaps understand this poem if we think of a typical Chinese landscape with a tiny figure in one corner of it looking at the view. In this poem the little figure is Tu Fu himself, who, far from solipsistically shrinking the landscape to his own dimensions, lends grandeur to it by contrasting it with his own slightly comical triviality.

FORM

Heptasyllabic Regulated Verse.

EXEGESIS

1. *Fēng jí tiān gāo yuán xiào āi*
   Wind keen sky high apes scream mourning

2. *Zhŭ qīng shā bái niăo fēi huí*
   Islet pure sand white birds fly revolving

3. *Wú biān luò mù xiāo-xiāo xià*
   Without limit falling trees bleakly-bleakly shed

4. *Bú jìn cháng jiāng gŭn-gŭn lái*
   Not exhaustible long river rolling-rolling come

5. *Wàn-lǐ bēi qiū cháng zuò kè*
   Myriad-li melancholy autumn constantly be traveller

6. *Bǎi-nián duō bìng dú dēng tái*
   Hundred-years much sickness alone ascend terrace

7. *Jiān-nán kǔ-hèn fán shuāng-bìn*
   Difficulties bitter-regrets proliferate frosty temples

8. *Liáo-dǎo xīn tíng zhuó jiǔ bēi*
   Despondent newly stop muddy wine cups

TRANSLATION
'From a Height'

The wind is keen, the sky is high; apes wail mournfully. The island looks fresh; the white sand gleams; birds fly circling. An infinity of trees bleakly divest themselves, their leaves falling, falling. Along the endless expanse of river the billows come rolling, rolling. Through a thousand miles of autumn's melancholy, a constant traveller racked with a century's diseases, alone I have dragged myself up to this high terrace. Hardship and bitter chagrin have thickened the frost upon my brow. And to crown my despondency I have lately had to renounce my cup of muddy wine!

34

登岳陽樓

Dēng Yuē-yáng lóu

昔聞洞庭水

1. Xī wén Dòng-tíng shuǐ,

今上岳陽樓

2. Jīn shàng Yuè-yáng lóu.

吳楚東南坼

3. Wú Chǔ dōng nán chè,

乾坤日夜浮

4. Qián-kūn rì-yè fú.

親朋無一字

5. Qīn-péng wú yí zì,

老病有孤舟

6. Lǎo-bìng yǒu gū zhōu.

戎馬關山北

7. Róng-mǎ guān-shān běi,

憑軒涕泗流

8. Píng xuān tì-sì liú.

TITLE AND SUBJECT

Dēng: 'climb'.

Yuē-yáng: a town at the north-eastern corner of Lake Tung-t'ing, Yo-chou.

Lóu: 'tower'. Here the gate-tower in the walls of Yo-chou looking westwards across the lake.

Tu Fu left K'uei-chou in the spring of 768 and sailed 250 miles downstream to Chiang-ling, where he and his family stayed for a number of months. In the autumn he set off for Yo-chou, intending to proceed onwards from there to the junction of the Yangtze and the River Han. He planned to return to the North, to which he had so long been a stranger, by sailing up-river along the Han. News of a Tibetan invasion made him alter his plans. Although he reached Yo-chou that autumn, he was to spend all the rest of his life in the South.

This poem begins with the poet on top of a high building looking at a view which he has been longing to see for years, and ends with him collapsed on the parapet in sobs. Some critics have found it difficult to establish a connexion between the first and second halves of the poem, particularly between the magnificent fourth line, in which the whole universe appears to be floating in the ever-moving waters of the vast lake, and the comparatively more trivial fifth line in which the poet complains of the lack of news from his family and friends in the North. The difficulty is due to the rapidity with which one mood succeeds another in the course of the poem. Elation at achieving the long-expected view is followed by awe at its immensity, then by a feeling of isolation and loneli-ness, then by patriotic worry about the Tibetan invasion and its threat to the metropolitan area, and finally by the tearful break-down of the last line.

The result of compressing so many mental happenings into so exiguous a form is that the actual wording of the poem becomes a kind of shorthand from which the poet's full meaning has to be reconstructed. Poetry like this, in short, invites us to share some of the process of composition with the poet. That is why much of Tu Fu, particularly 'late Tu Fu', *reads* rather badly but *recollects* wonderfully well.

FORM

Pentasyllabics in Regulated Verse. Notice that in this poem, as in No. 6, not only the two central couplets but also the opening couplet are in parallel arrangement (*Xī* balancing *Jīn*, *wén* balancing *shàng*, and *Dòng-tíng shuǐ* balancing *Yuè-yáng lóu*). This gratuitous bit of extra formalism in a poem which is so heavily loaded with meaning suggests that the creative writer in China cannot have found his elaborately formal medium quite so cramping and inhibiting as is sometimes suggested by iconoclastic modern critics.

EXEGESIS

1. *Xī wén Dòng-tíng shuǐ*
   In-past hear-of Tung-t'ing's water

2. *Jīn shàng Yuè-yáng lóu*
   Now ascend Yo-yang tower

3. *Wú Chǔ dōng nán chè*
   Wu Ch'u east west split

4. *Qián-kūn rì-yè fú*
   Heaven-and-earth day-night float

Qián and *kūn* are the names of the first two hexagrams in the divination scripture of the Confucian canon: they are the symbols of sky and earth; used together here as a compound word they form a poetic synonym for *tiān-dì*, 'the world', 'the universe'.

5. *Qīn-péng wú yī zì*
   Relatives-friends not one word

6. *Lǎo-bìng yǒu gū zhōu*
   Old-ill have solitary boat

Lǎo-bìng: it should not be thought, from the rather frequent references to ill health which occur in his poems, that Tu Fu was a hypochondriac. During the occupation of Ch'ang-an he contracted malaria and some chronic respiratory disease, suffered from rheumatism a great deal during his stay in Ch'eng-tu (the 'river city'), and after his move to K'uei-chou was, at any rate for a time, paralysed in his right arm. Also while in K'uei-chou he became deaf in one ear and lost all his teeth.

7. *Róng-mǎ guān-shān běi*
   War-horses passes-mountains north

8. *Píng xuān tì-sì liú*
   Lean-on railing snivel-tears flow

Róng-mǎ: reference to the Tibetan invasion. In October 768 the Tibetans invested first Ling-wu and then Pin-chou, and a state of emergency was declared in the capital. The Tibetan invasion had been successfully stemmed by the time Tu Fu wrote this poem, but it is unlikely that news of government successes had yet reached him in Yo-yang.

TRANSLATION

'On Yo-yang Tower'

Long ago I heard about the waters of Tung-t'ing, and now today I have climbed up Yo-yang tower. The lake cleaves the lands of Wu and Ch'u to east and south. Day and night the world floats in its changing waters. Of friends and family I have no word. Old and ill I have only my solitary boat. The warhorse stamps north of the passes. I lean on the railing and my tears flow.

35

江南逢李龜年
Jiāng-nán féng Lǐ Guī-nián

岐王宅裏尋常見

1. *Qí-wáng zhái-lǐ xún-cháng jiàn,*

崔九堂前幾度聞

2. *Cuī Jiǔ táng-qián jǐ-dù wén.*

正是江南好風景

3. *Zhèng-shì Jiāng-nán hǎo fēng-jǐng,*

落花時節又逢君

4. *Luò huā shí-jié yòu féng jūn.*

TITLE AND SUBJECT

Jiāng-nán: literally 'south of the Yangtze': in the T'ang period this was the name of a huge area containing all the southern provinces from the south-east borders of Szechwan eastwards to the sea. In fact this encounter is believed to have taken place in T'an-chou (the modern Ch'ang-sha) on the River Hsiang.

Féng: 'meet'.

Lǐ Guī-nián: Li Kuei-nien was one of the most accomplished singers at Hsüan-tsung's brilliant court and made so much money by his singing that he was able to build an imposing mansion for himself in Loyang. Like many other of the Emperor's entertainers, he fled south in the troubles following An Lu-shan's rebellion. He succeeded in returning to Ch'ang-an some time after Tu Fu's death.

This poem was written only a few months before Tu Fu's death (in the winter of 770), and is the last *chüeh-chü* he ever wrote. He died, probably of fever, while travelling alone by boat.

FORM

Heptasyllabic *chüeh-chü*.

EXEGESIS

1. *Qí-wáng zhái-lǐ xún-cháng jiàn*
   Ch'i-prince's home-in often see

2. *Cuī Jiǔ táng-qián jǐ-dù wén*
   Ts'ui Ninth's hall-before several-times hear

   Qí-wáng: Hsüan-tsung's younger brother Li Fan, Prince of Ch'i.
   Cuī Jiǔ: 'Ninth Brother Ts'ui' is Ts'ui Ti, a palace chamberlain.

3. *Zhèng-shì Jiāng-nán hǎo fēng-jǐng*
   Truly Chiang-nan good scenery

4. *Luò huā shí-jié yòu féng jūn*
   Falling flower season again meet you

   Luò huā shí-jié has a poignant second meaning: Tu Fu and Li Kuei-nien are both old men now, one of them very near his death. It also hints at the vanished glories of Hsüan-tsung's reign.

TRANSLATION

'On Meeting Li Kuei-nien in the South'

I often saw you in Prince Ch'i's house and heard you a number of times in the hall of Ts'ui Ti. It's true that the scenery in Chiang-nan is very beautiful. And here, in the season of fallen blossoms, I meet you once again.

VOCABULARY

The arabic numerals before the stop refer to the number of the poem and those after the stop to the number of the line: e.g. 3.4 means that the expression given occurs in the fourth line of No. 3 (*Lì-rén xíng*). The sign o following the stop refers to the title, so that the reference for *lì-rén* will be 3.0. '31 pref.' is a reference to the prose preface which comes between the title and the poem in No. 31.

The following abbreviations are used to distinguish differences of grammatical usage listed under the same entry:

s.	'substantive'.
v.	'verb'.
adj.	'adjective'.
adv.	'adverb'.
conj.	'conjunction'.
prep.	'preposition'.
distrib.	'distributive'.

I cannot pretend that my apportionment of these labels is always satisfactory, but the alternative to using these familiar names would have involved me in writing a Chinese grammar, and was therefore one that I was not prepared to contemplate.

The meanings I list are those that the words have in the context of these poems. Sometimes they are not the commonest meanings of the words; but this is a vocabulary and not a dictionary. I have indicated the etymology of many of the compound words by listing after the simple word any compounds appearing elsewhere in the vocabulary in which it features as the first element. Thus the reader may learn from the vocabulary that the *gōng-* of *gōng-chén* ('deserving minister') is the *gōng* elsewhere used on its own in the sense of 'achievement', but not the *gōng* meaning 'handiwork'. I have not hesitated to give separate entries for words of different meaning and no apparent semantic connexion which happen to be written with the same Chinese character, as, for example, *xíng* 'walk' and *xíng* 'ballad', nor have I bothered to mention derivations when the connexion between the two terms is too devious or obscure to be useful.

āi, v., to lament, grieve for 5.0, 7.0; s., sorrow 31.24; adj., mournful 33.1. *āi-yín, āi-zāi*

āi-yín, to sound mournful, make a mournful noise 3.19

āi-zāi, alas 5.27

ài, to love 24.25. *ài-xī*

ài-xī, to cherish, spare 25.6

ān, quiet, peace 22.8

ān-mǎ, saddle-horse 3.21, 24.1

àn, bank (of river, etc.) 32.1

bā, eight 30.0, 30.2. *bā-huāng, bā-qiān, bā-zhēn*

bā-huāng, lit. 'the eight wilds': the far quarters of the earth 26.4

bā-qiān, eight thousand 31.15

Bā-xiá, place-name: the Pa gorge 19.7

bā-zhēn, lit. 'the eight delicacies': rare and delicious foods 3.18

bǎ, to hold 2.18, 18.3, 20.6

bà, to stop, halt 31.8

bái, adj., white 2.13, 5.1, 6.7, 7.10, 11.3, 14.9, 23.37, 26.5, 31 pref., 33.2; s., whiteness 25.8. *bái-gǔ, bái-pín, bái-rì*

bái-gǔ, bleached bones, whitening bones 2.33

bái-pín, a water-plant: frogbit 3.23

bái-rì, in the daytime 19.5

bǎi, a hundred 5.11. *bǎi-cǎo, bǎi-nián*

bǎi-cǎo, lit. 'the hundred grasses': the grass 2.31

bǎi-nián, a hundred years, a century, life-time 33.6

bài-wǔ to perform the dance of obeisance 24.9

bàn, half 10.7

bàng, v.8.4 to draw alongside

bǎo, to protect, preserve 5.16

bǎo, treasure 24.31. *bǎo-jué*

Bǎo-gōng, person's name: the Duke of Pao 23.15

bǎo-jué, crescent-shaped ornament of jade worn at the girdle 5.7

bēi, s., sadness, grief 9.0; adv., sadly 22.3; adj., sad 33.5. *bēi-zhuàng*

bēi, cup 17.8, 18.3, 33.8

bēi-zhuàng, lit. 'sad and strong': stirring but sad 29.3

běi, in the north 2.10, 5.24. *běi-dǒu, běi-jí*

-běi, north of . . . 7.20, 17.1, 24.7

běi-dǒu, a constellation: the Dipper 26.7

běi-jí, the pole star 21.5

bèi, to sustain, endure, be the object of 2.21

bèi-hòu, at the back, on the back 3.9

bǐ-cǐ, lit. 'that this': mutually, on both sides 7.16

bǐ-jì, lit. 'brush traces': specimens of some one's painting or calligraphy 24.11

bǐ-lín, neighbour 2.30

bì, necessarily, certainly, whenever . . . always . . . 23.24

bì, emerald, bright green 16.3

bì, to escape, flee from 5.4

bì-gōng, shrine, temple 25.10

biān, frontier 11.2; limit, end 33.3. *biān-tíng*

biān, whip 5.5

biān-tíng, frontier station, outpost 2.14

biàn, conj., even 2.11; adv., then, next 19.8

biàn, to change, alter 21.4

biàn, to discern, elicit, determine 31 pref.

bié, s., separation 6.4; v., to part from, take leave of 9.0, 10.11, 18.1, 20.0, 20.2

bié-jià, title used in addressing or

referring to a Lieutenant-Governor 31 pref.

bīn-cóng, clients and attendants, retinue, following 3.20

bìn-chún, front edge of a woman's hair 3.8

bìn-fà, hair on the temples 10.6

bīng, soldiers 2.20; warfare 11.8. *bīng-chē*

bīng-chē, army-cart 2.0

bìng, to be ill 26.2

bō-làn, lit. 'waves and ripples': every little movement 31 pref.

bō-làng, waves 13.15

bó, cypress 12.22, 16.2, 24.33, 25.0, 25.1

bó, thin 12.23

Bó-dì, place-name: the City of the White Emperor, i.e. K'uei-chou 31.11

bó-zhòng, lit. 'elder and middle brothers': peers 28.5

bú-yì, in just the same way as . . ., just as if one were . . . 2.21

bǔ, repair 12.20

bù, not 2.5, 2.16, 2.32, 3.17, 8.5, 10.1, 10.21, 11.7, 12.14, 12.21, 13.10, 14.2, 14.6, 21.5, 23.7, 23.18, 23.31, 24.33, 25.19, 26.1, 26.12, 30.3, 31.25, 33.4. *bù-céng*, *bù-dé*, *bù-gǎn*, *bú-yì*

bù-céng, has not, has never, at no time in the past 17.3

bù-dé, to be unable to, fail to 5.6, 7.14, 12.8

bù-gǎn, not dare to 5.17

bù-kěn, be unwilling to . . ., refuse to . . . 5.9

bù-shēng, be unequal to the task of . . ., be inadequate for . . . 6.8

cái, timber, material, a pun on the word for 'talent' 25.24

cái-rén, name of a certain class of palace lady, maid of honour 7.9, 24.8

cǎi, to pluck, pick 12.22

cān, to meet, visit 25.4

cān, to feed on, make one's diet of 26.18

cān, to harness, put in the traces 31.6

cán, to be wasted away, consumed, spent 22.2. *cán-shēng*

cán-shēng, the remainder of one's life, one's declining years 18.8

cǎn-dàn, to take pains, travail 23.22

cǎn-shāng, to be grievously wounded 26.16

cāng, grey 10.6

Cáo jiāng-jūn Bà, person's name: General Ts'ao Pa 23.0, 24.0

cǎo, grass 16.3, 31.22, 32.1. *cǎo-mù*, *cǎo-shū*

cǎo-mù, grass and trees, vegetation 6.2, 12.4

cǎo-shū, 'grass writing': a type of calligraphy in which the strokes are made in a rapid, flowing manner 31 pref.

cè, side 7.8

cè, to measure, estimate 13.10

cè-cè, wretched, anguished 13.2

céng, once, on some past occasion 24.5

céng, layered 1.5

chā, to stick in, insert 12.21

chái-láng, jackals and wolves, ravening beasts 5.15

chán, to entangle, enmesh 23.40

chāng-hé, palace gates 23.20

cháng, once, to have . . ., on a past occasion or occasions 31 pref.

cháng, always 13.2, 14.5; often 23.9; constantly 33.5. *cháng-rén*

cháng, adv., for a long time 5.17; always 11.7, 13.6, 16.8; adj., lasting, of long duration 10.22; long, coming from afar 23.20, 33.4; tall 24.21; s., length 25.7. *cháng-jìn*

Cháng-ān, place name: Ch'ang-an, the capital of the T'ang empire

cháng-jìn, to make progress 31 pref.

cháng-rén, ordinary people 5.14

cháo, s., reign 16.6, 18.6; v., to pay court to 24.31. *cháo-tíng*

cháo-tíng, court 21.5

chē, cart 2.1

chè, to split 34.3

chēn, angry look, glare, ire 3.26

chén, dust 3.17, 7.19. *chén-āi*

chén-āi, dust 2.5

chèn, to fit, suit 3.10

chēng, to mention 10.19

chéng, city wall 5.1; city 6.2, 7.19, 7.20; wall of rock 31.22

chéng, to form, make 2.14, 10.12, 24.22; to be accomplished, perfected 30.2. *chéng-bài*

chéng-bài, lit. 'success or failure': success, fortune, outcome 26.17

chéng-ēn, to be a recipient of Imperial favour 23.10

Chéng-huáng, name of a mythical, earth-born horse 24.4

chéng-xiàng, Prime Minister, chancellor 3.26, 16.1

chī-mèi, mountain demon 15.6

chí-qū, to gallop 5.6

chǐ, unit of measurement, a Chinese foot 25.4

chì, to be red, to redden 26.6. *chì-chí*, *Chì-sōng-zǐ*

chì-chí, lit. 'red paving': palace court 23.19

Chì-sōng-zǐ, person's name: the Master of the Red Pine 26.13

chóng, again, a second time 10.10, 18.0, 18.3

chóu, s., sorrow 19.3; v., to be sad at, be made despondent by 31.26

chóu-cè, plans 28.3

chóu-chàng, downcast, crestfallen 23.28

chū, come from 2.27; emerge from 3.13, 12.18, 23.23; go out of 9.0, 14.9; come out 25.8, 31.24; stand out above 31 pref. *chū-kǒu*, *chū-rù*, *chū-shī*

chū, at first 19.2, 23.5, 31.16

-chū, at the beginning of . . . 9.0, 31 pref.

chū-kǒu, utter 5.26

chū-rù, lit. 'going out and coming

in': both in the field and at court 18.6

chū-shī, to lead out an army, to lead or send an expeditionary force 16.7

chú, hoe 2.18

Chǔ, place-name: Ch'u 34.3

chǔ-shì, a retired gentleman 10.0

chù, place 29.6

chuān, to traverse, make one's way through 19.7

chuán, to send word 19.1; to pass on, transmit 24.8, 31.10. *chuán-wèi*

chuán-wèi, to hand the throne to another, abdicate 5.23

chuáng, couch 26.2

chuī, to blow 5.19

chuī, cooked rice 10.18

chuí, to hang down 3.8, 32.3; overhang 28.1

chūn, spring 6.0, 6.2, 8.0, 10.17, 17.1. *chūn-fēng*, *chūn-rì*, *chūn-sè*

chūn-fēng, spring wind 27.5

chūn-rì, on a spring day, in spring 7.2

chūn-sè, v., to glow with the colours of spring, to bloom 16.3; s., spring's colours, nature's spring dress 21.3

chún, lip 31.9

cí, to decline, refuse 25.20

cí-miào, shrine, temple 21.7

cí-táng, the hall of a shrine 16.1

cǐ, adj., this 9.0, 9.1, 10.4, 24.30, 31.12; pron., this place, here 18.1; these (animals) 24.17; adv., thus, on this occasion 21.2

cóng, from (the age of) 2.10; from (the position of) 9.0, 18.1, 19.7; from (the date of) 11.3. *cóng-hé*

cóng-hé, whence, from what 2.27

cù-jīn, a heavy, rich material embroidered with gold thread, passement 3.6

cù-tà, to paw the ground, trample 24.21

cuàn, to lie hid in, lie low in 5.11

cuī, to hasten, speed up, hurry on 23.27, 29.1

Cuī Jiǔ, person's name: Ninth Brother Ts'ui 35.2

cuī-wéi, towering, lofty 25.11

cuì, kingfisher-coloured 3.13, 12.23. *cuì-huā, cuì-wēi*

cuì-huā, lit. 'the kingfisher flower': the Imperial banner

cuì-wēi, a greenish-blue colour, the colour of distant hills 3.8

cūn, village 2.17, 27.2

cún, survive 23.4

dá, to arrive, reach 11.7. *dá-guān*

dá-guān, high officials (ones who have 'arrived') 5.4

dà, great 3.12, 5.3, 25.17, 25.24, 32.4. *dà-míng, dà-niáng, dà-yǔ-jiàn*

Dà-lì, name of era 31 pref.

dà-míng, great name, fame 28.1

dà-niáng, title of eldest sister in family, Miss 31.0, 31 pref.

dà-yǔ-jiàn, 'great feather arrows': a kind of arrow favoured by the Emperor T'ai-tsung 23.14

dài, to wear, carry 7.9

dài, a substance used as eyebrow black, black 25.4

dài-yán, mats bordered with tortoiseshell, a luxurious banquet 31.23

Dài-zōng, Tai-tsung: name of the sacred mountain T'ai-shan 1.1

dān-qīng, painting 23.0, 23.7; paintwork 25.12

dǎn, courage, 'nerve' 9.3

dàn, only 2.9, 5.10, 12.15, 17.2, 23.6, 23.39

dāng, facing, by, at 3.22

dàng, heaving 1.5

dào, to arrive 15.3

dào, road 2.8, 9.1

dào, to tell 5.9, 5.10; to say 14.6

dào-yǐng, inverted image 26.10

dé, to be able to, succeed in 2.30, 26.22; to get, catch 13.16; to obtain 24.3, 24.11. *dé-dì*

dé-dì, to be firmly sited, hold one's ground 25.13

dēng, to climb, ascend 21.0, 33.0, 33.6, 34.0. *dēng-lín*

dēng-lín, to climb and look down from 21.2

dēng-zhú, lamp 10.4

dī, low 20.4. *dī-áng*

dī-áng, to undulate, move up and down 31.4

dí, to oppose, be a match for 24.17

dǐ, to be worth 6.6

-dǐ, under . . . 5.4

dì, place 13.3

dì, younger brother 11.5

dì-yī, first, number one 7.7, 31.16

dì-zǐ, pupil 23.29, 31.0, 31 pref., 31.10, 31.19

diǎn-xíng, to mobilize for service 2.9

diāo-sàng, lifeless, spiritless 23.32

dǐng, summit 1.7

dìng, to settle, establish 26.15, 28.6

dōng, winter 2.24

dōng, s., east 2.19, 24.28; adv., eastward, in the east 31.24, 34.3. *dōng-fēng, dōng-lái*

-dōng, east of . . . 25.9

dōng-fēng, the east wind 5.19

dōng-lái, from the east 5.20

dòng, to move, stir 3.17, 8.3, 23.15, 26.10, 31.2. *dòng-yáo*

dòng, often 10.2, 12.22

Dòng-tíng, lake Tung-t'ing 26.4, 34.1

dòng-yáo, to shake, tremble 29.4

dú, adv., alone 4.2, 12.14, 14.12, 18.7, 22.2, 31 pref., 33.6; only 24.2, 27.4; adj., lonely 32.2

duǎn, short 6.7, 29.1

duàn, v., to break off, interrupt 11.1; adj., broken 20.4. *duàn-zhé*

duàn-zhé, to be broken, snapped 5.5

duì, to face, partner in, oppose at 20.5

dùn, to stamp 2.6. *dùn-cuò*

dùn-cuò, sharply-defined, moving

with incisive gestures, striking 31 pref.

duō, many 3.2, 21.2; much 8.4, 14.7, 15.4, 25.14, 33.6

è, bad 2.28

È-gōng, a person: the Duke of O 23.15

è-yè, woman's head-dress 3.8

ér, son, boy 10.16. *ér-nǚ*

ér-nǚ, sons and daughters, children 4.3, 10.12

ér-yǐ, expression occurring at end of sentence: 'only' 31 pref.

èr, second 9.0, 31 pref.; two 24.15. *èr-bǎi*, *èr-qiān*, *èr-shí*

èr-bǎi, two hundred 2.16

èr-qiān, two thousand 25.4

èr-shí, twenty 10.9

fà, hair 12.21

fān-shēn, to bend back the body 7.11

fán, ordinary 23.24

fán, adj., numerous 9.2; v., to make numerous, multiply 33.7

fán-yuàn, to complain, be resentful 2.34

fǎn, contrariwise, contrary to expectation 2.29, 14.14, 23.37. *fǎn-zhǎng*

fǎn, to go back 13.12

fǎn-zhǎng, turning the hand, a flick of the hand, a twinkling 31.17

fáng, to guard, defend 2.10

Fáng tài-wèi, a person: Marshal Fang 20.0

fǎng, to inquire about 10.7

fàng-gē, to sing unrestrainedly 19.5

fēi, is not 13.9

fēi, adj., flying 3.17, 7.12; v., to fly 5.2, 24.6, 24.10, 26.5, 33.2. *fēi-qù*

fēi-qù, to fly away 3.24

fěi, is not 31 pref.

fēn-fāng fragrance 31.10

fēn-lún, busily weaving, moving industriously 3.16

fēn-míng, just as if 27.8

fēn-sàn, to be scattered 11.5

fén, grave-mound 20.2

fèn-fēi, to fly vigorously, struggle to fly 26.2

fēng, hump 3.13

fēng, maple 26.6. *fēng-lín*, *fēng-xiāng*

fēng, wind 8.6, 23.20, 24.34, 32.1, 33.1. *fēng-bō*, *fēng-chén*, *fēng-jǐng*, *fēng-liú*, *fēng-shā*

fēng-bō, wind and waves, rough water 14.7

fēng-chén, lit. 'wind and dust': troubles, disorders, turmoils 22.5, 31.18

fēng-huǒ, beacon-fire 6.5

fēng-jǐng, scenery 35.3

fēng-lín, maple woods 13.11

fēng-liú, style, elegance 23.4

fēng-shā, wind and sand, sand-storms, windy desert 24.18

fēng-shì sealed memorial 8.7

fēng-xiāng, liquidambar 26.18

féng, to meet 23.34, 35.0, 35.4

fèng-huáng, phoenix 26.8

Fèng-jì, place-name: Feng-chi 18.0

Fèng-xiáng, place-name: Feng-hsiang 9.0

fū, then; so 1.1

fū-xū, husband 12.11

Fū-zhōu, place-name: Fu-chou 4.1

fú, smooth out with the hands 23.21; brush against 24.28

fú, float 34.4. *fú-yún*

fú-chí, maintain, uphold, support 25.15

fú-róng, lotus 26.9

fú-yún, floating clouds 14.1, 21.4, 23.8

fǔ, prefecture 22.0

fǔ, ponder, reflect on, savour 31 pref., 31.14

fǔ, cauldron 3.13

Fǔ, proper name: Tu Fu.

fù, wife 2.18

fù, adv., again, furthermore 2.20, 24.16; once more 20.1, 24.32, 31.23; v., bring back, renew 18.2, 28.7

fù, cover 3.23

fù, be disappointed, frustrated in, forgo 14.0

fù, to come to 27.1

fù-guì, riches and greatness 23.8

fù-zhí, father's friend 10.13

gǎi, to change, alter 21.5, 26.16

gài, because 23.33

gài, to cover, spread throughout 30.1

gān, v., to dry 4.8; adj., dry 20.3

gān, to assail 2.7

Gān, see *Hán Gān*, 23.31

gān-gē, warfare 23.35

gǎn, to move, affect 3.19; respond to, be moved by 6.3, 10.22, 31.14. *gǎn-ji*

gǎn, to dare, presume 2.23, 26.17

gǎn-jí, to feel grateful 31 pref.

gāo, adj., high 12.7, 21.1, 33.1; s., height, high place 33.0. *Gāo-dì*, *gāo-tóu*

Gāo-dì, the 'High Emperor': alternative form of Kao-tsu, first emperor of the Han dynasty 5.11

gāo-tóu, lit. 'high-heads': familiar term for dancing-girls who frequently performed in the Imperial presence 31 pref.

gǎo, plain white silk (for painting) 24.18

gào-guī, to take leave, say goodbye 14.5

gē, to cleave, divide 1.4. *gē-jù*

gē, song 29.6

gē-jù, divided occupation (reference to the partitioning of the Han empire between the 'Three Kingdoms' of Wei, Shu, and Wu) 23.3, 28.3

gé, kind of building 29.0

gé, to be beyond, on the other side of, separated by 10.23, 16.4, 26.3, 26.21; come between, intervene 17.8

gè, each 2.3, 10.6

gēn, roots 25.2

gēng, watch (of the night) 29.3

gèng, even 6.7

gōng, lit. 'duke': used as pronoun 'you, sir' in addressing older men 23.38

gōng, achievement 30.1. *gōng-chén*

gōng, handiwork 25.16

gōng-chén, deserving minister, subject who has performed distinguished service 23.11

gōng-diàn, palace halls 7.3

gōng-jiàn, bow and arrows 2.3, 7.9

Gōng-sūn, surname: Kung-sun 31.0, 31 pref., 31.1, 31.16

gǒng, lit. 'join hands': interlace 31.21

gòng, v., to share 10.4; prep., with 15.7

gòng, to present as tribute 26.22

gòng-fèng, to be on call for the entertainment of officials (used of registered geishas) 31 pref.

gū, lonely, solitary 20.2, 34.6. *gū-gāo*

gū-gāo, standing in solitary eminence 25.14

gǔ, adj., old 25.0, 25.11; s., the ancients, antiquity 26.19. *gǔ-jì*, *gǔ-jīn*, *gǔ-lái*

gǔ, valley 12.2

gǔ, bone 23.31. *gǔ-ròu*

gǔ, drum 3.19, 11.1. *gǔ-jué*

gǔ-jì, ancient site, remains 27.0

gǔ-jīn, lit. 'antiquity and present-day': all time, eternity 21.4

gǔ-jué, drums and trumpets 29.3

gǔ-lái, from ancient times 2.33, 23.39, 25.24

gǔ-ròu, lit. 'bones and flesh'; body 3.4, 12.8; one's nearest and dearest, one's own flesh and blood 5.6

gù, to call, visit 16.5. *gù-shì*

gù-rén, old acquaintance 13.5

gù-shì, glances 24.24

gù-xiāng, native land, birthplace 11.4

gù-yì, friendly feelings 10.22

guān, to lead, surpass, overtop 31 pref.

guān, official post 9.6, 12.7, 32.6.
guān-jūn

guān, to look, watch 24.0, 31.0, 31
pref. *guān-zhě*

guān-gài, lit. 'hats and awnings':
officials 14.11

guān-jūn, lit. 'official army': the
Imperial army 19.0

guān-sài, passes 13.12, 22.6

guān-shān, mountain passes 34.7

Guān-xī, lit. 'West of the Passes':
the metropolitan area, Shensi
2.25

guān-zhě, spectator 31.3

Guān-zhōng, lit. 'Within the Passes':
the metropolitan area, Shensi
12.5

guǎn, pipes, flutes 31.23

guāng, light 10.4, 31.8. *guāng-huī*

guāng-huī, lustre, brightness 24.12

guī, adj., returning, homing 1.6; *v.*,
return 7.14, 9.5, 24.9, 27.6; make
one's way to 9.0. *guī-lái*, *guī-qù*,
guī-shùn

guī-lái, come back 2.13

guī-qù, go back 18.7

guī-shùn, lit. 'return to obedience':
make one's way to loyal territory
9.1

guī-zhōng, wife 4.2

guǐ ghost, 2.34, 10.7. *guǐ-shén*

guǐ-shén, the spirits 3.19

guì-qī, Imperial kinsfolk 24.11

gǔn-gǔn, rolling, seething 33.4

Guō-jiā, the Kuo household 24.14

guó, state, country 3.11, 6.1, 30.1.
guó-chū, *guó-jiā*

Guó, name of an ancient state 3.12

guó-chū, founding of the state,
beginning of the dynasty 24.1

guó-jiā, state, country 26.17

guǒ, to wrap 2.12

guò, to go past 8.2; to pass by, pass
that way 15.6; to surpass 23.6.
guò-zhě

guò-zhě, passer-by 2.8

hǎi-shuǐ, water of the sea, sea 2.14

hān, to be intoxicated, drunk with
23.16

hán, cold 4.6, 12.23, 22.1, 24.20,
25.8, 29.2, 31.20

Hán, name of an ancient state
26.14

Hán Gān, Han Kan, a well-known
T῾ang horse-painter 23.29

Hán jiàn-yì Zhù, person's name:
the Admonisher Han Chu 26.0

hán-xiào, with a smile on one's face
23.27

Hàn, name of dynasty 28.7. *Hàn-
dài*, *Hàn-jiā*

Hàn-dài, the Han dynasty 26.14

Hàn-jiā, the land of Han, China
2.16

háng, row 10.12

hǎo, good 2.29, 5.21, 19.6, 22.14,
35.3. *hǎo-yīn*

hǎo-yīn, having a beautiful voice
16.4

hào-chǐ, gleaming teeth 7.13

hào-dàng, tremendously, enormously 31 pref.

hé, adv., how? 3.21, 5.22, 12.7;
where? 7.13, 19.3; adj., what?
10.3. *hé-chù*, *hé-fāng*, *hé-shí*, *hé-
suǒ*, *hé-yǐ*

Hé, the Yellow River 2.10. *Hé-běi*,
Hé-nán, *Hé-xī*, *Hé-zōng*

hé, crops 2.19

Hé-běi, place-name: Ho-pei 19.0

hé-chù, where? 16.1

hé-fāng, what direction? what part?
10.14

hé-hūn, a tree, the *albizzia julibrissia* 12.13

Hé-nán, place-name: Ho-nan 19.0

hé-shí, when? 4.7

hé-suǒ, what? 3.7, 3.9, 32.7

Hé-xī, place-name: Ho-hsi, Chinese
Turkestan 31 pref.

hé-yǐ, how? 13.8

Hé-zōng, the River God 24.31

hè black, dark 13.12

hèn, *v.*, to hate, regret 6.4, 23.6,
30.4; *s.*, regret 30.4

hóng, red 3.24

hóng, swan 26.5. *hóng-yàn*

hóng-yàn, wild swan 15.3

hòng-tóng, in endless succession 31.18

hòu, behind, last 3.21; later, latterly 24.26. *Hòu-zhǔ*

Hòu-zhǔ, the Second Ruler (of Shu) 2.17

hū, to cry, caw, croak 5.2, 24.34; to call, shout 17.8

hū, suddenly 10.12, 19.1

hú, *s.*, barbarian, foreigner 5.4; *adj.*, foreign 27.7. *hú-jì*

hú-jì, foreign horsemen 7.19

hú-wèi, why? 26.21

hù-yǒu, doors and windows 25.12

huā, flowers 6.3, 8.1, 12.21, 20.7, 21.1, 35.4. *huā-jìng*, *Huā-mén*

huā-jìng, flower-strewn path-way 17.3

Huā-mén, place-name: Hua-men 5.25

Huá-liú, name of legendary horse 23.32

Huá-zhōu, place-name: Hua-chou 9.0

huà, to paint 23.30, 23.31, 23.33, 24.0, 24.1. *huà-gōng*, *huà-tú*

huà-gōng, painter 23.18

huà-tú, painting 27.5

huái, *v.*, to think of 15.0; *s.*, thoughts 27.0, 28.0, 32.0

huán, still 2.13, 21.7

huán-pèi, girdle-gems 27.6

huán-xiāng, to return to one's old home 19.6

huāng, wild 31.26

huáng-hūn, *adv.*, at twilight, in the dusk 7.19; *s.*, the dusk 27.4

huáng-jīn, yellow gold 7.10

huáng-lí, oriole 16.4

huáng-liáng, yellow millet 10.18

huáng-mén, palace eunuchs 3.17

huáng-tǔ, yellow earth, clay, earth 29.7

huǎng, curtain 4.7

huī, light, radiance 4.6

huī-huī, wide, broad-meshed 14.13

huí, to return 12.19; to turn back 25.18; to circle 33.2

huì-dāng, must, ought to 1.7

huì-miàn, to meet 10.19

hūn, to marry 10.11

hūn, *s.*, darkness 1.4; *v.*, to darken 31.8

hún, entirely, quite 6.8

hún, soul 9.4, 13.9, 13.11, 13.12, 27.6

hún-tuō, a dance 31 pref.

huò, some 2.10, 26.8

huò, to flash 31.5

jī, chicken 2.21

jī-fū, skin 5.12

jī-lǐ, complexion 3.4

jí, *adv.*, immediately 19.7; *conj.*, then, so 31 pref. *jí-jīn*

jí, *adv.*, urgently 2.26; *adj.*, urgent, insistent, shrill 31.23; keen 33.1

jí, to reach the summit, climax 31.24

jí, speed 31.26

jí, to assemble 26.7

jí-jīn, at present 23.35

jǐ, several 29.6. *jǐ-dù*, *jǐ-shí*

jǐ-dù, on several occasions, at several performances 35.2

jǐ-shí, what time? when? 10.5, 15.3, 18.3

jì, to send, post 11.7, 26.0

jì, having ... 31 pref., 31.13

jì, to, down to 31 pref.

jì, plan 16.5

jì, to remember 31 pref.

jì, juncture, time 23.35

jì, to clear (of weather) 29.2

Jì-běi, place-name: Chi-pei 19.1

jì-fāng, training schools at which geishas were registered 31 pref.

jì-huì, to meet 25.5

jì-liáo, to be melancholy, distressed 29.8

jì-mò, *adj.*, forlorn 14.16; *adv.*, in solitude, quietly 18.8; *v.*, to be at rest, to be still 31.9

jiā, home, household 11.6, 17.6, 29.5. *jiā-shū*

jiā-qì, auspicious influence 5.28

jiā-rén, beautiful woman 12.0, 12.1, 31.1

jiā-shì, distinguished man 23.34

jiā-shū, letter from home 6.6

jià, to marry 2.30

jiān, to be killed 28.8

-jiān, during 24.21, 28.5, 31.17

jiān-nán, difficulties 33.7

jiān-wèi, variety of dishes 17.5

jiǎn, to cut 10.17. *jiǎn-fá*

jiǎn, calloused 31.26

jiǎn-fá, cutting down, lopping, and felling 25.20

jiàn, sturdy, strong 2.18. *jiàn-ér*

jiàn, sword 20.6

jiàn, to sprinkle 6.3

jiàn, to see 2.5, 2.32, 3.9, 12.15, 14.4, 17.2, 20.7, 24.4, 24.33, 28.5, 31 pref., 35.1

jiàn, to mix with 10.18

jiàn-dào, by by-ways, by unfrequented paths, secretly 9.0

jiàn-ér, reservists, regular troops, veterans 5.21

Jiàn-gé, place-name: Chien-ko 7.15

Jiàn-qì, name of a dance 31.0, 31 pref., 31.2, 31.16

Jiàn-wài, name of a province 19.1

jiāng, about to 23.7. *jiāng-lǎo*

jiāng, general, soldier 23.14. *jiāng-jūn*

jiāng, river 30.3, 32.4, 33.4. *jiāng-chéng, jiāng-cūn, jiāng-hǎi, jiāng-hú, jiāng-huā, Jiāng-nán, jiāng-shuǐ, jiāng-tóu*

jiāng-chéng, the River City (Ch'eng-tu) 22.2

jiāng-cūn, river village 18.7

Jiāng-dū-wáng, the Prince of Chiang-tu 24.2

jiāng-hǎi, rivers and seas 31.8

jiāng-hú, rivers and lakes 14.7, 15.4

jiāng-huā, river flowers 7.18

jiāng-jūn, general 23.1, 23.12, 23.21, 23.33, 24.3, 24.9

jiāng-lǎo, ageing 14.14

Jiāng-nán, name of province: Chiang-nan 13.3, 35.0, 35.3

jiāng-shuǐ, river water 7.18, 24.32

jiāng-tóu, river-bank 7.0, 7.3

jiàng, purple, dark red 31.9

jiāo, water-dragon 24.32. *jiāo-lóng*

jiāo-fáng, lit. 'pepper chambers': the Empress's apartments 3.11

jiāo-lóng, water-dragons 13.16

jiāo-qú, crossroads 5.17

jiāo-yuán, suburban plain 25.11

jiǎo, superb, high-riding 31.6

jiē, steps 16.3

jiē, to link up with 25.7

jiē, all 11.5, 23.28, 24.30; both 17.1, 24.17

jié, victory 16.7

jié-yú, lady in waiting 24.8

jiě, to understand 4.4

jiè-wèn, I venture to ask 24.25

jīn, adv., now 5.22, 7.13, 13.7, 17.4, 23.4, 26.1, 31 pref., 34.2; s., the present 24.15. *jīn-nián, jīn-xī, jīn-yè*

jīn, cloth 3.24

jīn, front of gown, bosom 16.8

jīn, adj., golden 5.5; s., tael of silver 6.6. *Jīn-guāng-mén, Jīn-sù-duī, jīn-yuè*

jīn-gǔ, sinews and bones 24.30

Jīn-guāng-mén, the Gate of Golden Light 9.0

jīn-nián, this year 2.24

Jīn-sù-duī, the Hill of Golden Grain 24.33, 31.21

jīn-xī, this evening 10.3

jīn-yè, tonight 4.1, 11.3

jīn-yuè, lit. 'brazen tracery': palace doors 8.5

Jǐn-guān-chéng, the City of the Brocade Officer: Ch'eng-tu 16.2

Jǐn-jiāng, the Brocade River 21.3

Jǐn-tíng, Brocade River Pavilion 25.9

jǐn-yī, brocade dress 31 pref.

jǐn-yīn, brocade (i.e. patterned) carpet 3.22

jìn, distrib., all 5.13; *v.*, to finish off 17.8; to be exhausted, run dry 33.4; *auxiliary v.*, completely, all 24.34

jìn, adj., recent 20.3; *v.*, to be near to 21.1. *jìn-qián, jìn-shì, jìn-shì*

jìn-qián, to approach, draw near 3.26

jìn-shí, recently, in modern times 24.14

jìn-shì, in close attendance, in the Emperor's retinue 9.5

jìn-xián-guān, a sort of hat 23.13

jīng, to sustain, endure 25.22. *jīng-yíng*

jīng, thorn-bush 2.17. *jīng-jí*

jīng, to be startled 6.4, 25.19. *jīng-hū*

jīng-hū, to give a startled cry 10.8

jīng-huá, the capital 14.11

jīng-jí, thorns, 'briers and brambles' 5.11

Jīng-mén, name of a mountain: the Gate of Ch'u 27.1

jīng-qí, banners 26.9

jīng-yì, the capital 9.5

jīng-yíng, to plan, design 23.22

jǐng, well 22.1

jǐng, daylight 29.1

jìng, to pay respects to, honour 10.13

jiǒng, far off, in the distance 23.20, 24.20

jiū-jiū, (onomatopoeic) to make a twittering sound, of ghosts 2.35; of birds 8.2

jiǔ, for a long time 3.15, 14.2, 24.16, 31.4

jiǔ, nine 5.5, 24.23, 31.5. *jiǔ-chóng, jiǔ-xiāo*

jiǔ, wine 17.6, 33.8. *jiǔ-jiāng*

jiǔ, chives 10.17

jiǔ-chóng, lit. 'the ninefold': the sky 23.23

jiǔ-jiāng, wine 10.16

jiǔ-xiāo, lit. 'nine welkins': the sky 8.4

jiù, adj., old (opp. of 'new') 2.34,

17.6; *s.*, former acquaintances 10.7. *jiù-dū, jiù-rén*

jiù-dū, former capital 5.20

jiù-rén, former wife 12.16

jiù-zhōng, amongst them 3.11

jū, to spy on 5.26

jú, grasp, hand 12.22

jú-cù, to be flurried, in a hurry 14.5

jǔ-sàng, to be lost, bewildered 31.3

juān-juān, beautiful 26.3

juān-sù, plain silk (for painting on) 23.21

juǎn, to roll up 19.4. *Juǎn-máo-guā*

Juǎn-máo-guā, horse's name: Curly-haired Dun 24.13

jué, adj., bursting, straining 1.6; *v.*, to be broken, blighted 28.8

jué, adj., extreme, final, topmost 1.7; *v.*, to be cut off, interrupted 22.5. *jué-dài, jué-lún*

jué, to feel, be aware of 24.12

jué, horn, bugle 22.3

jué-dài, surpassing all others in one's day, peerless 12.1

jué-lún, without a match, unrivalled 3.25

jué-niè, to champ the bit 7.10

jūn, you 2.16, 2.32, 10.11, 13.7, 14.3, 17.4, 24.33, 35.4; your 14.4; lord, master 7.8, 26.11. *jūn-chén, jūn-zǐ*

jūn-chén, prince and minister 25.5

jūn-wù, military activities 28.8

jūn-zǐ, your 10.10, 15.2

jùn-xún, to advance hesitantly or disdainfully 3.21

kāi, to open 17.4; to reveal, disclose 23.12; to open out into 24.18. *kāi-biān, kāi-jì, kāi-yuán*

kāi-biān, opening-up of frontiers, territorial aggrandizement 2.15

kāi-jì, founding and maintaining 16.6

kāi-yuán, name of an era 23.9, 31 pref.

kǎn-lǎn, frustration, difficulties 23.40

kàn, to see, look 4.2, 19.3, 22.4, 23.39

kāng-kǎi, to be moved, excited, elated 31 pref.

kē, branch 25.2

kě, can be, could be 3.25, 13.10, 31 pref. *kě-lián*

kě-lián, pitiful, poor 5.8, 21.7; lovable, admirable 24.23

kè, visitor 17.0, 17.3, 20.8, 21.1; traveller 33.5

kěn, to be willing 17.7

kōng, *adv.*, in vain, to no purpose 3.16, 16.4, 18.2, 27.6; *adj.*, empty 12.2; *s.*, the sky 20.4, 24.20; *v.*, to be void, annulled, effaced 23.24; to be empty, deserted 25.12

kǒng, to fear, suspect 13.9, 14.8; to suspect, believe that 26.4

Kǒng-míng, person's name: K'ung-ming 25.1

kǒng-què, peacock 3.6

kòng, saddle 3.17

kòu-dào, raiders 21.6

kū, to weep 2.6, 2.7, 2.34, 7.1, 12.16, 29.5. *kū-shēng*

kū-shēng, sound of weeping 2.7

kǔ, *adv.*, bitterly, ruefully 14.6; *adj.*, bitter 25.21. *kǔ-hèn*, *kǔ-xīn*, *kǔ-zhàn*

kǔ-hèn, bitterness, regret 33.7

kǔ-xīn, earnestly, conscientiously (lit. 'with bitter heart') 24.25

kǔ-zhàn, lit. 'bitter warfare': keen fighting 2.20

kuáng, to go mad, be mad 19.4

kuàng, even more, particularly, especially 2.20, 11.8, 31 pref.

Kuí-fǔ, place-name: K'uei-chou 31 pref.

kùn-kǔ, distress 5.10

kuò, broad 13.5, 32.3

là-jù, wax candle 22.2

lái, *v.*, to come 3.21, 10.14, 13.11, 17.2, 24.28, 25.7, 31.7, 31.24, 33.4; to bring, conjure up 21.3; *s.*, coming 14.6, 23.16

lán-dào, to stand in the way 2.6

láo, to be in vain, to be labour lost 28.8

lǎo, *s.*, old age 23.7; *adj.*, old 25.1. *lǎo-bìng*, *lǎo-chén*, *lǎo-fū*, *lǎo-rén*

lǎo-bìng, *s.*, old age and sickness 32.6; *adj.*, old and ill 34.6

lǎo-chén, old minister 16.6

lǎo-fū, old fellow 31.25

lǎo-rén, old man 26.20

lè, bridle 7.10

lè, pleasure 26.1, 31.24

léi, to produce in succession, do successively 10.20; to become implicated, get into trouble 14.14

léi-tíng, thunder 31.7

lěi-luò, multitudinous, thronging 24.29

lèi, tears 6.3, 7.17, 16.8, 20.3. *lèi-hén*

lèi-hén, tear-stains, traces of tears 4.8

lí, plough 2.18

lí, hedge, fence 17.8

lí-miàn, to slash the face 5.25

Lí-yuán, the Pear Garden academy 31 pref., 31.19

-lǐ, in 7.7, 24.33, 35.1

Lǐ Bó, Li Po 13.0, 14.0, 15.0

Lǐ Guī-nián, Li Kuei-nien 35.0

Lǐ shí-èr-niáng, Li Shih-erh-niang, Twelfth Sister Li 31 pref.

lǐ-zhèng, village headman 2.12

lì, strength, might 25.15

lì, to stand 5.18, 23.20

lì-rén, lovely woman 3.0, 3.2

lián, to pity 4.3

lián, to continue, go on for successive days, months, years, etc. 6.5; to extend continuously 27.3

liáng, good 23.13. *liáng-jiā-zǐ*

liáng-dòng, beams and rafters 25.17

liáng-fēng, cold wind, north-west wind 15.1

Liáng-fù-yín, name of a song 21.8

liáng-jiā-zǐ, son or daughter of good family 12.3

liǎng, *adv.*, on both sides 10.24; *adj.*, two 16.6; *distrib.*, both 31.9

liáo, to intend to, wish to 21.8, 31 pref.

liáo-dǎo, to be despondent 33.8

liǎo, to end, come to an end 1.2

liè, rank, row 24.22. *liè-jùn*

liè-fēng, fierce wind, keen wind 25.14

liè-jùn, linked provinces, adjoining provinces 18.5

lín, woods 20.7

lín, *prep.*, overlooking 5.17; *v.*, to look down on 8.3

lín, scales 3.14

lín-lín, to rumble 2.1

lín-wēng, old neighbour, old man next door 17.7

Lín-yǐng, place-name: Lin-ying 31 pref., 31.11

líng, to surmount 1.7. *Líng-yān*

líng-luò, leafless, stripped, stricken 12.4

líng-píng, amidst trials and tribulations, through many vicissitudes 22.7

Líng-yān, name of a gallery 23.11

liú, *v.*, to flow 7.15, 30.3, 34.8; *s.*, flow, flowing water 32.4. *liú-xuě*

liú, to remain 27.4. *liú-zhì*

liú-lí, flowing style 31 pref.

Liú-shì, (member of the) Liu clan 26.15

liú-xuè, flowing blood, blood shed 2.14

liú-zhì, to delay 26.19

liǔ, willow 7.4

liù, to be washed with 25.3

lóng, dragon 5.15, 23.23, 31.6. *Lóng-chí*, *lóng-méi*, *lóng-zhǒng*

Lóng-chí, Dragon Pool 24.6

lóng-méi, dragon's messenger (horse) 24.34

lóng-zhǒng, seed of the dragon 5.14

lóng-zhǔn, prominent nose 5.13

lǒng-mǔ, field edges 2.19

lóu, tower 21.0, 21.1, 34.0, 34.1

lóu-yǐ, ant 25.21

Lǔ, name of a land 1.2

lù, road 13.10, 25.9. *lù-yú*

lù, dew 11.3, 25.19

lù-shì, official title: Recorder 24.0

lù-yú, corner of road 5.8

luán-dāo, belled knife 3.16

luán-fèng, phoenix 25.22

lún, to take into consideration 12.7; to discuss 27.8

luó, to lay, set out 10.16

luó, creeper, vine 12.20

luó-wǎng, net 13.7

luò, hamlet 2.17

luò, *v.*, to fall 3.23, 20.7, 31.5; to sink, set 13.13; to droop 26.9; *adj.*, which are shedding their leaves 33.3; falling 35.4

luò-luò, widespread 25.13

Luò-yáng, place-name: Lo-yang 19.8

luò-yì, successively 3.18

lǚ, frequently 23.36

lǚ, travel 32.0

lǚ-qiē, lit. 'threadlike cutting': fine carving 3.16

lǜ, green 7.4

mǎ, horse 2.2, 5.5, 7.10, 23.24, 23.30, 24.15, 24.23. *mǎ-guān*, *mǎ-tú*

mǎ-guān, groom 24.22

mǎ-nǎo, agate 24.7

mǎ-tú, horse-painting 24.0

mái-mò, to be buried amidst 2.31

mài, to sell 12.19

mǎn, to fill 5.20, 7.19, 13.13, 14.11; to cover 16.8, 19.2

màn, carelessly 19.4; vainly 29.8

máng-máng, to be obscure, lost to sight 10.24

máo-fà, hair 23.15

máo-wū, thatched cottage 12.20

mào, *s.*, likeness, portrait 23.18; *v.*, to paint a likeness of 23.36, 24.5

měi, beautiful 12.12. *měi-rén*

měi-rén, beautiful woman 26.3, 26.21, 31.11

mén, gate, door 7.3, 9.0, 14.9

měng, fierce 23.14

mèng, v., to dream of 13.0, 14.0, 14.3; s., dream 13.5

Mì-luó, name of river: the Mi-lo 15.8

mì, to look for 20.6

miǎn, to avoid, escape 25.21

miàn, face 27.5

miào, marvellously, wonderfully well 31.12

miào, temple 25.1

míng, fame 14.15, 30.2; name, reputation 24.3, 32.5

míng, adj., bright 11.4; v., to show clearly, prove, demonstrate 13.6. *Míng-fēi*, *míng-móu*

Míng-fēi, the Bright Concubine 27.2

míng-míng, at a remote height, obscured with distance 25.14, 26.5

míng-móu, bright eyes 7.13

míng-rì, tomorrow 10.23

míng-zhāo, tomorrow morning 8.7

mìng-dá, success in life 15.5

mò, do not 21.6, 25.23; is not 31 pref.

mò-mò, wide, vast 24.18

mù, tomb 20.0

mù, to become evening 8.1. *mù-chūn*

mù, tree 31.21, 33.3

mù-chūn, late spring 3.5

mù-fǔ, headquarters 22.1

nǎ, how? 12.16

nǎi, being, as 10.15, 11.8

nài, to endure, be capable of 2.20

nán, to the south 34.3. *Nán-chán-yú*, *Nán-jí*, *Nán-xūn-diàn*, *Nán-yuàn*

-nán, south of 7.20, 17.1, 31.21

nán, male, son 2.28, 2.31

nán, s., difficulty 10.19, 21.2; v., to be difficult 22.6; adv., with difficulty, hard to, impossible to 25.24, 28.7

Nán-chán-yú, the Southern Ch'an-yü 5.24

Nán-jí, name of constellation 26.20

Nán-xūn-diàn, Hall of Southern Fragrance 23.10

Nán-yuàn, the South Park 7.5

nèi-fǔ, the Inner Treasury 24.7

nèi-rén, 'Insiders': class of entertainers chosen to appear before the Emperor 31 pref.

néng, to be able 10.5, 23.30, 25.20

ní-jīng, rainbow banner (borne before the Emperor's coach) 7.5

nián, year 22.7, 31 pref., 31.17

niǎn, Emperor's carriage 7.9

niǎo, bird 1.6, 6.4, 8.2, 24.34, 33.2

níng, to congeal, freeze 31.8

niú, ox 25.18

nóng, gorgeous 3.3

nú, slave 5.10

nǚ, girl, daughter 2.29, 2.30. *nǚ-yuè*

nǚ-yuè, female entertainer 31.20

ōu-gē, songs 18.5

pán, dish 3.14, 17.5, 24.7, 24.9. *pán-jù*

pán-jù, broadly based, encompassing like a coiled snake 25.13

páng, v., s., side 26.12

-páng, beside 2.8

pēi, brew, vintage 17.6

péi, to accompany, keep company 20.5

péng-mén, rustic gate 17.4

pī-lì, thunder and lightning 24.6

pí, skin, bark 25.3

pí-pá, balloon guitar 27.7

pǐ, unit of horses 24.19, 24.29

piāo-bó, vagrant, drifting 23.35

piāo-piāo, drifting 32.7

pín, poor 17.6, 23.38

pín, adj., frequent 2.9; adv., repeatedly 14.3. *pín-fán*

pín-fán, frequent troubling, importunity 16.5

píng, level 32.3

píng, to lean on 34.8

píng-shēng, adj., living 13.9; s., life-time 14.10

píng-zhàng, screens 24.12

pò, to be ruined, broken 6.1, 9.3

pú, reeds 7.4

qī, seven 24.19

qī-zǐ, wife and children 2.4, 19.3

qí, their 23.40; her 31 pref.; his 31.25. *qí-yú*

qí, a board game: *wei-ch'i* 20.5

qí, to ride, bestride 26.8. *qí-zhàn*

Qí, name of a land 1.2

qí-lín, mythical beast, unicorn 3.6, 26.8

Qí-wáng, Prince of Ch'i 35.1

qí-yú, the remaining 24.19

qí-zhàn, mounted warfare, cavalry engagements 24.17

qǐ, to beg 5.10

qǐ, thorn tree 2.17

qǐ, damask 24.10

qǐ, how? surely not? 7.18, 9.6, 25.21, 26.17, 32.5

qǐ, to rise, raise 15.1, 29.6

qì, to weep 5.8

qì, spirit 23.32, 24.24; vapours 25.7

qì, springiness, elevation 31 pref.

qiān, thousand 2.17, 7.3, 27.7, 29.5. *qiān-jīn*, *qiān-mén*, *qiān-qiū*

qiān, to drag 2.6, 12.20. *qiān-lái*

qiān-jīn, thousand taels (of silver) 5.16

qiān-lái, to lead forward 23.19

qiān-mén, lit. 'thousand doors': palace 9.8

qiān-qiū, lit. 'thousand autumns': lasting a thousand years, imperishable 14.15

qián, previously 24.26

-qián, before, in front of 7.9, 23.26, 24.33, 25.1, 35.2

qián-kūn, the universe 34.4

qián-xíng, to make one's way furtively 7.2

qián-yuán, name of an era 9.0

qiáng, mast 32.2

qiǎng, perforce 22.8

qiáo-cuì, wretched, miserable 14.12

qiě, and 3.3

qiě, let me, I will 5.18. *qiě-rú*

qiě-rú, take for example 2.24

qiè-wén, I have heard (polite form) 5.23

qīn, kin, kinswoman 3.11. *qīn-gù*, *qīn-péng*

qīn-gù, near and dear 9.0

qīn-péng, relations and friends 34.5

Qín, name of land 2.20, 3.12

qín, to sleep 8.5

qīng, to collapse 25.17

qīng, clear 4.6, 7.15, 12.17, 22.1; cold 31.8; clean 33.2. *qīng-gāo*, *qīng-mén*

qīng, light 24.10. *qīng-bó-ér*

qīng, green 1.2, 5.7, 13.11, 18.2, 26.6. *qīng-chūn*, *Qīng-hǎi*, *qīng-niǎo*, *qīng-zhǒng*, *qīng-tóng*

qīng-bó-ér, philanderer, faithless man 12.11

qīng-chūn, green spring 19.6

qīng-gāo, noble, sublime 24.24, 28.2

Qīng-hǎi, Kokonor 2.32

qīng-mén, a poor man, in humble circumstances 23.2

qīng-niǎo, blue bird 3.24

qīng-tóng, green bronze 25.2

qīng-zhǒng, the green grave (of Wang Chao-chün) 27.4

qíng, feelings, emotion 7.17, 18.2. *qíng-qīn*

qíng-qīn, affection, concern 14.4

qǐng, to ask leave to 5.25

qióng, to exhaust, cover the whole range of 23.30. *qióng-tú*

qióng-jiāng, drink of the Immortals 26.11

qióng-tú, desperate straits 23.37

qiū, maple 24.21

qiū, autumn 11.2, 22.1, 33.5. *qiū-shuǐ*

qiū-shān, mountains 25.18

qiū-shuǐ, autumn water 15.4, 26.3, 26.21

qū, bend 7.2. *Qū-jiāng*

qū, body 5.16

qū, to drive, chase 2.21, 10.16

Qū-jiāng, the Serpentine 7.2

Qú-táng, the Ch'ü-t'ang Gorge 31.22

-*qǔ*, verbal suffix 17.8

qǔ, tune, melody 27.8, 31.12, 31.23

qù, to go, depart 2.12, 7.16, 24.34, 27.3

quán-mén, powerful families 24.11

quán-shuǐ, spring water 12.17, 12.18

quǎn, dog 2.21

què, to turn back 19.3; take back, remove 23.25

qún-dì, lords of the sky 26.7, 31.6

qún-ōu, flocks of gulls 17.2

qún-shān, many mountains 27.1

rào, to run round, to wind round 25.9

rè, to warm 3.25; to inflame 10.8

rén, man, person 7.7, 15.6, 23.36, 25.6, 31.15. *rén-jiā, rén-jiān, rén-shēng, rén-shì, rén-xíng*

rén-jiā, homes 5.3

rén-jiān, amongst men, in the world 24.4

rén-shēng, human life 7.17, 10.1

rén-shì, human affairs 29.8

rén-xíng, travel 11.1

rěn, to endure, to bear to 22.7, 23.32

rěn-rǎn, interminable, long-continuing 22.5

rì, s., day 5.11, 24.6, 31 pref.; sun 26.5, 31.5, 31.20; *adv.*, daily 9.7. *rì-mù, rì-rì, rì-yè*

rì-mù, evening 12.24, 21.8

rì-rì, every day 17.2

rì-yè, day and night 34.4

róng, to harbour, to hold 25.21

róng, glorious 18.6

róng-mǎ, war-horse 34.7

ròu, flesh 23.31

rú, like 10.2, 23.18, 25.2, 31.3, 31.5, 31.6, 31.7, 31.8, 31.19; as 12.12, 23.38; if 25.17. *rú-hé*

rú-hé, what like? 1.1, 8.8, 15.2

rù, to enter 1.6, 3.22, 13.5. *rù-shì*

rù-shì, lit. 'having entered the room': an adept, a successful

pupil 23.29

ruò, as if 14.10, 24.20; if 28.6

sà-shuǎng, grim, forbidding 23.16

sān, three 6.5, 14.3, 16.5, 18.6. *sān-fēn, sān-rì, sān-shí, sān-wàn, sān-xiá, sān-yuè*

sān-fēn, tripartite 28.3, 30.1

sān-rì, third day 3.1

sān-shí, thirty 24.3

sān-wàn, thirty thousand 24.29

sān-xiá, the Three Gorges 29.4

sān-yuè, the third month 3.1

sàn, to scatter 31.19

sāng-luàn, to fall into disorder, fall to the rebels 12.5

sāo, to scratch 6.7, 14.9

sǎo, to sweep 17.3

sè, colour 25.4; countenance 31.3. *sè-nán*

sè-nán, to be revolted by 26.18

sēn, in rows, ranks, clusters 24.22. *sēn-sēn*

sēn-sēn, thick, luxuriant, dense 16.2

shā, sand 33.2. *shā-ōu*

shā-lù, to kill, put to death 12.6

shā-ōu, seagull 32.8

shà, hall 25.17

shān, mountain 12.7, 12.18, 18.2, 23.18, 31.3, 31.26. *shān-dōng, shān-hé, shān-yuè*

shān-dōng, East of the Mountains 2.16

shān-hé, mountains and rivers 6.1

shān-hú, coral 5.7

shān-yuè, the peak 10.23

shàn, well 5.16; good at, skilled at 23.33, 31 pref.

Shāng, name of constellation 10.2

shāng, to wound, hurt 21.1

shāng, cup 10.20, 10.21

shàng, to ascend 23.10, 34.2

-*shàng*, on 5.2, 10.10, 23.25, 23.26

shàng, even, yet 12.13; still 23.4, 27.2, 31 pref.

shǎo, to be short of, lack 23.11

Shào-líng, place-name: Shao-ling 7.1

shào-zhuàng, youth 10.5
shè, to shoot 7.11, 24.32, 31.5
shè, house 17.1. *shè-dì*
shè-dì, my younger brother 11.0
Shēn, name of constellation 10.2
shēn, deep 6.2, 7.15, 13.15. *shēn-wěn*
shēn, body, person, self 3.10, 14.14, 16.7, 23.40, 26.2, 28.8. *shēn-hòu*, *shēn-shàng*, *shēn-shǒu*
shēn-hèn, to tell one's grievances 2.23
shēn-hòu after death, posthumous 14.16
shēn-shàng, on one's person 5.12
shēn-shǒu, soldiering, military skill 5.21
shēn-wěn, deep-seated 24.24
shén, adj., divine 1.3, 23.33; *s.*, spirit 26.16, 31.12. *shén-jùn*, *shén-miào*, *shén-míng*
shén-jùn, mettlesome 24.23
shén-miào, divine inspiration, genius 24.2
shén-míng, divine providence 25.15
shèn-mò, mind you don't . . . 3.26
shèn-wù, mind you dòn't . . . 5.26, 5.27
shēng, to be produced, generated 1.5; to grow 2.17, 2.19; to give birth to 2.28, 2.29, 2.30, 2.31; to put on, acquire, show, produce 7.6, 23.20, 24.12. *shēng-bié*, *shēng-miàn*, *shēng-zhǎng*
shēng, sound 2.7, 2.35, 11.2, 22.3, 29.3
shēng-bié, parting of the living 13.2
shēng-miàn, fresh appearance, new look 23.12
shēng-zhǎng, to be born and bred, grow up 27.2
shěng, verbal modifier implying time past 27.5
shèng-dé, Imperial favour 5.24
shèng-míng, fame, famous name 23.39
Shèng-wén-shén-wǔ-huáng-dì, titles of Hsüan-tsung 31 pref.
shèng-yán, a woman's looks at their best, in the prime of beauty 31 pref.
shī, lit. 'to lose': to leave nowhere, overshadow 28.6; to fail to 30.4. *shī-zhuì*
shī, to have as one's teacher, train under 31 pref.
shī, wet 2.35, 4.5
shī, poem 15.8. *shī-shū*
shī-shū, poems and writings 19.4
shī-zhuì, to sink, to capsize 14.8
Shī-zǐ-huā, name of a horse: Lion Dapple 24.14
shí, ten 10.20, 10.21, 22.7, 24.6. *shí-jiǔ*, *shí-wǔ*, *shí-yuè*
shí, truly, certainly 3.20
shí, time 2.12, 12.13, 25.5; the times, the age 6.3, 31 pref., 31.14. *shí-jié*
shí, rock, stone 25.2, 30.3, 31.22
shí-jié, season 35.4
shí-jiǔ, nineteen 31 pref.
shí-wǔ, fifteen 2.10
shí-yuè, tenth month 31 pref.
shǐ, to let, cause 13.16, 16.8, 23.32
shǐ, for the first time 17.4, 24.12
shì, the world 25.19. *shì-qíng*, *shì-shàng*, *shì-shì*
shì, affair, business, thing 14.16, 22.7; event 31 pref., 31.14
shì, to serve, attend, wait on. *shì-bēi*, *shì-nǚ*
shì, power 3.25
shì, market 17.5
shì, this 31 pref. *shì-rì*
shì, is 2.29, 11.4, 25.15, 26.14
-shì, of the . . . clan 26.15, 31 pref., 31.1
shì-bēi, servant-girl 12.19
shì-nǚ, woman in attendance 31.15
shì-qíng, the world's opinion, the way of the world 12.9
shì-rì, lit. 'this day': one day 23.19
shì-shàng, in the world 23.38
shì-shì, the world's affairs 10.24
shì-zhě, connoisseur 24.16
shōu, to recover 2.33, 12.8, 19.0, 19.1; to gather up 31.7

shŏu, head 14.9, 25.18, 31 pref.
shòu-chāng, long life and fame 26.20
shū, s., letter 11.7; calligraphy 23.5; v., to write 32.0. *shū-tiè*
shū, different 5.14, 23.30. *shū-jué*
shū, to be careless 5.27
shū-jué, utterly different, out of the ordinary, remarkable 24.19
shū-tiè, specimens of calligraphy 31 pref.
shú, who? 14.13
shú, pure, refined 3.3
shŭ, to reckon, to count as 24.2
Shŭ, name of a country 16.0
shù, commoner 23.2
shù, garrison 11.1. *shù-biān*
shù-biān, garrisoning the frontier, frontier duty 2.13
shù-mù, trees 25.6
shuāi-lăo, old and decrepit 9.7
shuāi-xiē, finished, decayed, having had one's day 12.9
shuāng, pair 4.8, 7.12
shuāng, frost 24.21, 25.3, 26.6. *shuāng-bìn*, *shuāng-xuě*
shuāng-bìn, frosty temples, greying hair 33.7
shuāng-xuě, frost and snow
shuí, who? 7.4, 22.4, 24.25, 25.20
shuĭ, water 13.15, 17.1, 24.1. *shuĭ-biān*, *shuĭ-jīng*
shuĭ-biān, water-side 3.2
shuĭ-jīng, crystal 3.14
shuò, often 8.8, 23.10, 31 pref.
Shuò-fāng, the Northern Command 5.21
Shuò-mò, the Gobi Desert 27.3
sī-rén, this man 14.12
sī-xū, a little while, a moment 5.18, 23.23
sī-yăng, stable-boy 24.22
sĭ, to die 5.5, 16.7. *sĭ-bié*, *sĭ-shēng*
sĭ-bié, partings caused by death 13.1
sĭ-shēng, dead or alive 11.6
sì, it seems that 26.13; is like 31.17, 32.7
sì, four 18.0. *sì-fāng*, *sì-shí*
sì, to think of 26.1

sì, to be presented to, bestowed on 24.9. *sì-jīn*, *sì-míng*
sì-fāng, on all sides 31.2
sì-jīn, payment, money bestowed by Emperor as reward for service rendered 23.27
sì-míng, to confer titles on 3.12
sì-shí, forty 2.11, 25.3
sōng, pine 24.33
sòng, to see off, 2.4, 18.0, 18.1, 20.8; to send, bring 3.18; to bear away 25.20
sú, common, vulgar 23.37
sù, to spend the night 8.0, 12.14, 22.0, 22.2; to roost 25.22
sù, white 3.14; plain silk ground 24.18
sù, awe-inspiring 28.2
suī, although 2.22, 23.3, 25.13
suí, along of, among 2.31; to follow 7.8, 12.10, 26.15
suì-mù, end of the year 29.1
sūn, food 17.5
suŏ, that which 26.19; whom 31 pref.; whither 31.25
suŏ, to seek 2.26, 24.8
suŏ, metal tracery 7.3

tā-rén, someone else 5.26
tā-xiāng, lit. 'another place': far from home 20.1
tà, couch 23.26
tái, terrace 33.6
tài, appearance 3.3
tài-pú, Chief Groom 23.28
Tài-zōng, the Emperor T'ai-tsung 24.13
tàn-jiē, to sigh 24.16
táng, hall 10.10, 35.2
téng-xiāng, to canter 24.29
tí, hoof 24.21
tí, to cry 20.8
tì-lèi, tears 19.2
tì-sì, tears 34.8
tiān, sky 2.35, 7.11, 22.4, 24.28, 25.4, 26.6, 33.1; weather 12.23. *tiān-dì*, *tiān-mò*, *tiān-qì*, *tiān-xià*, *tiān-yá*, *tiān-zĭ*

tiān-dì, heaven and earth, earth and
sky 21.3, 31.4, 32.8

tiān-mò, the world's end 15.0, 15.1

tiān-qì, weather 3.1

tiān-xià, the world, the empire 16.5

tiān-yá, the world's end 29.2

tiān-zǐ, the son of heaven, the Emperor 5.23

tīng, to hear 8.5

tíng, to stop, give up 33.8

tíng, court 23.36

tōng, to communicate with 25.8

tóng, adv., together 5.6, 18.4; adj.,
the same 23.18, 24.30; v., to
share, to have the same . . . 25.10.
tóng-niǎn

tóng-niǎn, sharing the same carriage
7.8

tóng-zhì, little boy 31 pref.

tóu, to throw in, drop 15.8

tóu, head 2.12, 2.13, 6.7. *tóu-shàng*
-*tóu*, shore 2.32; top 5.1

tóu-shàng, on the head 3.7, 23.13

tú, picture 24.15, 24.30, 30.0, 30.2

tǔ, earth, soil 20.3

tūn, to swallow 30.4. *tūn-shēng*

tūn-shēng, to sob 7.1, 13.1

tuó, camel 3.13

tuó-tuó, camel 5.20

wài, outside 31 pref.

-*wài*, outside 16.2

wán, whole, intact 5.12

wán, satin 24.10

wǎn, late, late in life 31.10

wàn, ten thousand 2.17, 6.6, 24.17,
25.18. *wàn-fāng*, *wàn-gǔ*, *wàn-
hè*, *wàn-hù*, *wàn-lǐ*, *wàn-shì*,
wàn-suì, *wàn-wù*

wàn-fāng, everywhere, every quar-
ter 21.2

wàn-gǔ, of all times, of all ages
23.24, 28.4

wàn-hè, ten thousand valleys 27.1

wàn-hù, ten thousand doors (of the
palace) 8.3

wàn-lǐ, ten thousand li 33.5

wàn-shāng, regret, pain 31.14

wàn-shì, all things, this world's
affairs 12.10

wàn-suì, ten thousand years, eternity 14.15

wàn-wù, all creatures, creation,
everything 7.6

wáng-shì, the royal house 31.18

wáng-sūn, lit. 'king's grandson':
young prince 5.0, 5.8, 5.16, 5.18,
5.27

Wáng yòu-jūn, a person: Wang
Hsi-chih 23.6

wǎng, to go towards 7.20, 31.25

wǎng, net 14.13

wǎng-shì, the past 9.0

wàng, to gaze at 1.0, 6.0, 7.20, 9.8,
26.4

wéi, tall 32.2

wéi, girth 25.3

wéi, fine 32.1

wéi, only 20.7, 23.31

wéi, to become 5.10; to be 10.7,
23.2, 25.6, 25.24; to make 21.8,
31 pref.

Wéi Fèng, a person: Wei Feng
24.0, 24.26

wéi-wò, lit. 'tent': strategy, policy
26.16

wèi, has not, not yet 1.2, 2.15, 2.25,
3.15, 4.4, 9.4, 10.11, 10.15, 11.8,
16.7, 23.38, 25.20, 26.16

Wèi, the river Wei 7.15

wèi, for the sake of, for the benefit
of 5.18, 7.4, 17.4; because of, as
a result of 31.4

wèi, exuberance, brilliance 31 pref.

wèi, to tell 23.21

Wèi fū-rén, the Lady Wei 23.5

Wèi-wǔ, Emperor Wu of Wei 23.1

wén, v., to hear 2.16, 12.16, 19.0,
19.2, 35.2; hear of, about 26.13,
29.5, 34.1; s., hearing 20.8

wén-cǎi, cultural brilliance 23.4

wén-zhāng, literature 15.5, 32.5;
embellishment 25.19

wěn, firm 3.10

wèn, to ask 2.8, 2.22, 5.9, 8.8, 10.14,
11.6, 31 pref. *wèn-dá*

wèn-dá, question and answer 10.15, 31.13

wǒ, me 10.14, 23.8; my 13.5; I 13.6, 26.1

Wò-lóng, Sleeping Dragon: i.e. Chu-ko Liang, who lived on Sleeping Dragon Hill 29.7

wū roof 5.3, 5.4. *wū-liáng*

wū, crow 5.1

wū-liáng, beams, rafters 13.13

Wū-xiá, the Wu Gorge 19.7, 25.7

Wú, name of a land 30.4, 34.3

wú, I 26.17

wú, the *wu-t'ung* tree: *sterculia platanifolia* 22.1

wú, there is not, are not 2.19, 7.16, 13.4, 17.5, 20.3, 34.5; may there not be 5.28; not have 11.6; do not 13.16; did not, have not 23.6, 24.32; without 33.3. *wú-cái, wú-rén, wú-shí, wú-yǒu*

wú-cái, lacking in talent 9.7

Wú-rén, native of Wu 31 pref.

wú-rén, no one 2.33

wú-shí, at no time 5.28

wú-yǒu, have not 5.12

wǔ, five 31 pref. *wǔ-gēng, Wǔ-líng, wǔ-shí*

wǔ, dance 31.0, 31 pref., 31.2, 31.12. *wǔ-nǚ*

wǔ-gēng, fifth watch 29.3

Wǔ-hóu, the Martial Marquis (posthumous title of Chu-ko Liang) 25.0

Wǔ-huáng, the Emperor Wu 2.15

Wǔ-líng, lit. 'Five Tumuli': the Imperial tombs 5.28

wǔ-nǚ, dancing girl 31 pref.

wǔ-shí, fifty 31.17

wù, to hate 12.9

wù, mist 4.5

xī, formerly, previously, in the past 5.22, 7.5, 9.1, 10.11, 12.5, 24.27, 26.15, 31.1, 34.1. *xí-rì, xí-zhě*

xī, evening 10.3

xī-rì, former times, of an earlier age 24.13

xī-zhě, some time ago 31 pref.

xī, to regret, deplore 18.5, 26.19

xī, to roost, perch 8.2. *xī-xī*

xī, west 2.11, 2.19. *xī-jiāo, xī-shān*

xī-jiāo, the western suburbs, outskirts 9.2

xī-shān, the Western Mountains 21.6

xī-shǎo, few 26.12

xī-xī, to come to rest, come to roost 22.8

xī-zhù, chopsticks of rhinoceros horn 3.15

xǐ, v., to delight in, be happy at 15.6; s., happiness, joy 19.4

xì, thin, fine 7.4, 24.10, 32.1. *xì-nì*

xì-nì, delicate 3.4

xiá, red glow of sunrise or sunset 24.20

xià, to dip 3.15; to go down to 7.5, 19.8; to fall 33.3. *xià-bǐ, xià-mǎ -xià*, under 23.19, 23.39

xià-bǐ, to set to work with one's brush 23.12

xià-mǎ, to dismount 3.21

xiān, before, first 16.7. *xiān-dì, Xiān-zhǔ*

xiān-dì, the late Emperor 23.17, 24.5, 31.15

Xiān-zhǔ, the First Ruler (of Shu) 25.10

xián, to hold in the beak 3.24

Xián-yáng-qiáo, the Hsien-yang Bridge 2.5

xiàn, to offer, present 24.31

xiàn-guān, district officers, local magistrates, *hsien* officials 2.26

Xiāng, the River Hsiang 26.10

xiāng, fragrant 4.5, 25.22

xiāng-duì, facing, sitting face to face with 17.7

xiāng-jiàn, to meet, see one another 10.1

xiāng-qīn, to invade 21.6

xiāng-sòng, to see off 2.4

xiāng-xiàng, to face each other 23.26

Xiāng-yáng, a place: Hsiang-yang 19.8

xiāng-yì, to think about someone 13.6

xiāng-zhuī, to follow in close succession 24.10

xiáng, to soar 31.6

xiǎng, to fancy, imagine 8.6

xiàng, to go towards 5.3, 19.8, 24.28; to face 7.11, 27.4

xiàng, minister, chancellor 16.0, 23.13, 23.30

xiāo, poetic word for the sky 29.2

Xiāo, the River Hsiao 26.10

xiāo, flute 3.19

Xiāo Cáo, Hsiao Ho and Ts'ao Shen, Han statesmen 28.6

xiāo-sè, withered, bleak 31.22

xiāo-tiáo, desolate, bleak 22.6

xiāo-xī, news 7.16, 13.4

xiāo-xiāo, to whinny (of horses) 2.2; to rustle (of falling leaves) 33.3

xiǎo, little, small 1.8

xiǎo, dawn 1.4

xiǎo, to understand 31 pref.

xiào, to hoot, scream 33.1

xiào, to laugh, smile 7.12, 12.15

xiě-zhēn, to make a likeness, paint a portrait 23.34

Xiè fù, Grand Tutor Hsieh 20.5

xīn, heart, mind 6.4, 16.6, 21.1, 25.21

xīn, new 2.34, 3.1, 7.4, 10.18, 24.15, 33.8. *xīn-rén*

Xīn-fēng-gōng, the palace at Hsinfeng 24.27

xīn-rén, the new wife 12.12, 12.15

xìn, really, truly, for sure 2.28

xīng, star 8.3, 32.3. *xīng-gōng, xīng-hé*

xīng-fǔ, stinking, putrid 26.18

xīng-gōng, starry palace, paradise 26.11

xīng-hé, Milky Way 29.4

xíng, kind of ballad 2.0, 3.0, 25.0, 31.0

xíng, to serve, bring 3.14; to move 14.1; to walk 18.4. *xíng-lù, xíng-rén, xíng-yì*

xíng-lù, to travel 22.6, 23.36

xíng-rén, service-man 2.3, 2.8, 2.9

xíng-yì, to be on one's travels 20.1

xìng-míng, name 5.9

xiōng, chest, bosom 1.5

xiōng-dì, brothers 12.6

xiū, to demobilize 2.25, 11.8; to resign, retire from 32.6

xiū, long, tall 12.24

xiù, sleeve 12.23, 31.9

xiù, the flower, the cream, the best of, beauty 1.3

xiù-luó, embroidered silks 3.5

xū, empty 4.7

xū, must, should 19.5

Xú-jūn, the Lord of Hsü 20.6

xuān, balustrade, railing 3.22, 34.8

xué, to learn, study 23.5

xuě snow 3.23, 24.20. *xuě-shān*

xuě-chǐ, to wipe out a disgrace 5.25

Xuě-shān, the Snowy Mountains 25.8

xuè, blood 2.14. *xuè-wū, xuè-xīng*

xuè-wū, blood-stained 7.14

xuè-xīng, stink of blood 5.19

xún, to look for, seek 16.1

xún-cháng, *adj.*, ordinary 23.36; *adv.*, often 33.1

xún-xìng, Imperial progress 24.27

yà-yāo-jié, kind of garment worn by women 3.10

yān, how? 10.9, 26.22

yān, smoke, mist 31.19. *yān-wù*

yān-hóng, dark red 24.7

yān-wù, mist 26.9

Yán-gōng, Duke Yen 18.0

Yán-qiū-mén, the Gate of Autumn 5.2

yán-sè, colour, hue 7.6, 23.11; face 13.14

yǎn, eye 23.37

Yǎn-chéng, place-name: Yench'eng 31 pref.

yàn, wild goose 11.2

yàn-yù, sated, satiated 3.15

yáng, sunny side 1.4

yáng-huā, willow-down 3.23

yáng-yáng, animated 31.12

yǎng, to look up to 7.11

yǎng, to maintain, support 18.8

yāo, waist 2.3. *yāo-jiān, yāo-xià*

yāo-jiān, at the waist 23.14

yāo-xià, at the waist, below one's belt 5.7

yáo, to stir, agitate 26.10

yáo, far away 4.3

yáo-tiáo, dark, hidden, remote 25.12

yào, to require 25.17

yào-jìn avenue of power, key position 3.20

yè-niáng, father and mother, parents 2.4

yě, particle of predication 31 pref.

yě, the wilds 5.15; countryside 29.5, 32.3. *yě-lǎo*

yě-lǎo, old countryman 7.1

yè, night 5.2, 8.8, 10.17, 14.3, 22.3, 29.0, 32.0, 32.2

yé, leaf 16.4, 25.22, 26.6

Yè-xiàn, place-name: Yeh-hsien 31 pref.

yī, one 7.12, 11.2, 22.8, 24.17, 28.4, 31.2, 32.8, 34.5; once 27.3. *yī-jǔ, yī-lǎn, yī-rén, yī-xǐ*

yī, to accord with, be like, depend on 12.4

yī, clothes. *yī-shāng*

yī-jǔ, at one go 10.20

yī-lǎn, at a single glance 1.8

Yī Lǚ, I Yin and Lü Shang 28.5

yī-rén, alone, the only one 31 pref.

yī-shāng, clothes 3.5, 19.2

yī-xǐ, efface all at a single stroke 23.24

yí, barbarian, foreign 29.6

yí, to be doubtful, half expect 13.14

yí, to transfer, shift 9.0, 9.6, 22.8, 28.7

yí, remaining, surviving 30.4. *yí-xiàng*

Yí-chūn, name of academy 31 pref.

yí-rán, merrily, cheerfully 10.13

yí-xiàng, likeness of dead person, surviving portrait 28.2

yǐ, reason, cause 31.13. *yǐ-lái*

yǐ, to lean against, lean 4.7, 12.24

yǐ, v., to be finished, be over 2.15, 10.15; to conclude, make an end of 13.1; *adv.*, already 5.23, 10.6, 22.7, 25.5, 25.19, 31.21. *yǐ-jīng, yǐ-yǐ*

yǐ, final particle 31 pref.

yǐ-jīng, already 5.11

yǐ-lái, since 24.1

yǐ-yǐ, over and done with, a thing of the past 23.3

yì, even 10.21, 31 pref.; also 23.30, 23.34, 24.19

yì, on high, loftily 23.26

yì, notions 2.15; thoughts 3.3, 15.2; mind 14.4. *yì-jiàng*

yì, to think of, remember, call to mind 4.4, 7.5, 11.0, 24.27, 25.9

yì, easy 14.6

Yì, name of legendary archer 31.5

yì, or 26.8

yì, wing 7.12

yì, bosom 7.17

yì, post-station 18.0

yì, city 5.15

yì-fū, service-man 2.23

yì-jiàng, creative mind, artist's mind 23.22

yì-yuán, partition wall, inner wall 8.1

yīn, on, borne on 8.6; because 9.0; due to, owing to 25.16

yīn, dark side 1.4; dark, overcast 2.35. *yīn-yáng*

yīn-shū, news, letters 22.5, 29.8

yīn-yáng, lit. 'dark and light': forces of nature 29.1

yín, silver 3.6

yín, a kind of ballad or tune 23.0

yín, shade, shadow 8.1

yǐn, to drink 17.7

yǐn-jiàn, to introduce, bring to court 23.9

yìng, must 9.4; ought 15.7; promises, augurs 26.20; owing to 32.6

Vocabulary

yīng, heroic 23.16. yīng-xióng

yīng, oriole 20.8

yīng-tián, to work on an army farm, military colony 2.11

yīng-xióng, hero, man of heroic stamp 16.8, 23.3

yíng, to fill 12.22

yǐng, shadow 26.10, 29.4

yìng, to shine on 16.3, 31.20

yǒng, long 22.3

yǒng, to bob on, float on 32.3

yǒng, to sing, celebrate in song 27.0, 28.0

yǒng-ruì, bold and keen 5.22

yòng, to make use of 25.24

yōu-jū, to live obscurely, in hiding, in retirement 12.2

yōu-rén, person living in obscurity or retirement 25.23

yóu, still 2.30, 9.3, 13.14, 25.6

yóu-hún, wandering soul 7.14

yóu-lái, antecedents 31 pref.

yóu-zǐ, wanderer 14.2

yǒu, to have, to be, there is, there are 2.18, 2.22, 3.7, 7.17, 8.7, 9.0, 9.4, 11.5, 12.1, 13.8, 20.4, 23.33, 23.38, 24.15, 24.26, 25.1, 27.2, 31.1, 31.10, 31.13, 34.6

yòu, also 5.3; again, once more 24.4, 35.4

yū, to tie up, entangle 28.3

yú, I 31 pref.; me 31.13

yú, foolish 5.22

yú, at 23.8, 31 pref. yú-jīn

yú-zī, fading looks 31.20

yù, remaining, left over 17.8. yú-zī

yú-jīn, now, nowadays 23.2

yú-qiáo, fishing and fuel-gathering 29.6

yǔ, for, on behalf of 2.12; from 5.14, 9.0; with 17.7, 24.30, 25.5, 31.13

yǔ, and 2.21, 3.12, 10.2

yǔ, v., to speak 5.17, 15.7; s., speech 27.7

yǔ, rain 2.35, 10.17, 25.3

yǔ-máo, feather 28.4

yǔ-rén, stable-boys 23.28

yǔ-rén, winged immortal 26.12

yǔ-yì, wings 13.8

yǔ-zhòu, universe 28.1

yù, will be 6.8; want, intend 7.20, 26.2; about to 19.4, 26.6

yù, jade 12.12. yù-bì, Yù-huā (Yù huā-zōng), yù-jīng, yù-kē, Yù-léi, yù-mào, yù-táng

yú-bì, jadelike arms 4.6

yù-chú, Imperial kitchen 3.18

Yù-huā, see Yù-huā-zōng, 23.25

Yù-huā-zōng, name of horse: Jade Flower Mane 23.17

yù-jīng, City of Jade 26.7

yù-kē, jade bridle-bells 8.6

Yù-léi, name of mountain: the Jade Fort 21.4

yù-mǎ, Imperial horse 23.17

yù-mào, jadelike face 31 pref.

yù-tà, Imperial couch 23.25

yù-táng, jade hall 26.22

yuān-hún, wronged ghost 15.7

yuān-yāng, mandarin duck 12.14

yuán, originally, actually 25.16

yuán, subordinate official in provincial government 9.0

yuán, ape 33.1

yuán, because of 17.3

Yuán Chí, person's name: Yüan Ch'ih 31 pref.

yuǎn, far, distant 3.3, 13.10, 17.5, 18.1

yuàn, garden, park 7.6

yuàn-hèn, resentment 27.8

yuàn-jiē, to cry out in resentment, exclaim at one's wrongs 26.23

yuē, to say 31 pref.

Yuè, one of the Five Peaks 1.0

yuè, moon 4.1, 8.4, 11.4, 13.13, 18.4, 25.8, 26.5, 31.24, 32.4; month 6.5. yuè-sè, yuè-yè

Yuè-mǎ, 'Horse Leaper': nickname of Kung-sun Shu 29.7

yuè-sè, moon, appearance of the moon 22.4

Yuè-yáng, place-name: Yo-chou 26.1, 34.0, 34.2

yuè-yè, moonlit night 4.0, 11.0, 27.6

yún, to say 2.9, 12.3, 14.13

yún, well-proportioned 3.4

yún, cloud 1.5, 7.11, 20.4, 25.7. *yún-huán, yún-mù, yún-xiāo*

yún-huán, cloud-like hair 4.5

yún-mù, cloud-embroidered bed-curtains 3.11

yún-xiāo, the heavens, the clouds (poetic word for 'sky') 2.7, 28.4

yùn, cycle, fortune's wheel 28.7

yùn, rhyme 18.0

zá, to mix, to mingle 24.20. *zá-tà*

zá-tà, thronging, numerous 3.20

zǎi, year 9.0, 10.9, 24.3, 27.7, 31 pref.

zài, prep., in 5.15, 12.2, 12.17, 31.11; on 26.2; *v.*, to exist, survive 6.1; to be situated, be in 7.13, 13.7, 19.3

zān, hatpin 6.8

zāo, to encounter 12.6, 23.37

zǎo, early, long ago 23.29

zào-huà, the Creator 1.3, 25.16

zēng, to increase 31.14

zèng, to hate 15.5

zèng, to present 10.0, 15.8, 23.0

zhái, house, residence 24.0, 31 pref., 35.1

zhān, to wet 7.17

zhàn, fighting 2.20, 23.16. *zhàn-fá*

zhàn-fá, war 29.5

Zhāng Liáng, person's name: Chang Liang 26.14

Zhāng Xù, person's name: Chang Hsü 31 pref.

zhǎng-zhě, title of respect used in addressing superior 2.22

zhàng-lì, malarial, pestilential 13.3

zhāo, to summon 9.4

Zhāo-yáng-diàn, the Chao-yang Palace 7.7

zhào, to shine on 3.5, 4.8, 13.14. *Zhào-yè-bái*

zhào, Imperial summons 23.21, 24.8

Zhào-yè-bái, name of horse: Night Shiner Grey 24.5

zhé, to pluck, pick 12.21

-zhě, one who 24.25, 31 pref.

zhēn, true 3.3, 23.23, 24.4

zhèn, formation 30.0, 30.2

zhèn-nù, rage 31.7

zhēng, to vie in 24.23

zhèng, straight and true, fairly and squarely 7.12; just as that moment 9.2. *zhèng-shì, zhèng-zhí*

zhèng-shì, truly is 35.3

zhèng-zhí, straight, upright 25.16

zhī, particle of determination 3.13, 3.14, 23.1, 23.9, 24.15, 26.11, 28.5

zhī, him 5.9, 26.22; it 31.4

zhī, branch 22.8. *zhī-gān*

zhī, to know 2.28, 10.9, 12.13, 23.7, 31 pref., 31.25

Zhī Dùn, person's name: Chih Tun 24.26

zhī-gàn, branches and trunk 25.11

zhí-shàng, to go straight up, ascend to 2.7

zhǐ, only 4.2, 17.6

zhǐ-huī, control 28.6

zhì, ambition 14.10, 28.8. *zhì-shì*

zhì, to place 26.22

zhì, to reach, attain 2.11; to arrive 14.2, 17.0, 23.7. *zhì-jīn, zhì-zūn*

zhì, to record 27.5

zhì-dé, name of an era 9.0

zhì-jīn, up to the present 9.3

zhì-shì, man of ambition 25.23

zhì-shǒu, to warm one's hands 3.25

zhì-zūn, the supremely honoured one: i.e. the Emperor 9.6, 23.27

zhōng, middle 22.4. *zhōng-chǎng*

-zhōng, in 7.6, 24.32, 27.8; during 23.9; in the midst of 23.22

zhōng, end 21.5, 25.22, 28.7, 29.7, 31.23. *zhōng-jí, zhōng-rì*

zhōng, to concentrate 1.3

zhōng-cháng, bowels, inside, heart 10.8

zhōng-jí, to come to an end 7.18

zhōng-rì, all day long 14.1; all one's days 23.40

zhòng, weight 25.18

zhòng-shān, multitudinous mountains 1.8

zhōu, prefecture 2.16

zhōu, boat 32.2. *zhōu-jí*

zhōu-jí, boat 14.8

Zhōu-nán, name of region: Chounan 26.19

zhū, pearl 3.10, 12.19, 31.9

Zhū-gé, a surname: Chu-ko 28.1

zhú, lamp 12.10

zhú, bamboo 12.24

zhú-kè, exile 13.4

zhǔ, host 10.19

zhǔ, islet 33.2

zhù, to stay 7.16

zhù, famous, distinguished 32.5

zhù-mǎ, to rein one's horse 9.8, 20.2

zhuǎn, to turn 12.10; to roll 30.3

zhuǎn, increasingly 31.26

zhuàng, to be impressed by 31 pref.

zhuì, to fall 7.12

zhuó, to peck 5.3

zhuó, muddy 12.18, 33.8

zhuó, to wash 26.4

zī, looks 23.16

zī, this 31 pref.

zǐ, your 10.22

zǐ, purple, red 3.13. *zǐ-tái*

zǐ-sūn, lit. 'sons and grandsons': descendants 5.13, 23.1

zǐ-tái, crimson terraces (of Imperial palace) 27.3

zì, word, character of Chinese writing 34.5

zì, eye-sockets, rims 1.6

zì, naturally, of course 5.14, 25.15

zì, from 9.0, 31 pref. *zì-cǐ, zì-cóng*

zì, self 12.3, 16.3. *zì-yǔ*

zì-cǐ, from here 31 pref.

zì-cóng, ever since 24.31

zì-yǔ, to speak to oneself 22.3

zōng-chén, revered statesman 28.2

zòng, even if 2.18

zòng-jiǔ, to drink with abandon 19.5

zǒu, to run 2.4, 5.4

zū, rent 2.26. *zū-shuì*

zū-shuì, taxes 2.27

zú, troops 2.25

zú, foot 2.6, 26.4, 31.26

zú, sufficient 12.7

zuì, drunk 10.21, 26.11

zūn, jar 17.6

zuó, yester(year) 25.9. *zuó-yè, zuó-zhě*

zuó-yè, last night 5.19, 18.4

zuó-zhě, a while ago, the other day 26.13

zuǒ-shěng, the Chancellery 8.0

zuǒ-zhí-yí, Remembrancer of the Left 9.0

zuò, to make 27.7; to be 33.5. *zuò-bàng*

zuò, fortune (of royal house), line 28.7

zuò-bàn to accompany 19.6

INDEX